MODULAR CURRICULUM

MODULAR CURRICULUM

Edited by
BOB MOON

P·C·P
Paul Chapman
Publishing Ltd

Paul Chapman Publishing Ltd
London

British Library Cataloguing in Publication Data

Moon, Bob
    Modular curriculum.
    1. Education—Great Britain—Curricula
    I. Title
    375′. 00941   LA632

ISBN 1–85396–008–X

Typeset by Inforum Ltd, Portsmouth
Printed and bound by St Edmundsbury Press,
Bury St Edmunds, Suffolk

CONTENTS

CONTRIBUTORS

Tim Brighouse held a number of local authority posts in Monmouth, Buckinghamshire and the ILEA before becoming Chief Education Officer for Oxfordshire.

Bob Gregory worked in industry before taking up science teaching in Somerset. He helped establish the Somerset TVEI scheme before becoming Director of TVEI for Sheffield.

John Hart was Assistant Rector of Falkirk High School before being seconded to the Scottish Education Department to work on the Scottish *Action Plan*. He is now Assistant Director, SCOTVEC.

Henry Macintosh was Secretary to the Southern Regional Examinations Board before becoming assessment and accreditation consultant to the MSC TVEI unit.

Bob Moon taught at Tulse Hill School in the ILEA and was Head of Bridgewater Hall School, Stantonbury Campus, Milton Keynes and Peers School, Oxford before becoming Professor of Education at the Open University.

Gareth Newman was Head of Ysgol Emrys ap Iwan, Abergele before becoming Adviser for Secondary Education in Coventry. He is now Head of Ruffwood School, Kirkby.

Pat O'Shea, after teaching in comprehensive schools in Gloucestershire, became tutor in English at the University of Oxford Department of Educational Studies. She is currently Deputy Head of Peers School in Oxford.

Peter Seazell was the officer responsible for the development of the unit based schemes within the West Midlands Advisory Council for Further Education. He is now Manager of the Training Services Unit at Handsworth Technical College.

Christine Southall was a primary school teacher before teaching languages at Peers School in Oxford, where she became Director of the Sixth Form. At present she is Vice Principal of Lord William's School, Thame.

Martin Taylor was Deputy Head of Peers School before obtaining the headship of T.P. Riley Community School in Walsall.

Bob Willars taught in secondary schools and teacher education before becoming Head of Resources at Bosworth College in Leicestershire. He was seconded from this post to work on the development of the Leicestershire modular framework. He now works for PERA as Head of Information Services.

FOREWORD

The educational world, especially in secondary schools, is divided into the followers of Copernicus and Ptolemy. The contributors to this book are unrepentant Copernicans. I shall over-simplify in my explanation.

Imagine the world before Copernicus. It was flat and those who inhabited it were convinced of Ptolemy's wisdom. If you sailed too far, quite simply you would fall off the edge of the world. The truth of that perception was enforced with every ship that failed to return to port and sometimes even by those who did. The establishment of the day did not encourage Copernicans: such uncertainty threatened their hegemony. Indeed in due course the discovery of the new world quite upset the balance of power in the old.

Those of Ptolemaic persuasion support the unchanging order of the secondary curriculum and school organization and believe in a largely unchanging or fixed curriculum, expressed in terms similar to those in the Education Reform Bill . . . Science, Maths, English, History, Geography, and so on.

They have been largely influenced, indeed usually made profit by the rationing of education, whether in school (grammar or secondary modern) or in assessment systems such as the eleven-plus, streaming or norm referenced examinations at GCE/CSE. The fixed navigational points in such a system owe a great deal to a view of human ability and intelligence that is at once monocular, general, inherited and largely unchangeable. It is also ungenerous in the sense that it is remorselessly predictable. To some extent it owes much to and in a sense has been operated as a result of the work of Sir Cyril Burt who had an enviable capacity to find sets of identical twins brought up in apparently dissimilar environmental circumstances. Moreover the support he received for the theories based on the study of such statistically unlikely samples came on occasion from a number of shadowy academics through the British Psychological Journals, of which he was once the editor.

The flavour of this book is different. The educators who have contributed to it are not fatalists but optimistic realists. They seek human talent as multifaceted and the role of the teacher as a key one in unlocking and developing that talent. They represent the latest in a comparatively short line of curriculum developers and educational reformers who have chafed at the constraints of the Ptolemaic educators and their predictably preordained few successes and the many failures who found their way as obedient citizens to the unskilled and semi-skilled work stations which kept their bodies if not their souls together.

The line of educational reform and curriculum development is short because universal schooling itself is young in the context of the thousands of years of human existence and even the many hundreds in different periods during which it is claimed to be civilized. During the last forty years in particular there has been a flowering of curriculum reform within the system which distinguishes it from the 'Adventures in Education' chronicled in a book of that name by William Van Eycken published in the 1960s. His review underlined how many advances were achieved earlier in the century outside the mainstream in places like Summerhill, and so on.

What distinguishes the protagonists of change in this book from those of most other fundamental curriculum development is that they challenge neither the followers of Ptolemy nor those of Copernicus. You can be an educational conservative, an unrepentant traditionalist: you will still see the sense of breaking down the syllabus and programmes of study into more manageable, shorter-term objectives as an aid to teaching and learning. After all, they claim, it provides a clearer map to the learner with shorter-term staging posts for ascertaining the mastery of learning along the route: the motivational gain for the youngster is obvious. Indeed the evidence of gain for those, whatever their discrete talent, in the middle of the ability range is impressive.

Moreover, those at the more progressive end of the educational spectrum will argue that to break down the overcrowded curriculum into smaller units helps to avoid unnecessary overlap in common skills and concepts between separate subjects: at the same time it enables a more comprehensive coverage of the curriculum tailored to the individual and different needs of the particular youngster.

From whichever wing you approach modular developments, therefore, there are the encouraging common features of enthusiastic teachers, learners who display increased motivation and confidence as they can see more clearly their achievements, and a closer and more sharply focused dialogue between teacher and learner.

The editor, Bob Moon, would claim how fortunate he has been in Peers Upper School close to the car works in Oxford, where the staff have hammered out and given practical expression to a changed curriculum based on a modular approach. The effect on the behaviour, achievement, and most important of all the confidence of the students has been impressive. Bob Moon has been a little more than 'fortunate': he has worked unstintingly with inspiration, perception and engaging self-mockery to bring together and encourage the best from a group of talented colleagues.

The book represents a store of ideas and practical detail which will serve as a starting point for those about to sail uncharted waters and a compass for those voyagers in mid-journey.

Their particular curriculum development is different because it addresses the implications of whole school organization as well as enlivening the discrete parts of the syllabus. Fortunate the youngsters who encounter teachers engaged in it: I am convinced that in consequence they have an increased chance to develop their many talents and contribute to the future health of our society.

Tim Brighouse

EDITOR'S INTRODUCTION

What exactly is the modular approach? Can you show me a module? What is so different about teaching in a modular structure? These, and dozens of other questions, have become familiar to anyone leading teacher discussions on the introduction of a modular curriculum. There is, of course, no one answer to the first question posed. Modular initiatives now cover the whole spectrum of curriculum reform from small, school-based schemes to major local authority changes involving hundreds of teachers and lecturers.

This work is a source book for those who wish to gain some insight into both the general characteristics of modular approaches and examples of the approach in practice. Numerous examples of modules and schemes have been included in the text, in part as a response to repeated requests for specific information and details as well as general accounts. It is, therefore, a practitioner's book with emphasis on the secondary years where the modular approach promises so much.

This is even more significant as schools begin to formulate strategies for implementing the National Curriculum. Curriculum planners were always faced with the proverbial problem of fitting a quart into a pint pot. This has been vividly illustrated by the strident claims from many subject areas for inclusion into a nationally prescribed curriculum. The modular approach, as typified for example through the Technical and Vocational Education Initiative (TVEI), has been one way of responding to competing interests. Given the extension of TVEI, the National Curriculum elements of modular structures are likely to be developed in the majority of schools.

The first chapter explores the context in which a widespread interest in modular curriculum has been generated. The case is argued for a critical review of existing organizational structures prior to contemplating modular innovation. A summary is made of the main concerns that experience suggests teachers will bring to discussions of such curriculum change.

These general points are reflected in six case studies of modular reform. Chapter 2 examines the experience of one comprehensive upper school that, over the period 1983–6, introduced a significant element of modular organization into the curriculum. Chapters 3, 4 and 5 provide examples of local-authority-based initiatives, one of the most important sources of inspiration for the modular approach. Chapters 6 and 7, whilst outside the mainstream of secondary schooling, provide an invaluable insight into the work of further education in England and in Scotland. The Scottish *Action Plan* represents one of the boldest and most imaginative unifying frameworks for providing coherence in the curriculum post-16. It has proved an inspiration for countries throughout the world both for its simplicity and for the flexibility it allows students in negotiating courses. The new initiative in the West Midlands reflects a similar ambition. Both provide potential pointers for the school system as we move into a period when social, economic and technological changes may open out the constrained organizational patterns familiar to us today. The impact of ideas about lifelong education in a wide range of learning environments is inevitably going to create a reconsideration of the structure of the school day, week and year.

The third section of the book examines some issues that are of general significance for modular reform. Assessment looms large following the introduction of GCSE, records of achievement and a reconsideration of the post-16 structures, including A-levels. Modular approaches lead almost inevitably to banking arrangements both for the student and for the teacher; a banking arrangement in two senses, as Chapter 9 makes clear. The potential for promoting collaborative working amongst teachers, schools and colleges is enormous and represents one of the most exciting developments sparked by the modular debate. Finally, the practical challenge of timetabling modular schemes is explored.

In much of this book the word *module* is invariably used and it now has common currency in the curriculum development world. It is not, however, the most friendly of terms and a number of people argue, as some of the chapters show, for a word such as *credit* that emphasizes achievement. Whatever the terminology, however, the approach will be characterized now by a period of sustained development. The accounts of practice in this book provide one starting point for those involved.

ACKNOWLEDGEMENTS

All the contributors are deeply involved in applying the ideas and priorities they describe here. I am indebted to them for finding the time to reflect upon this and in a form appropriate to this book.

In more personal terms I would want to express profound gratitude to the staff of Peers School, Oxford, who have provided the critical forum in which practice has been refined and evaluated. Veronica Brown patiently typed and retyped parts of the manuscript and dealt, with her usual skill, in maintaining the network of communications required by this collaborative writing venture.

Bob Moon
Oxford 1987

ACKNOWLEDGEMENTS

PART 1

INTRODUCTION

1
INTRODUCING THE MODULAR
CURRICULUM TO TEACHERS
Bob Moon

INTRODUCTION

In recent years, the concept of modular curriculum has been extensively discussed in secondary schools. The growth of interest has been prodigious, assisted in part by increased opportunities for teachers to visit local authorities and schools that have implemented modular schemes. National and regional conferences organized by the Schools Curriculum Development Committee in the mid 1980s were heavily oversubscribed. Subsequent courses run by local advisory teams, or organizations such as the Association for the Study of Curriculum, have proved equally popular with teachers. The main focus of this book is the secondary school, and in this chapter many of the issues frequently raised by teachers about the modular curriculum are considered. The organization of this chapter might well reflect the way a debate in a school contemplating modular approaches is planned. First, the structure and organization of the existing curriculum arrangements is examined critically; second, the characteristics and advantages of a modular approach are reviewed; finally, the genuine worries and concerns often expressed by teachers are explored, bearing in mind the increasing availability of evidence about modular schemes now in practice.

Modular curriculum, of course, can mean many different things. A paper produced within one local education authority (Oxfordshire County Council, 1986) contrasted the minimal and maximal ways schools could use a modular structure under GCSE:

School A The home economics syllabus is revised using modules established within a module bank. A member of the department had helped the previous year with new curriculum units to go into the bank.

School B Science and technology subjects are given a block on the timetable
   rather than across option columns. The syllabus is planned around
   modules from a module bank accumulated over a three-year period,
   13–16.
School C Two new programmes of creative arts and personal and social
   education (PSE) are developed. Both involve progression through credits
   from the bank. In the four cases there is a wide range of choice for students
   from a variety of credits. The PSE course involves a progression through a
   range of compulsory units.
School D A TVEI style of programme is introduced into the fourth-year
   curriculum. Courses are built up around modules already established in a
   module bank. The school in advance develops three modules in agri-
   culture and horticulture in recognition of the particular needs of the
   locality.
School E In this school, following an extensive curriculum review process,
   all areas of the curriculum (except English and mathematics) plan programmes around the credit accumulation process. In science, technology
   and humanities, students are offered a range of choice between modules;
   in the remaining areas a linear progression is established. A particular
   feature of this school is the link with the local further education college,
   which contributes to the module programme within the technology and
   business studies areas.

For many years, modular structures have equally been used in a variety of
subject areas: the movement of students from one area to another in a design
or physical education department on a termly or half-termly basis can be
seen as an embryonic form of modular planning. In further education and to
a lesser extent in higher education modular structures have existed for a very
long time, and secondary school teachers working in the early TVEI
schemes, or newly-formulated 16–19 programmes, have come into contact
with the theories and principles of a modular curriculum.

THE ORGANIZATION OF
THE EXISTING CURRICULUM

The surge of interest in recent years has been directed towards the older age
range in the compulsory years of schooling up to 16. It was here that many
teachers, and other observers, perceived major problems of both student
motivation and attainment. It was in this area that the performance of
comprehensive schools was being most critically evaluated. In the vast
majority of schools, the form of curriculum organization adopted in the final
years is quickly summarized. All students take English, mathematics, PE

and RE. They then choose, always in the third year of secondary schooling, a further range of subjects. The choices are made from option columns and in most schools there will be six. In an increasing number of schools the choice of subjects is constrained to ensure, for example, that everyone selects a science or creative subject from somewhere in the options. The shortcomings of this form of organization are now well documented. Ann Hurman, in her study of option choice in Midlands' comprehensive schools (Hurman, 1978), discovered that for many students choices existed theoretically rather than in practice. Considerable inventiveness was used in schools to direct students towards particular groups of subjects. The perceived attainment level of the student was the single most important factor in giving guidance. In 1979, the major HMI survey of secondary schools, *Aspects of Secondary Education* (DES, 1979), was almost polemical in denouncing the incoherence and fragmentation manifest in the curriculum choices of so many students.

The case against the option structure is a powerful one. It does, however, sustain many vested interests and it is important to be clear about the problems. The following represent the eight most frequently cited:

1. Students make final, irrevocable choices at far too early a stage. Most do so midway through the third year of schooling. It is hard to substantiate the case for such final decisions being made, on average, at 13½. Careers guidance and advice is distorted to fit into this pattern. The negative impact on the teaching and learning of 'dropped' subjects in the second half of the third year can be considerable.

2. Important areas of curriculum experience disappear from the curriculum of many students after 14. Many point to the irony that the major leisure-time interest of young people is in the subject area with one of the highest drop-out rates, namely music. Another subject area where many drop out – modern languages – is the subject most sought after in adult education. There are further criticisms. Can a student choosing biology be regarded as receiving a science education? Can we accept that the arts should have such a minimal representation in the school experience of the older adolescent?

3. The option structure predetermines the number of subjects that all students take. Six options – plus English and mathematics – lead, at least, to an eight-subject examination curriculum. In 1985 in England and Wales, DES statistics recorded the average subject-holding per student as 5.6 subjects. The non-examination students increase in number as two-year courses progress. Schools rarely have the resources to provide additional groups and so growing levels of drop out and failure create problems of motivation and classroom organization. In an individual

curriculum everything becomes directed to external assessment and students rarely have the flexibility to select those parts of the courses they study that they wish to submit for examination certification.

4. The two-year course has dominated the evolution of curriculum development. Interesting initiatives piloted under Newson, ROSLA and, more recently, the Low Achieving Pupils Project (LAPP), appear inevitably transformed into two-year subjects often for four periods of the week and adding up to approximately 150 hours of study. Frequently these courses are pale reflections of established academic subjects: European studies for those it was thought could not continue with French; environmental studies rather than geography; and motor mechanics in place of physics. Although in theory the status of subjects within the options is equal, in practice sharp divisions emerge. The presentation of the option lists in many schools still shows the high-status subjects (physics, chemistry, biology, history, geography and French) out of alphabetical order across the tops of the columns. Certain subjects, from a very different tradition, are frequently listed well down. Where new subjects were not certificated through CSE the status distinction becomes even greater.

5. Option columns inhibit allowance being made for syllabus overlap between subjects. The student taking control technology and physics will often repeat similar course-work in each of the subjects.

6. A structure that organizes choice on the basis of two-year-long, 150–80-hour subject courses is insufficiently flexible to tackle gender stereotyping in subject choices. Attempts to persuade girls to do a two-year course in CDT or boys to take parentcraft are proving less than successful whatever the publicity and associated promotions that go with option choices.

7. The option columns arrangement disperses curriculum teams across the timetable. Teamwork and collaborative working becomes difficult unless by chance the size of a year group can support, say, two or even three sets in chemistry in one column. Heads of department often have the invidious choice of clustering the sets together in one column to promote co-operation or spreading the sets across the columns in the hope of attracting greater student take up.

8. In terms of staff resources, subject choices at 13 begin a two-and-a-half-year cycle of commitment to a staffing structure. The offer has to be protected through that period whatever changes take place in the school. There are frequent anomalies in the size of subject groups with low figures for options such as German or music and maximum figures for social studies or home economics.

A school undertaking a curriculum review would do well to carry out some research into each of these areas. What is the average overall subject drop-out rate? What percentage of students drop out of major areas of curriculum experience? Are there significant differences in group sizes between subjects and does this create markedly variable working conditions from one teacher to another? If the roll is falling look at the numbers in each subject and set within the options and take off the proportional number represented by the fall in roll over the coming years. What curriculum decisions would this require and how much forward planning rather than *ad hoc* timetabling is required? Could the school make explicit some of the tensions between departments when the option arrangements are agreed?

These problems have been set out in some detail because they do become major issues for a staff discussing change. To make these criticisms is not to challenge the nature and importance of the subject-based curriculum. It is a challenge, however, to the way in which the two-year course structure has come to determine the organization and style of the whole curriculum for all students. The historical antecedents are clear to see. It was against the style and stature of the grammar schools that the first comprehensive schools were established. This was as true of curriculum as any other feature of the new schools. The first building blocks, therefore, of the curriculum were represented by the high-status subjects of the selective system – hence their so frequent listing at the top of the option columns. Over more than two decades attempts have been made to build under this edifice a curriculum for all. However, as the discussion so far indicates, the structure is now proving problematic – not least in the way that the organizational decisions about the arrangement of subjects in the columns, the amount of time allocated for each subject and the nature of the guidance given to students can stimulate debilitating inter-departmental conflicts. The territorial imperative dominates teacher organization and the fourth and fifth-year curriculum represents one of the major areas of its expression.

CHARACTERISTICS AND ADVANTAGES OF A MODULAR APPROACH

At this point enthusiasm for modular arrangements begins to make sense. A modular approach has the advantage of not being overtly ideological in concept and as an organizing principle it is neutral. It avoids, therefore, some of the heat generated by alternative strategies prepared over the years. Integrated courses, mixed-ability teaching and mini-schools are three recent examples that have fallen foul of both media misrepresentation and – more seriously – the concern of the secondary school teacher to hold on to some form of subject identity. Modular structures do not necessarily change the outcome in subject terms. They do, however, provide an alternative style of organization that is more responsive and flexible than the arrangements existing in most schools today. Some sceptical commentators have used the term 'bandwagon' to describe teacher interest – always a pejorative description with the implication of unthought-through acceptance of new-fangled ideas. Experience of in-service events suggests that the process is quite the reverse, with ideas being rigorously tested and argued over.

Many teachers new to the idea ask the simple question, 'What is a module?' The examples in this book provide specific answers. In general terms the word *module* – or *unit* or *credit* – describes a unit of teaching activity and learning expressed as an approximate number of hours of study. The module will be self-contained although certain combinations of modules may represent a progression through the curriculum. At the least, as the examples at the beginning of this chapter indicate, a single subject may be broken down into a sequence of modules. Most of the interest, however, is focused on a restructuring of the secondary school curriculum to allow teams of teachers in related disciplines to offer a range of modular courses within blocks of curriculum time. The main characteristics and suggested advantages of this are illustrated as follows.

Credit Accumulation

In a conventional timetable students follow courses or subjects over a two-year period. The possibility of a change of direction is minimal. Credit accumulation through modular schemes works very differently. Students choose units or credits in a way that allows them to build, Lego-like, an individually designed course. The designers of the scheme will make choices and decisions about how directed these routeways will be. The inadvisability of studying *Structures II* before *Structures I* is clear. More significantly, however, curriculum planners will make some decisions about essential, core modules to be taken by all, and areas where student choice can be expressed across the full range of the offer. Information about progress is normally given formally at the end of the module and recorded within an overall assessment framework. The assessment process can be diagnostic allowing targets to be reformulated whilst safeguarding the value of credits already completed. The certificating of modular programmes leads in many schemes to a programme of credit banking.

Credit Transfer and Dual Certification

This follows from the banking concept mentioned above. Students can carry credits forward from one institution to another in building an individual curriculum programme. A number of schemes have been established in higher education, and in schools the idea of credit transfer could become central to establishing coherent 14–18 curriculum progression. Advocacy for this has come in statements from both the National Association of Head-teachers and the Secondary Heads Association.

A number of modular schemes are now developing dual certification arrangements. Students can use a module for the requirements of, say, an RSA or BTEC certification in wordprocessing and/or as partial fulfilment of a GCSE subject certificate in Business Studies.

Short-term Goals

The end of the two-year examination course can seem a long way off for the 13- or 14-year-old. The syllabus as a whole can be a daunting document. A key organizing principle of modular schemes is the explicit statement – for the teacher, student and parents – of short-term goals established for that unit of study. These will be conceived within the long-term aims for the programme of study but for the student motivation is seen to come from a more limited statement about what they are aiming at. Many teachers working in modular schemes report on the improvements in attitudes that follow from this and the Welsh Joint Education Committee has produced some complementary, although as yet unpublished, evidence on improvements in grade scores for students on modular as opposed to two-year courses. Motivation appears to be further enhanced where students have a degree of choice between alternative curriculum routes.

Curriculum Overcrowding

The list of subjects and issues competing for inclusion in the secondary school curriculum is formidable. The lobbies for technical, vocational, creative personal, political and social curriculum elements are becoming difficult to resist as are the groups working to safeguard areas such as modern languages or history. If the curriculum remains structured around two-year subject courses then an increasing number of subjects will be offered each with a limited allocation of time. Broadly-based modular courses in, say, the humanities or the sciences provide a framework in which new skills and contexts can be introduced in a coherent way.

Gender Stereotyping

Girls and boys find it easier to opt for shorter units in subject areas they traditionally avoid. A 30-hour module in technology or dance is less daunting than a two-year GCSE course. Again, as with curriculum over-crowding discussed above, the movement towards a modular structure requires the reconsideration of subject titles on the fourth- and fifth-year curriculum. The new Secondary Examinations Council (SEC) criteria, *The Sciences : Double Award* due for publication in 1988, are likely to lead to further developments of modular schemes and this may have significant implications for the take up of the physical sciences by girls.

Linking Academic and Vocational Activities

TVEI schemes have sought to introduce a more practical and applied vocational element into the curriculum. Many schemes have chosen a modular structure to achieve this. It can take a number of forms. Pro-grammes leading towards well-known subject titles may include one or more modules that cover new content perhaps reflecting a local study relevant to the objectives of the course. A business studies course, for example, may include as a module a case study of a local commercial organization. Using credit banks individual schools may develop modules specific to their locality whilst adopting more broadly-based core modules for the majority of the time. Alternatively, outside GCSE students may select modules the outcome of which can be recorded on a record of achievement – and/or certificated through a vocational validating body.

Mixed-age Grouping

A curriculum that is divided into free-standing modules with clear learning outcomes enhances the possibility for mixed-age classes. At present, mixed-age groups are common post-16, in further education and adult education classes, for example, but hardly exist at all in secondary schooling. The arbitrary structure of the academic year and the division of children into age bands according to date of birth is coming under increasing criticism as the move towards criteria rather than normative-based assessment develops. In schools the creation of mixed-age groupings is usually dependent upon a review of the way the school day is organized.

Safeguarding the Teacher's Specialist Identity

Modular schemes have the very significant advantage of safeguarding the teacher's specialist identity. Within a modular science or humanities programme, for example, the chemist or historian can make a purely specialist contribution or – if they wish – teach modules in related or integrated areas. The modular structure allows teachers who wish to experience teaching in other areas to do so but on short-term rather than year-long courses. Experience in modular schemes indicates that this helps build confidence. The majority of teachers in the teaching teams begin to explore teaching possibilities across the range of their curriculum areas.

Teacher Organization

Modular schemes allow for considerable flexibility in the planning of teaching teams. Teachers can experiment over a limited period of time with new activities or in new subject areas. Specialists can be borrowed from other subject areas for specific contributions to a subject programme. The curriculum offered can be adjusted unit by unit to take account of the teaching skills available. Teachers can work collaboratively over the span of one module unit and independently for subsequent units. Teaching teams can be given a large measure of autonomy in formulating the overall plans for teacher time.

CRITICISMS OF THE MODULAR APPROACH

A critique of existing arrangements and the advantages to be gained from moving to modular structures has so far been set out in this chapter. It is the fate of innovation, however, to be evaluated against criteria far stricter than those applied to previous circumstances. Equally inevitably, innovation is always evaluated against the best of the previous arrangements. Experience of many debates and discussions suggests that the following concerns are likely to be prominent:

Modular structure leads to fragmentation and breaks up the coherence of the subject curriculum. In the modular plans that have been implemented there is no evidence that this has happened. The worry is based in part on assumptions that need questioning. Just how coherent the established curriculum is, particularly from the students' viewpoint, needs questioning. The way the syllabus is taught is frequently up to the wishes and predilections of individual teachers. Rarely, for example, have we asked questions about the sequence of study of a geography or a business studies syllabus. In some areas a sequence of units or modules may be highly appropriate as skills and concepts are built up. In other areas a degree of free choice may be more desirable. Core modules for all in business studies may be followed by free choice amongst a range of modules covering different practical applications of skills previously learnt. By exploring the skeleton of a subject, the module planner can create greater coherence and less fragmentation. The skill of the curriculum developer has to be applied whatever the organizational structure.

Modular structures represent an alternative to subject teaching. This unspoken worry can cause confusion and misunderstanding. Many who have advocated a degree of modularization are critical of the way in which an eight or nine-subject curriculum taught over two years inhibits alternative forms of teaching and learning. This is not to criticize the subjects themselves or the values they bring to school experience – the worry represents a confusion between means and ends. Modularization as a concept represents a structure. How teachers use structure will reveal a host of different intentions. The document mentioned earlier in this chapter (Oxfordshire County Council, 1986), used by an LEA in talking to headteachers, shows how at a minimal level modular innovation can alter the teaching organization of one subject. On the other hand, a modular structure can be used to plan the whole curriculum. Opponents of the modular structure have sometimes made unfavourable comparisons with the structure of the American high-school credit system. In most schools, however, the unit of credit is used in flexible ways to provide progression and sequence where appropriate, and the opportunity to pursue, for some percentage of the curriculum time, personal, and even idiosyncratic, interests. The examples in this book are mostly drawn from British experience. However, it is interesting to see in the example passages of the curriculum handbook given at the end of this chapter the thought and planning going into a credit-based curriculum. At the other extreme it could, as in Newton North High School, represent the style of delivery for the whole curriculum. It seems likely that with the advent of GCSE and records of achievement the majority of school courses will still be targeted on subject outcomes. What is likely is that new titles will appear to meet, for example, the needs of TVEI and that a number of broadly-based titles in the sciences and humanities will allow greater student choice within a coherent framework of skills and concepts.

Modular structures inhibit the integrated development of processes and skills within the curriculum. Curriculum planning involves the implementing of a range of different teaching styles. Curriculum planners can combine both in developing new strategies. It has already been noted that most schools currently using a modular structure do so for only a proportion of the curriculum. In any case, the concept of integration can still be represented in a sequence of modules. The danger in the secondary schools is that integration, perhaps through a pre-vocational course, requires a group of students separated from their peers who follow a subject-based route. More often than not such groups represent the lowest attainers. Nationally, the LAPP project has many examples of this. Modular structures sensitively organized avoid such changes and stereo-typing.

Modular structures are more appropriate to some curriculum areas than others. In a number of subject areas syllabus design has reflected a modular perspective. Science, particularly, has long been associated with such plans. TVEI has tended to promote modular innovation in certain subjects. Technical and vocational activities in modular form have also been a feature of pre-vocational initiatives in schools. Evidence of modular planning, however, now exists in all subject areas although schools tend totally to eschew modular structures.

Modular structures negate grounded relationships between teachers and students. This is, perhaps, a more frequently expressed concern than any other. It can only be said that the practice belies the worry. Contrary to this concern, there are frequently comments about improved motivation and attitude. One explanation suggests that student application to clearly defined tasks creates motivation that in itself leads to good relationships. In other words, good relationships can be both the end product and starting point for learning, and curriculum planners could do well to think about the intergration of both in their plans.

Modular structures do not really change what happens in classrooms. Improvement is more likely to come from a reform of the process of teaching and learning rather than structures. The evidence of improved motivation suggests that structure can have a significant impact on process. Modular curriculum planners appear to take infinite pains to ensure a range of activities and resources within the individual units of work. There is some evidence of an increase in the amount of practical and applied work within the students' curriculum. Modularization in itself does not lead to a change in classroom processes. It is attractive, however, as a planning approach and seems conducive to teachers working collectively to introduce an improved curriculum. The base for curriculum reform in the past was syllabus design. Teachers report favourably on the focus that a unit structure gives to curriculum development activities.

Modularization leads to over-assessment, creating unnecessary pressures for both teachers and students. Some schools have reported problems in assessment design. Modularization clearly leads to a more explicit organization of assessment. Assuming that testing and evaluation existed under the previous arrangements, although in a rather *ad hoc* way, it is difficult to know whether modularization overall actually leads to an increase in the amount of assessment. A number of schemes have now moved away from an end-of-module assessment and have attempted to integrate the process throughout the module. Moves in this direction have in part been linked to curriculum initiatives within the development of records of achievement. Papers published by the examining groups for GCSE are a source of information on developments nationally, although these do reflect some of the rather unique problems of fulfilling the national criteria.

Modular schemes have become rather chaotic because of the different lengths of time in which module units are planned. This point has become particularly interesting following the reform of 16-plus examinations. Existing or planned schemes include three to seven modules per subject each, of anything from 20 to 60 hours long. The most common module length appears to be 20 to 30-hour units. As the move towards criteria rather than normative-based assessment proceeds some would argue that the number of hours devoted to a module is irrelevant. In other words, if the student completes the task and displays sufficient evidence of a good level of understanding then there is no need to worry about the allocation of hours. At present, schools allocate widely varying amounts of time to subject curricula without any apparent consequences for examination outcomes. It is becoming apparent that a more pertinent question relates to the number of credits or modules that will accumulate to a subject outcome. Schemes being planned vary, although the range is usually between four and six. Increasingly five credits for a GCSE title is the most common choice.

Modules lead to an instrumental view of student learning. The specification of learning outcomes is seen by many to inhibit a curriculum approach that allows spontaneity of responses by students as interests develop in the classroom. Against this two points need making. First, not all modules need to be seen in a mastery context. In a number of schools modules that are totally student based and experential, perhaps with a title such as *Project Assignment*, co-exist with more precisely structured units as *Gears and Gearings* in a science course. Students can, as well, be sequenced through modules if this is seen to be desirable. Second, this concern raises a philosophical question about the extent to which teachers reveal their curriculum plans to students. It is increasingly argued that students and their parents are entitled to a much clearer explication of what they are expected to achieve. Legislation in England and Wales is reinforcing this more consumer-oriented approach. The sort of detail given by Newton North High School to students and parents could be a model for development on the British side of the Atlantic.

Modules cannot be implemented without an excessive stage of curriculum development and in-service training. Judging by the number of INSET courses associated with modular developments, the providers are working at full stretch to meet demand. It would be wrong, however, to suggest that the move to modular structure required a complete reworking of the curriculum. A great deal of the existing curriculum, with associated textbooks and resources, can be easily adapted for modular purposes. Working within the new structure, teachers will see opportunities for improvement and change but on an incremental basis as the time and resources become available. Modular structures do expose technical issues of assessment that may well require specific in-service support. The move, however, from assessment that ranked students in comparison with each other to a system based on assessing individuals against specific criteria is common to modular and non-modular schemes. It represents a very significant challenge that will require the acquisition of new professional skills.

The response to these ten concerns represents, nationally, an increasing level of experience. It would be wrong to suggest that implementing modular schemes is without its problems and pitfalls. Many teachers, for example, report the need to review the administrative organization of a school when modular schemes are implemented. The use of the computer to produce group lists and to process assessment information can place additional burdens on ancillary staff. And it is not always possible, in advance, to anticipate the new demands that the system will place on existing arrangements. In a number of schools new posts have been established to promote whole-school assessment policies, or to ensure that the storage and retrieval of continually assessed work is efficiently organized. In the transition from one approach to another difficulties inevitably arise and it is unlikely that all these can be foreseen in the planning stages.

INITIATIVES TO THE MODULAR CURRICULUM

It is important, however, to stress that the worries about modular developments have now been answered, in practice, in a good number of secondary schools. Outside secondary schools, in further and higher education, concern has moved on from 'Shall we or not?' to a systematic improvement of schemes within a framework of agreed principles. It is towards this stage that many secondary schools are now moving. In the process an attempt is being made to integrate a range of related initiatives. The future of modular schemes, for example, must be related to the development nationally of records of achievement. A number of schemes are now looking at the way curriculum statements can be made that give more precise information about a student's attainment than is possible with subject titles or grades. Most records of achievement stress the need to involve the student in discussing or negotiating learning goals at frequent intervals throughout the secondary years of schooling. Modular schemes provide an explicit structure for this. There is also a move to use records of achievement as a framework for reporting beyond the compulsory years of schooling. With the rapid decline in employment opportunities at 16, and the associated growth of training schemes, there is the need to establish points of contact and linkage between the myriad of educational and training opportunities. Increasingly, the compulsory school years will become one stage in a progression of learning experiences. Schools, therefore, have to be seen as unfinished business with a comprehensive report of achievements prepared for the next phase of learning. The stress on continuity between the primary and secondary phases of schooling will be extended to cover the secondary to tertiary experience.

The need to provide routeways between traditionally separate educational experience will require the concept of equivalence to be explored in some detail. In higher education in the Manchester region, for example, some interesting planning by all the providers has focused on this problem. At the secondary and tertiary stages of education, SEC and the National Council for Vocational Qualifications (NCVQ) are beginning to discuss the way GCSE, A- and A/S-levels can be seen in relation to complementary vocational accreditation. A number of TVEI schemes are pressing for this. The possibilities of a unit accreditation structure that allows equal value between academic and vocational activities is an attractive proposition.

The attempt to establish more permeable boundaries between different sectors within the educational system is likely to bring into question a number of further areas of secondary school organization. The rather rigid nature of the school day, for example, is not conducive to the more flexible deployment of staffing and resources that may be required to service the newly-emerging curriculum structures. Why not, for example, plan a school day that extends to take in the provision of adult education opportunities in the evening? Is it essential for all students, particularly the older adolescent, to all be learning at precisely the same time? The way in which students are excluded from certain activities because of the crammed compression of everything into 22 to 25 hours a week works against the provision of a broadly-based range of opportunities. More and more we may be thinking about a central core of foundation activities around which the student can develop a personal curriculum profile. Early morning or evening courses may be considered in lieu of certain morning or afternoon classes. At present legal requirements of schools would make this difficult. There is, however, increasing pressure, not least from chief education officers, for some flexibility to be introduced.

One characteristic of nearly all modular initiatives is the way they are usually based on groups of schools and colleges working collaboratively. Most of the TVEI projects work on a co-operative basis if only to maximize the use of scarce resources. The potential for inter-school group development is considerable, however, and in establishing modular credit-based schemes provides both the best use of resources and the stimulus that comes from collaborative activity. A number of teachers have reported how refreshing it is to move outside a particular institutional context in development work of this kind.

Where this is linked to GCSE and records of achievement, new styles of working are being developed not only for teachers but also for those in the examination groups. Again the emphasis is on collaborative working relationships. The days when teachers prepared a new syllabus and sent it off to be judged by anonymous examination board officers are increasingly likely to disappear. A number of local authorities have set up projects with examination groups. Joint appointments between local authorities and examining groups are being made.

Across the country, therefore, there is a range of fascinating developments linked to the growth of modular curriculum initiatives. One very experienced protagonist in curriculum affairs, working at a national level over many years, observed recently that he could think of no similar reform proposal that had attracted such extensive, broadly-based and sustained interest. It is a challenge that offers schools the opportunity of revitalizing curriculum arrangements in ways that may transform the experience of schooling for many young people. The evidence to date suggests that both motivation and attainment can be improved with well-designed and coherent schemes. If secondary schooling is to develop with confidence and commitment, securing the confidence of the community at large, this is one organizational opportunity worthy of very careful consideration.

REFERENCES

Department of Education and Science (1979) *Aspects of Secondary Education in England: a survey by HM Inspectors of Schools*, London, HMSO.

Hurman, A. (1978) *A charter for choice*, NFER Publishing Company, Slough.

Oxfordshire County Council (1986) unpublished document available from the Oxfordshire Examinations Syndicate, TVEI Centre, Cricket Road, Cowley, Oxford.

Secondary Examinations Council (forthcoming) *The Sciences: Double Award*, London, available from the Secondary Examinations Council.

NOTES AND ILLUSTRATIONS
Newton North High School

Sample passages from Newton North High School's *Curriculum Handbook* (Newtonville, near Boston, Mass.).

GRADUATION REQUIREMENTS

You must take English and physical education each year.

You must earn a total of 100 credits.

You must meet the following distribution requirements:

20 credits in English
5 credits in a biological science
5 credits in a physical science
15 credits in social studies (including 5 in U.S. History)
10 credits in mathematics
5 credits in the arts or "hands on" subjects (art, music, theatre, home economics, typewriting, or technical/vocational)
7 credits in physical education.

Some inter-disciplinary courses fulfill departmental requirements:

Mini Courses

The following courses meet once or twice a week. They are for students interested in social studies who might have time for a minor course. These courses may be used to fulfill part of your social studies requirement.

480L CLOSE UP: Seminar in * X,XI,XII L 1 period 1 credit
     Government
The CLOSE UP program offers an ususual opportunity to visit Washington, D.C., for a week, usually in March, to observe the workings of government. As preparation and follow up students will meet once a week throughout the spring semester to discuss American government and politics. The one-week trip to Washington is an optional part of the course. The cost of the trip must be met by students.

481 Russian History * X,XI,XII full year 2 periods 2.5 credits
This course investigates Russian and Soviet culture since the mid-19th century. How much did the great revolution of 1917 actually change Russia, and how much remains the same? Reading includes Russian drama and fiction as well as historical source readings.

801L Foods and Nutrition 2 * IX,X L 4 periods 2.5 credits
After reviewing basic cookery principles, you will use advanced techniques to prepare breads, eggs, meat, soups, salads, gelatins, and desserts for dinner meals. Consumer and nutrition issues will be related to food additives, convenience foods, energy considerations, fad dieting, and exercise.

802F Foods and Nutrition 3 * XI,XII F 4 periods 2.5 credits

This course will take you on a culinary tour of the United States, from New England, to the South, to the West, and on to Alaska and Hawaii. The course is oriented to food preparation and to the historical and cultural whys and wherefores. It emphasizes appreciating our American heritage.

803L Foods and Nutrition 4 * XI,XII L 4 periods 2.5 credits

You will take a culinary tour of seven countries. The foods, customs, cultures, and culinary heritage of Italy, France, China, Mexico, Greece, Ireland, and the Mid-East region will be investigated. You will prepare food, using the techniques and equipment unique to each country.

623 Physics II II XI,XII full year 5 periods 5 credits

This is primarily a laboratory course. Most topics will be introduced by experiments or "hands-on" experiences. The lectures will serve mainly to pull together what is learned in the laboratory and to decide what new experiments to do. Mathematical requirements are not as demanding as for 613, but algebra is desirable and may be taken at the same time.

The principal topic is energy and how we know it exists in its many forms. Specific experiments will deal with heat, temperature, heat capacity, electrical work, simple electrical circuits, gravitational potential energy, kinetic energy, energy on the atomic scale, the law of conservation of energy, radiant energy, photons, and applications of energy principles to technical problems.

The basic text is *Energy, An Experimental Approach.*

619 Human Physiology I I XI,XII full year 4 periods 5 credits

Prerequisites: successful completion of a curriculum 1 biology course and approval of the teacher.

This course provides an in-depth survey of all normal human systems, their chemistry, and some pathology. There will be laboratroy work and class discussion. Human Physiology is particularly recommended for students entering various areas of medicine.

The text is *The Human Body* by Morrison.

629 Human Physiology II II XI,XII full year 4 periods 5 credits

Prerequisites: successful completion of a high school biology course and approval of the teacher.

Physiology is the study of living systems such as a cell, a particular organ, a group of organs, or an entire individual. Physiology logically follows a course in biology, and relates to the understanding of the normal (healthy) human body. Numerous and interesting laboratory exercises parallel and give practical application to topics discussed.

Your text will be *The Human Body* by Morrison.

630 General Physical Science II XI,XII full year 4 periods 5 credits

This course is limited to students who have not successfully completed the physical science requirement for graduation. Much of the class work goes on in the laboratory, with individual study modules in many areas. Discussion of social issues relating to science, films, trips, guest lectures, and demonstrations helps you examine various aspects of physics, chemistry, and geology.

The text is *Individualized Science Instruction System (ISIS) Series.*

668 Marine Biology I I XI,XII full year 2 periods 2.5 credits

Open to students who have successfully completed a general biology course and have the consent of the teacher giving this course. Enrollment limited.

The course is divided into two parts. The first part includes the geology and physiography of the oceans, the theory of Continental Drift, and the physical and chemical properties of sea water. The second part is devoted to study of marine organisms and marine ecology. Included in the course are field trips, speakers, and a large number of laboratory experiences.

632F Weather/Astronomy * XI,XII 4 periods 2.5 credits

This is basically a no-lab course. All materials are presented in instructional units called mini-courses. Each mini-course has its own study guide and consists of self-paced instruction. The student can move ahead or return to resource material, films, or slides.

Topics to be covered are the following. The Atmosphere, Weather Elements, Weather Prediction, Aeronautical Meteorology, The Solar System, The Moon and Space Travel, The Universe.

PART 2

THE MODULAR CURRICULUM IN PRACTICE

A CASE STUDY: PEERS SCHOOL, OXFORD

Pat O'Shea and Christine Southall

THE SCHOOL

Peers School is a 13–18 mixed comprehensive upper school in Oxford. It is situated in the south east of the city, just outside the ring road, close to the Cowley car works. The school serves the large estates in this part of the city. Peers currently has 950 on roll, and like all local schools has experienced a drop in numbers, in Peers' case from approximately 1,200. About a quarter of the parents whose children come to Peers work in the car industry – this used to be a major employer for school-leavers but now takes very few. Instead, many students leave to work in service industries, particularly those such as catering, where both the university and the tourist industry are large employers.

The school was formed from the merger in 1968 of a grammar school and a secondary modern school that were already on the same site, with some purpose-built additions. In 1981 a nearby school closed because of falling numbers, and these students now come to Peers. Despite this expansion of the catchment area the overall numbers have dropped markedly. However, this fall in roll has been turned to advantage and has facilitated change of two kinds. First, rooms no longer needed as teaching space have been adapted to various other uses and in many cases are available both to the school and to members of the community. Examples include a crèche, a computer centre, a training restaurant, a health and fitness centre, a staff curriculum development room, and a room housing students' work and records of achievement. Second, the fall in roll concentrated the minds of staff who saw that many of the subjects that had been offered could no longer be sustained under the option system. This was an important factor in setting the context for curriculum reform.

Over the past few years, Peers has developed closer links with the community, both by opening up the school facilities and by making the curriculum more responsive to the community's presence. One important example of the former is the joint-use scheme negotiated with the local district council, which has enabled the building of a well-equipped sports and arts centre on the campus. The emphasis on the importance of community links implies a commitment to communicating as openly and fully as possible with parents, and to making the school accessible to them.

THE CONTEXT

Several local developments in the LEA were important in providing a context for curriculum change in the school.

Appointment of a New Head

In the autumn of 1982 Bob Moon – formerly head of Bridgewater Hall, Stantonbury Campus, Milton Keynes – became headteacher. Any such new appointment creates the expectation of change.

Oxfordshire Self-evaluation Scheme

Schools in the authority undergo a process of self-evaluation in a four-yearly cycle. Peers completed its evaluation in spring, 1982. The result of this was to clarify for staff, and for the incoming head, the direction of future developments.

The Oxfordshire School Day

At about the same time a debate was initiated by the Chief Education Officer, Tim Brighouse, about the timing of the school day. Peers, in common with other schools, did not implement the most radical of the proposals, but it did make a significant shift in extending the length of the morning session and reducing that of the afternoon. At the same time the length of teaching periods was increased and their number reduced. This obviously has implications for the kinds of teaching methods and learning styles that are most appropriate.

Oxford Certificate of Educational Achievement

Tim Brighouse was also a key figure in setting up the Oxford Certificate of Educational Achievement (OCEA), a record of achievement scheme instituted by the Oxford Delegacy for Local Examinations with a group of LEAs including Oxfordshire. Peers has been involved with the OCEA from its earliest stages and is now a pilot school for the project. This is an opportunity to improve assessment, recording and reporting systems, and for students to be clearer about their learning and achievements.

Secondment

The provision of teacher secondment in Oxfordshire has been very generous over the last five years, and Peers has benefited from this. For example, staff have been seconded to develop community links, to work on the Oxfordshire Skills Project, and as part of the INSET programme for the OCEA.

DISESTABLISHING THE OPTIONS

Students join Peers from the fourth year of their middle school. The intake year (13–14-year-olds) is therefore called the upper fourth. The next two years (in most schools called the fourth and fifth years) are termed lower fifth and upper fifth. This terminology is used throughout this chapter.

In 1982 students in the lower and upper fifth studied Christian ethics (*sic*), English, mathematics, physical education and six further subjects from the option columns. Previously there had been five options – the move to six was in response to a perceived need to allow students both to exercise choice and to continue study in all the major areas of experience. Guided choice was the dictum and the aim was a balanced programme for all that included courses from the humanities, sciences and practical or creative areas. In practice there was often little balance. Exceptions were continually made for individuals to take three sciences, two humanities and a language, for example. A number of students were placated with several practical subjects and double social studies courses. In addition, a vocational skills course extended across four option columns, corralling dissenters in anticipation of their dissatisfaction with the system.

The new head quickly convinced the staff that the options could not continue. The school's roll was due to halve by 1988. In a memorable staff meeting shortly after his arrival, he showed a table of the numbers of students opting for various subjects in 1982 and, assuming that the pattern of choice remained broadly similar, the predicted numbers for 1988. A remarkable proportion of option subjects would fail to attract a dozen or so students. It was clear that the 20 subject departments would shortly be locked in a bitter struggle for survival in the option columns. As numbers fell in successive years, inter-departmental strife would grow, peaking at option time, when subjects failing to recruit sizeable groups would be given the *coup de grâce* by the timetabler. Fifteen teaching posts were to be shed between 1982 and 1984, and the balanced curriculum, already more illusory than real, would quickly succumb as it became the battlefield of teachers' livelihoods.

There was growing determination among the staff at Peers to forestall such a turn of events. (Ironically, the situation they managed to avoid in their own workplace was later enacted on a wider front as teachers were drawn into inter-institutional competition by the struggle among the Oxford City upper schools for a viable intake.) Teachers at Peers were, by tradition, generously predisposed towards innovation. They were also apprehensive that the new head would impose a model based on the structure of his previous school without regard for the circumstances indigenous to Peers, its locality and populace. In this atmosphere of insecurity and expectation a plan emerged.

STRUCTURAL CHANGE

In January 1983 the head and the director of studies put forward a proposal for a new structure designed to ensure a balanced programme for all students without exception. The 20 departments were re-grouped into teams with co-ordinators organizing four areas of experience: community studies with languages; English and creative arts; mathematics; and science and technology. The former subject membership of the areas is shown in Figure 2.1. Table 2.1 shows the areas of experience that have an invariable hold on every student's weekly timetable throughout the 13 to 16 period of schooling. This immutable time allocation, coupled with whole-year blocking in community studies and science and technology, has two liberating effects on the curriculum for both students and teachers. Management makes value judgements defining the proportion of time students spend in an area and establishing the principles of whole-school curriculum design. Thereafter:

1. teams of *teachers* from an area of experience are given scope to make decisions about the content and delivery of the curriculum;
2. *students* exercise a considerable degree of control over how they use their time in an area.

Science and technology	*Community studies with languages*
Woodwork	Commerce
Metalwork and technical studies	Economics
Biology	Geography
Chemistry	History
Physics	Physical education
	Religious education
	Home economics and catering
	Needlecraft
	Modern languages (has separate co-ordinator)
English and creative arts	*Mathematics*
Art	Mathematics
Drama	Computer studies
English	
Music	

Figure 2.1 Composition of curriculum areas in 1982–3

Area	*Number of sessions*	*Percentage hold on student week*
Community studies with languages	6	30
English and creative arts	5	25
Mathematics	3	15
Science and technology	5	25
Tutorial	1	5
Total	20	100

Table 2.1 Areas of experience on students' weekly timetable

The publication of the proposal was followed by clarification sessions and 18 curriculum development meetings were held in the spring term of 1983 to look at the overall structure and the possibilities it afforded. The science and technology area was the first to take up and explore the idea of a modular arrangement.

Quarts into Pint Pots: a Credit-based Approach Emerges

The problem confronting the science and technology area was as follows. The single-subject sciences, technology, materials and craft subjects were all pressing their entitlement to curriculum time. Could competing claims be reconciled? Could new technological courses be introduced without displacing established courses? If every field of study required a two-year course,

	Sept. – Nov.	Nov. – Feb.	Mar. – June
SA	Basic technology Dyes & dyeing Elements & compounds Feeding Gears and gearing Graphics Health & science Jewellery Microbes Microelectronics Minerals Physics of movement Social biology Woodwork	Body maintenance Design Dyes & dyeing Earth science Gears and gearing Health science Materials Microelectronics Molecular picture of matter Practical electricity Properties & structure of matter Respiration & homeostasis Social biology Woodcraft	Basic technology Feeding relationships Fibres & fabrics Fieldwork Graphics Health & hygiene Jewellery Materials Medical science Microelectronics Molecular picture of matter Planet Earth Science of crime Structure of matter
SB	Basic technology Domestic electricity Energy resources Feeding Fibres & fabrics Graphics Health science Jewellery Microbes Photography Physics of movement Science of crime detection Textile technology Woodwork	Design Domestic electricity Energy resources Fibres & fabrics Health science Jewellery Materials Molecule picture of matter Practical electronics Photography Respiration & homeostasis Science of crime detection Social biology Textile technology	Basic technology Energy Fibres & fabrics Food science Gears & gearing Heart & circulation Life cycles & genetics Our health Physics of movement Materials Mechanisms Structural design Textile technology Woodcraft

	Sept. – Feb.	Mar.
SC	Astronomy Body maintenance Elements & compounds Feeding relationships Food science technology Graphics Jewellery Microbes Microelectronics Our health Photography Physics of movement Textile technology Woodwork	Dyes & dyeing Domestic electricity Energy Food science Health & hygiene Life cycles Medical science Microelectronics Minerals Mol. pic. matter Prop. & Struc. matter Respiration & excretion Structural design Textile technology

Figure 2.2 Two-year modular scheme for science and technology area
(Each box contains 14 27-hour credits. Students select one credit from each box and complete 15 over a two-year period)

June – Oct.	Oct. – Jan.	Jan. – May	

Body maintenence
Computer-aided design
Earth science
Electicity & magnetism
Electronics
Gears & gearing
Human genetics
Life cycles & genetics
Mechanisms
Microelectronics
Social biology
Structural design
Textile technology
Water & aqueous
   solutions
	Applied science project
	Chemical change
	Fuels
	Gears & gearing
	Geographical science
	Greenhouse
	Human genetics
	Mechanisms
	Microprocessor or control
	Movement & co-ordination
	Pollution
	Textile technology
	Variation, evolution, etc.
	Waves, atoms &
	   radiation
		Brain & senses
		Chemical change
		Digital microelectronics
		Fire & safety
		Further design
		Jewellery project
		Meteorology
		Microelectronics
		Movement &
		   co-ordination
		Pollution
		Science & society
		Technology project
		Textile technology
		Waves, atoms & radiation
			SA

Applied science project
Carbon chemistry
Electricity & magnetism
Electronics
Food & microbes
Geographical science
Health & hygiene
Information
   communication
Life cycles
Mechanisms
Movement &
   co-ordination
Photography
Structural design
Textile technology
	Design
	Electricity & magnetism
	Electronics & logic
	Graphics
	Human genetics
	Life cycles & genetics
	Mechanisms
	Microelectronics
	Microprocessor control
	Photography
	Practical electronics
	Science & society
	Social biology
	Technology project
		Biology project
		Brain, sense &
		   movement
		Digital microelectronics
		Greenhouse
		Information
		   communication
		Jewellery project
		Medical science
		Microelectronics
		Movement &
		   co-ordination
		Photography
		Practical electronics
		Science & society
		Systems
		Waves, atoms & radiation
			SB

Oct.	Oct. – May		
	Brain, sense & movement Computer-aided graphics Electricity & magnetism Fibres & fabrics Graphics Horticulture Life cycles & genetics Mechanisms Meteorology Microelectronics Practical electromagnetics Social biology Water & aqueous solutions Working with materials		**SC**

Figure 2.2 (*Cont.*)

	Sept. – Nov.	Nov. – Feb.	Mar. – June
CA	Beliefs Community projects Health-related fitness Inequality Infancy People and communication Persecution and prejudice Recreational activities Starting work in a large kitchen The community The sewing machine and its use for creative work	Beliefs Community projects Design and sewing for children Health-related fitness Inequality Mass media Persecution and prejudice Recreational activities Running a restaurant Teenagers Word-processing and typewriting	Beliefs Community projects Design and making for the teenager Food and beverage service Health-related fitness How business works People and power Persecution and Prejudice Recreational activities The family
CB	Community projects Health-related fitness Law and order Persecution and prejudice People and communication Recreational activities Starting work in a large kitchen The wider world I The world turned upside down War	A study of tyranny Community projects Health-related fitness Persecution and prejudice Recreational activities Running a restaurant The family The wider world II War Word-processing and typing	Community projects Food and beverage service Health-related fitness How business works Pollution and conservation Recreational activities The European Community I The family War and peace
CC	Beliefs Health-related fitness Holiday or holy day? Inequality Recreational activities Services to people I Starting work in a large kitchen The community The family The wider world I	Beliefs Dirge or disco? Food preparation Health-related fitness Mass media People and power Recreational activities Running a restaurant The new century The wider world II Travel	Beliefs Child development Food and beverage service Health-related fitness Oh What A Lovely War Persecution and prejudice Recreational activities The European Community I To do or *not* to do? Tourism

Figure 2.3 Two-year modular scheme for community studies curriculum area (Students select one credit from each box and complete 18 over a two-year period)

June – Oct.	Oct. – Jan.	Jan. – May	
Business and personal finance Community projects Creating fabrics – weave and colour Further food services Health-related fitness People and work Recreational activities Retirement	Beliefs Catering for special groups Community projects Health-related fitness Information processing Modern office equipment People and power Persecution and prejudice Recreational activities Specialized cooking Textiles V – examination design brief	Beliefs Business enterprise Choice and use of fabrics for home Community projects From garden to table Health-related fitness People and power Persecution and prejudice Practical restaurant work	**CA**
Business and personal finance Community projects Eyeball to eyeball Further food services Health-related fitness People and work Recreational activities The European Community II	America in the modern world Catering for special groups Community projects Consumer affairs Health-related fitness Law and order Modern office equipment/ information processing Recreational activities The British Isles I The family	Business enterprise Community projects Consumer affairs Health-related fitness Law and order Practical restaurant work Recreational activities The British Isles II The wind of change War	**CB**
Dancing to the dole Further food services Health-related fitness People and work Putting others first I Recreational activities Services to people II The European Community II	Beliefs Care of handicapped Catering for special groups Food services I Health-related fitness Inequality Make do and mend Persecution and prejudice Putting others first II Recreational activities The British Isles II	Care of the elderly Consumer affairs Food services II From the cradle to the grave Health-related fitness Law and order Pollution and conservation Porridge Practical restaurant work Recreational activities The British Isles II	**CC**

Figure 2.3 (*Cont.*)

then the co-ordinator would have the impossible task of pouring quarts into pint pots. If, on the other hand, new fields and subjects were introduced in units of 25 hours and existing courses could be adapted to modular form, then a solution to the overload problem seemed possible. The result of experimenting with this idea was a modular scheme that, in its first two years of operation, offered students the opportunity to select 15 credits from a scheme of over 70. Students submitted their best eight credits for CSE Mode III Science and Technology. They could also combine credits leading to CSE Mode I and GCE O-level examinations in Biology, Chemistry, Control Technology and Physics. This was possible because credits that derived from what might be described as punctuated mode I syllabuses co-existed with free-standing units from 1984 to 1986. The co-existence of two-year courses and free-ranging modular programmes was an important stage in the change: it enabled the school to proceed sensitively, taking note of parental response and teacher evaluation in refining the approach. The advent of GCSE in September 1986 presented the opportunity to develop the potential of the modular structure more fully, and Oxfordshire's projected credit bank (described later) is intended to provide the optimum means of certificating a modular approach under GCSE.

Community Studies and Science and Technology from 1986

Written accounts of how the modular schemes operate at Peers make the system sound more complicated than it actually is. This section should be read with frequent reference to Figures 2.2 and 2.3.

In science and technology all students in the lower and upper fifth study 15 credits over a two-year period, which they select from a total scheme of 68. Of these, 65 are GCSE credits. They are engaged on three credits at any given time. Credits are based on about 27 hours of class time and last for 11 weeks on two lessons a week, although credits in SC (see Figure 2.2) last for 22 weeks on one lesson a week. There are three GCSE titles available: Science and Technology; Biological Science with Technology; and Physical Science with Technology. Students may submit their best seven credits for GCSE Mode III Science and Technology. They may follow a more constrained route through the scheme and submit 14 credits for certification: seven for GCSE Mode III Physical Science with Technology and seven for GCSE Mode III Biological Science with Technology. Examples of routes leading to single and double certification are as follows, for two students following the scheme in Figure 2.2.

1. Seven credits submitted for GCSE in Science and Technology:
   Gears and gearing

Science of crime detection
Fibres and fabrics
Photography
Social biology
Textile technology
Graphics
Plus a further eight credits taken but not submitted for GCSE.
2. Seven credits submitted for GCSE Biological Science with Technology:
Feeding relationships
Respiration, excretion and homeostasis
Life cycles and genetics
Movement and co-ordination
Elements and compounds
Basic technology
Electronics
3. Seven credits submitted for Physical Science with Technology:
Physics of movement
Properties and structure of matter
Water and aqueous solutions
Electricity and magnetism
Mechanisms
Technology project
Microelectronics
Plus one credit taken but not submitted for GCSE.

The possible permutations of credits are very numerous indeed and individuals may combine theroretical, applied, vocational, general interest and pre-A-level credits in constructing their programmes.

In the community area all students study 18 credits over a two-year period. Each credit of 27 hours lasts for 11 weeks on two lessons a week. Central to community studies is an integrated humanities programme for all. Five credits lead to GCSE Integrated Humanities: three are compulsory (beliefs, people and work, and persecution and prejudice) and the remaining two are selected from a scheme of nine. Students may use their remaining 13 credits to build programmes in a number of ways. They may select freely from the scheme (see Figure 2.3) and submit their best five credits for GCSE Mode III Community Studies. They may use some to do more credits from the integrated humanities programme and choose their best five for GCSE. Some may aim at one or two of a number of mode I GCSE examinations:

● Catering

- Geography
- History
- Home Economics: Food and Nutrition
- Home Economics: Textiles
- Office Studies and Information Processing
- Religious Studies
- Mode III Services to People.

These subject-based examination targets predetermine to a much greater extent the student route through the modular scheme. Sport and recreation has now been incorporated into the modular offer in community studies, and the possibility of GCSE accreditation is being explored. This move has been accompanied by a curricular shift away from compulsory games for all. Rather, all students now take two units of health and fitness, where they learn about diet, exercise and body maintenance. This has proved highly popular and motivating – and modules of recreational activity are available for those who want to do more. Examples of credit choices in community studies leading to different examination outcomes are, for three students following the scheme in Figure 2.3, as follows.

1. (a) Five credits for GCSE Integrated Humanities:
        Beliefs
        Persecution and prejudice
        People and work
        Law and order
        Inequality
    (b) Five credits for GCSE Community Studies (History):
        The world turned upside down
        A study of tyranny
        The European Community I
        War and peace
        People and power
        Plus two credits in health and fitness and six other credits not submitted for GCSE.
2. (a) Five credits for GCSE Integrated Humanities:
        Beliefs
        Persecution and prejudice
        People and work
        The family
        The community
    (b) Five credits for GCSE Catering:

Starting work in a large kitchen
Running a restaurant
Food and beverage service
Further food services
Practical restaurant work
(c) Five credits for GCSE Community Studies:
America in the modern world
From the cradle to the grave
Teenagers
Child development
Care of the handicapped
Plus two credits of health and fitness and one other credit not
submitted for GCSE.
3. (a) Five credits for GCSE Integrated Humanities:
Beliefs
Persecution and prejudice
People and work
The community
Consumer affairs
(b) Five credits for GCSE Business Studies in the TVEI scheme:
Word processing
How business works
Business and personal finance
Information processing
Business enterprise
(c) GCSE French taken as a two-year course instead of the six credits
available in CB (see Figure 2.3).
Plus two credits of health and fitness.

In all of the mode III schemes and in Mode I Integrated Humanities
assessment is by course-work or a combination of course-work and end-of-
credit tests. The predetermined or constrained route to end-examined mode
I GCSE is likely to recede as more modular schemes are designed and
approved. Another significant feature is that some textiles credits are
common to the science and technology and community areas. This disen-
gagement of credits from subjects anticipates the construction of student
programmes across areas of experience, and also represents the first steps in
teachers using their specialisms in different curriculum areas. We are here
confronting a problem endemic in the training of teachers – that they are
rooted in a small number of 'subjects' that are no longer discrete and
autonomous in the secondary curriculum.

CHANGING TEACHER TASKS AND ROLES

The shift from many subject departments to few areas of experience has had far reaching consequences for teachers at Peers School. Two are as follows:

1. Teachers had to adjust to working under the guidance of a co-ordinator who was not necessarily a specialist in the teacher's own subject as previously conceived.
2. They were encouraged to regard themselves as participants in a wide collaborative venture and to identify and to commence the tasks associated with the introduction of a modular system.

The credit-based system has created new tasks, as any new system does. It also needs new skills. In a credit-based curriculum structure, there may be no clear role for a head of, say, chemistry, but there still needs to be someone responsible for the chemistry input to the whole science and technology curriculum.

The new tasks are of two kinds: curriculum development and the administration of the modular scheme.

1. The curriculum development work consists of writing mode III syllabuses and designing their constituent credits. A diagram outlining this process is shown in Figure 2.4.
2. The modular system has thrown up new administrative tasks. In each year group and area teachers have been designated who are responsible for assigning students to groups on the basis of their choice of credit. With the assistance of the computer they collect and distribute all the data pertaining to credit choice, completion and summative assessment. The use of GCSE funding to employ computer ancillaries to do some of the routine clerical work associated with keying in grades and compiling the lists following the allocation of students to credits is intended to alleviate the teacher's administrative load.

In addition there are advisers. An adviser is responsible for overseeing the progress of students of a tutor group in the adviser's curriculum area. Students meet their advisers at the end of each credit. The subject adviser's task is threefold:

1. to provide additional explication of forthcoming credits;
2. to monitor the student pathway through the scheme and to check that credit choice matches the agreed examination targets; and
3. to supervise formative assessments and to communicate with the teachers of each successive credit.

Assessment	Pedagogy	Curriculum
1. Statement of assessment objectives with relative weightings.*	1. Development of teaching syllabus in which activities, materials and time are used to provide coverage of curriculum aims and assessment objectives:	1. Statement of aims and intended outcomes of credit.
2. Statement of modes of assessment and their relationship to assessment objectives.*		2. Credit content defined as knowledge, skills, processes.
3. Design of assessment components to include any of the following:	(a) Design of tasks and activities to facilitate learning and assessment opportunity.	3. Simplified credit description for inclusion in booklet for parents and students.
(a) Tests at one or more levels.	(b) Allocation of student time to learning and assessment; division of teacher time between teaching and assessing.‡	
(b) Bank of test items.†		
(c) Design projects.	(c) Selection of learning resources.	
(d) Worksheets testing sectional work of credits.	2. Statement of targets for student. Targets are aims and assessment objectives as mediated to students.	
(e) Interpretation of general profile of practical attainment in terms of the specific credit. Precise statements of performance required for each level of practical attainment, expressed as a profile sentence.†		
4. Compilation of bank of statements for reporting student achievement.†		
5. Design of forms for reporting student evaluation of learning in credit.		

* Linked to the parent GCSE syllabus.
† In early stages of development or the focus of in-service training.
‡ A desirable future development would be that credits contain a grid similar to the grid showing the relationship of assessment objectives to assessment components, showing the maximum time allocation to assessment.

Figure 2.4   An illustration of credit design as it operates in Peers Science and Technology GCSE Mode III: how to construct a credit

All these and other tasks have meant changes in job specifications for many staff. An analysis of the teaching staff in 1982 and in 1986 reveals that 41 teachers have remained in the school over that period. Twenty-four of these are now doing a job substantially different from the one they did in 1982. Oxfordshire's generous secondment programme has given 29 of the 41 the opportunity to spend at least a term on in-service training. It is only through this kind of 'time out' that teachers can reflect upon their classroom practice, adapt to changed tasks and do the developmental work connected with mode III submissions, credit writing, community projects and information management.

The implementation of the credit-based approach strengthens the craft skills of teachers and improves their confidence in addressing numerous aspects of educational practice. Where curriculum development is a matter of designing or revising a 25-hour unit of work it becomes a manageable affair and is likely to happen. Teachers have 'adopted' credits, often corresponding to their own specialist interests – because they teach and reteach them a number of times in a two-yearly cycle they are continually refining their design and delivery and producing detailed teaching syllabuses. The pressure on teachers to teach and to assess a credit in 25 hours has highlighted pedagogical issues. In science and technology, for example, activities must be carefully selected to allow students to demonstrate the practical skills that comprise 40 per cent of the assessment in each credit and that are recorded by means of a detailed criterion referenced profile for each student. Many visitors to the school ask if the modular approach, which is largely a structural change, has had an impact on the kinds of learning taking place. The answer is that structure does impinge on process, for many teachers have long recognized the need to revise educational objectives and to employ more effective learning strategies – what they have lacked until now was a manageable base for experimentation and innovation. In community studies, for example, much time and energy has been devoted to the development of learning materials: simulations, games, resource booklets and the use of computer software to make the compulsory integrated humanities programme a worthwhile and stimulating core experience.

The Teachers' Dispute over Pay and Conditions of Service

The modular schemes were introduced in September 1984 and early in the spring term of 1985 the majority of teachers at Peers Schools began 'prepare, mark, teach' action, withdrawing their support from all curriculum development except that associated with the TVEI. Work on the OCEA was postponed. The modular schemes were fully operational in an organizational sense, and to revert to the previous system was no longer possible. Teachers found themselves, therefore, working to new mode III syllabuses where the module content was only sketched in and had to be developed and taught simultaneously. Under these circumstances curriculum development and lesson preparation were one and the same. More than one teacher would argue that the quality of 'acts of learning' actually improved during that phase of the industrial dispute.

STUDENT GUIDANCE AND COUNSELLING

Under the previous system, the student was counselled at the end of the upper fourth year and chose six subjects, in addition to the core subjects, that he or she would follow as options. If a student was allocated to a non-examination subject or group within a subject, then the subsequent two-year course held no prospect of a rewarding outcome and motivation suffered. The system found it difficult to take account of changing aspirations or interests, or of mistakes – both students and teachers were locked into a two-year relationship, frequently unproductive and inappropriate.

In the present arrangements, with a credit-based system, students do not have to opt for a small number of subjects to the exclusion of others and commit themselves for the next two years. They are, however, guaranteed a balanced curriculum in which their time is spent in an equitable way in the various curriculum areas, regardless of their level of attainment, their gender, or their age (see above).

As in an option system, the counselling a student receives is critical, but unlike such a system, counselling is not focused intensively in the second part of the upper fourth year but has to be continuously available.

The first stage takes place during their upper fourth year (13–14 years). This is target-setting – establishing what examination outcomes the student is aiming for. This process takes account of the view of each curriculum area as to the potential and present level of attainment of each student. High-attaining students across the board, for example, would be encouraged to aim for double GCSE certification in Science and Technology and not to give up a modern language. The tutor and the student work together to set the targets in the light of these assessments, and they also have available advisers from each of the curriculum areas, as explained above. Any one tutor group, therefore, has a small team of five advisers, including the tutor.

Target-setting will include decisions such as the following:

1. Will the student be aiming for GCSE in Science and Technology (seven

best credits out of the 15 to be taken) or for double certification in Physical Science and Technology (seven credits) and Biological Science and Technology (seven credits)?

2. In community studies, where each student takes 18 credits and has to submit five from a specified range for Integrated Humanities GCSE, will the remaining credits be used for a mixed programme, of which the best five will be submitted for GCSE Community Studies, or will they be put together in more constrained ways to produce one or two subject-based outcomes? If the student aims for one of these subjects, it is still possible to follow a varied programme and submit the remaining credits accumulated for Community Studies GCSE.

3. Given that all students will study English in each year, will the student be aiming for GCSE English Literature as well as GCSE English?

4. Does the student want to be part of the TVEI cohort? If so, is his or her vocational preference – for science and technology – Business Studies or Services to People? (See below for more about TVEI.)

The target-setting involves a discussion between student and tutor in the light of information from the curriculum areas. A card setting out proposed targets is signed by parents and represents a negotiable contract. If, subsequently, interests or likely outcomes change, the card is amended during the lower fifth and upper fifth years.

The next stage is to choose the first units to be studied, with a provisional choice for the second set of units. A booklet with descriptions of each credit helps the choice, and the curriculum advisers are available for consultations if difficulties arise in matching target outcome to credit choice. Curriculum areas are currently placing 95 per cent of students in the unit of their first choice. If their first choice is oversubscribed it is usually available later, and the disappointed student has priority then. Choices are therefore made every 22 weeks, for the next two units. Flexibility is thus built in, for student and teacher alike. The offer can vary to meet student demand or to respond to changes in staffing: if a teacher leaves and one with different skills is appointed, the offer of credits can be modified very quickly, while maintaining the overall balance of disposal of time.

Some examples of the kinds of counselling that happen during the lower fifth and upper fifth years are as follows:

1. A student aiming for double certification in science and technology has to submit 14 out of 15 credits taken. Though some of the credits on offer are not validated for GCSE, they still have 65 different credits from which to select their 14 for GCSE. If students have science A-levels in mind their choice may be more carefully directed to credits containing foundation A-level content.

2. Students identified as members of the cohort supported by the NLI will not know that they have been so identified. (NLI – the New Learning Initiative – is Oxfordshire's LAPP project to enrich the curriculum of the lower 40 per cent of the attainment range.) But some credits have been designed with the needs of the NLI cohort in mind and incorporate elements of residential or community experience essential to the NLI programme. These students will be encouraged, as part of the counselling they receive, to select these units – though they are available to all and not one is designated an NLI unit. Indeed, they are among the most popular. One, community projects, comprises a weekly placement, undertaken within the school timetable, in a setting such as an old people's home, nursery or animal sanctuary supported by a classroom session studying community provision and the context of the placement.

3. Students who are aiming at subject-based examination outcomes as part of their community studies curriculum need to be counselled to ensure that they select the appropriate credits. In addition to integrated humanities, it is possible to take two subject-based GCSEs in this area, provided the right credits are accumulated. It is shown above how various outcomes can be achieved from the community studies curriculum.

4. Students who have joined the TVEI cohort have to be counselled to select the units that are designated as TVEI credits. (TVEI is oversubscribed at Peers and membership of the cohort is random after the need to have a group balanced in terms of gender, ethnic background and attainment level has been met.)

The length of each credit has recently been extended from ten weeks to eleven without adding to the teaching content. This increases classroom time by about 2.5 hours. The extra time has partly been facilitated by the later date of GCSE examination compared with CSE. The time is to allow for teacher assessment and student self-evaluation of the learning achieved in that credit, and for this to be discussed. It allows space, too, for discussion of the future choice of credit, and for teacher and students to visit the room where work and records of achievement are stored in individual student files. This room is attractive and comfortable with a carpet and a number of easy chairs. The files are brightly-coloured large ring-binders stored in tiers by tutor group on circular carousels. Students' files are labelled with their names and are their property to take away when they leave the school. In the files the work accumulates that will be moderated for GCSE. Also in the files is material relating to the students' personal records of achievement under the OCEA scheme. The outcome of each credit, in the form of a grade, is stored in the microcomputer system. A section of the OCEA certificate is given to the reporting of curriculum attainment. Students will receive a summary statement of each credit studied and eventually a more detailed profile of performance. Teachers are exploring the extent to which performance criteria can be predetermined and stored in statement banks on the microcomputer for use in the explicit recording of curriculum attainment.

ASSESSMENT

Assessment in modular schemes is a microcosm of GCSE, accentuating its positive and negative features. In each modular scheme, the mode of assessment varies to reflect the assessment objectives. In community studies the scheme of assessment varies from credit to credit, while in science and technology a pattern common to all credits has been established. In all cases, however, assessment is carried out within the time span of the credit. In this respect, the credits are free-standing, in contrast to the practice in some modular schemes where unifying modules or final tests account for a proportion of the marks.

In science and technology the assessment scheme is:

either	40 per cent end of unit test at two levels,
with	20 per cent assignment on sectional work of the credit or minor project;
or	60 per cent major technology project,
and	40 per cent assessment of practical competence based on the OCEA criteria.

The assessment of practical competence contributes to a profile for each student, which builds up over the 15-credit programme. Assessment opportunities are provided for students to demonstrate competence in each skill or process at four levels. Thus, within days of the commencement of GCSE, teachers at Peers were grappling with a major unresolved element of the new examination system. Whereas SEC was maintaining a cautious silence on grade criteria, teachers were battling on with performance criteria, anxious not to lose the ground won through painstaking work on the OCEA and graded objectives that was intended to make assessment a constructive, formative process for students. Teachers held internal moderation meetings to discuss how the criteria of practical performance applied to the learning in each particular credit and to achieve some consistency of interpretation. It is the authors' contention that this attempt by teachers to preserve and advance the spirit of assessment against explicit and meaningful criteria and to report progress in statements of positive achievement is a remarkable testimony to their professional integrity. It is all the more remarkable in the light of the evasiveness and pessimism on the subject at a national level.

A further feature of assessment at Peers, which owes its inception to the OCEA, is the emphasis on the students' own evaluation of their work. They are given the opportunity to comment on their own learning and experience in a credit, and to identify areas for their future development. These comments can be fed into the personal statement in their OCEA record of achievement. Students are also invited to select their best credits for certification alleviating the continuous pressure associated with some forms of continuous assessment. There is still much need for streamlining of the assessment. It seems to be the case that, in their desire to establish the rigour and validity of school-based assessment, teachers are paying excessive attention to assessing students and to ensuring that sufficient evidence of the right quality is available for the award of grades.

The difficulties of operating credit-based schemes arise from the fact that mode III regulations pre-date the large-scale development of modular schemes. For example, the mode III requirement that no test paper should be repeated within a two-year period is clearly obstructive to modular arrangements where a particular credit may be taught several times over that period in a single school. The Southern Examining Group is showing continuing willingness to help resolve incompatibilities of this kind.

ACCOUNTABILITY AND EVALUATION

In the credit-based system, the curriculum is described and documented making the secondary experience explicable to governors, management, parents, students and teachers. Parents are happy that feedback is available on request at the end of each credit and that the routeway through a course is subject to discussion and negotiation, no longer a once-and-for-all decision to the upper fourth as it was under options.

End-of-credit assessment and grading means that students are more directly accountable to teachers for their performance. At the same time, the fact that students can submit their best credits for final certification makes it possible for remediation and improvements to be acknowledged in the final grade.

It is true that some teachers in modular curriculum areas regret the loss of prolonged contact with students. Many others admit that this continuity was not always mutually fulfilling and maintain that the boost to student motivation as a result of short-term objectives is the outstanding advantage of the modular approach. The latter view is supported by such evidence as there is on completion of the first modular CSEs in 1986. The evidence is as follows:

1. The number of students leaving school with no examination certificate was halved as compared with the previous year.
2. Many more students obtained passes in humanities and in science and technology than was the case when those areas were not subject to modular arrangements. There was a large increase in numbers of students gaining grades 2 and 3 and a correspondingly large reduction in numbers gaining grades 5 and U.
3. Referral of students from the classroom for unacceptable behaviour has been substantially reduced in credit-based areas.
4. The creative arts area has opted for credit-based arrangements from 1986 so that students can continue to work in more than one medium.
5. The effects of sex stereotyping on course selection are severe in option systems. Under the system in operation at Peers every girl studies at least two technology credits. Boys have taken up textiles credits in large numbers – few would have been persuaded to select two-year needlecraft courses under the option system.

THE FUTURE: CREDIT BANKING

GCSE is likely to remain a central form of certification for some years. Modular approaches are gaining widespread recognition and will continue to do so provided that they colonize the central forms of accreditation, just as they must espouse the whole upper school population and the full spectrum of educational experience. If they are marginalized to cater for the low attainer, or to provide only the pre-vocational or the experimental, their impact on the stagnation in the curriculum will be weakened. For this reason the credit-based schemes at Peers School are certificated through GCSE and the discriminatory use of pre-vocational packaged courses has been avoided.

The next step is the development of unit accreditation and in 1986 Oxfordshire approached the Southern Examining Group with a proposal that the latter should empower an LEA consortium, called the Oxfordshire Examination Syndicate, to administer a bank of GCSE credits. The syndicate negotiates with the examining group the combinations of five credits that constitute a coherent programme of study, and a GCSE title. Schools, colleges and agencies of continuing education deposit credits in and draw credits from the bank – they are able to expand their curriculum offer, as credits and schemes developed in one institution become available to all the others in the syndicate. For students, too, the advantages are impressive: they bank their credits, build programmes of study before and beyond the age of 16 and submit their credits in clusters of five for GCSE. There now exists the real prospect that certain credits will carry the imprimatur of GCSE and RSA or an A/S-level or A-level exemption. If this is realized, then the academic–vocational gap that has been threatening to widen and deepen in the 14–18 age range, leaving young people trapped on either side of it, may well be closed.

Credit banking is consonant also with the changing role of the Southern Examining Group, which is committed to working in partnership with its constituent LEAs to ensure that assessment is genuinely curriculum led and extends across the 14 to 18 age range.

The modular scheme at Peers as originally devised incorporated science and technology and community studies – about half the students' week. As the advantages of the modular arrangement became apparent, other curriculum areas began to rethink their offer. Creative arts decided to join the other two areas in a fully modular programme, increasing the modular portion of the students' timetable to about two thirds. The remaining areas, English, maths and languages, while not choosing to adopt a modular structure, have each in different ways sought to build in some of the beneficial features that accompany modularization, in particular greater explicitness about learning objectives, emphasis on achievement of short-term goals, and a space for the student viewpoint on learning. In languages, this is done by using OMLAC, the Oxfordshire Modern Languages Achievement Certificate. Mathematics uses the OCEA achievement framework combined with a 100 per cent course-work GCSE syllabus. In English, students are taught by one teacher in a stable 'base group', but are re-grouped, according to choice or teacher advice, for intermittent short courses to focus on specific skills, texts or projects.

The school is thus working towards a coherent approach to learning and achievement, through a curriculum that will remain a mixed economy. The logical next step will be a revaluation of the curriculum of the intake year, looking at ways of combining common experience for students with some modular choice in that year. The modular structure lends itself to a number of other developments that the school has not yet explored, but that are possibilities for the future. Among these are mixed-age grouping, more flexible use of teachers' time and supported self-study. The structure is no more than a structure – how it is realized can vary according to circumstance and need. The implementation of a modular curriculum at Peers School has taken a particular form and by no means the only one possible. The forms it can take in the future, at Peers and elsewhere, are open to exploration.

3

LOCAL AUTHORITY
INITIATIVES: LEICESTERSHIRE
Bob Willars

INTRODUCTION

The current development of modular schemes represents a major educational initiative. Modular courses of study are not in themselves a novel feature of secondary education, but rather it is their organization in programmes of study for certification purposes that constitutes a radical development. That such schemes are evolving so successfully, without the support of a national curriculum body and extensive resources, is unusual. However, the degree of interest is less surprising when examined in the light of current educational trends.

New areas of study are vying for space within the curriculum. Influential developments such as TVEI have adopted a matrix approach, and the introduction of GCSE has been an ideal opportunity for curriculum reform. It would seem that the high degree of teacher commitment represents a form of grass-roots appreciation of the value of modular approaches. The motivational effects of short-term goals and negotiated choice, together with the organizational flexibility that modules permit are just a few of the oft-quoted advantages – but it is perhaps the degree of teacher involvement that has been central to the successful introduction of accredited modular schemes within schools and colleges.

This has certainly been the case in Leicestershire, where a large number of teachers have been involved in the formation of a mode III GCSE scheme entitled the Leicestershire Modular Framework Syllabus (Midland Examining Group, 1986). The scheme has not only fired the imagination of teachers in Leicestershire, but it has also attracted considerable attention from outside the county resulting in the inclusion of schools from four other authorities in the initial pilot arrangements with the Midland Examining Group (MEG).

What has particularly interested other education authorities about the Leicestershire framework is the combination of features that distinguish it from most, if not all, other modular syllabuses written for GCSE accreditation – fundamental principles that the scheme's originators felt had to be maintained. These include the equal weighting of all modules; the problem-solving approach and emphasis on process skills; the continuity resulting from common assessment objectives within each module; and the possibility within the scheme of cross-curriculum programmes of non-related modules, leading to a General Studies GCSE certificate. This 'pick-and-mix' approach, as it has been dubbed, has been fought for in terms of the value of effective student choice and the balance it can bring to an individual student's personal curriculum. In fact, it is probably this aspect of the scheme, together with the degree of LEA co-ordination that has been made available, that are the key distinctions between this and all other modular syllabuses to date.

THE EVOLUTION OF THE FRAMEWORK
Initial Developments

Early in 1984 a framework proposal was prepared by the Leicestershire TVEI Co-ordinator, and presented at a meeting of the authority's TVEI school co-ordinators. A significant decision was made by this group – that any such scheme should be more widely available to avoid the possible divisive effects of modular developments being restricted to TVEI students.

As a result, a joint inquiry was conducted by the authority's assessment and TVEI co-ordinators, and this revealed a high level of interest across its schools and colleges in various forms of modular curriculum provision. This led the authority's 14–19 Curriculum Group to commission a report (Burke and D'Hooghe, 1985) on the feasibility of an authority framework for modular curriculum developments. This was not intended to restrict any other developments, but to provide the assistance of the authority in seeking accreditation and a mechanism for sharing the effort of curriculum development.

The task of developing what they described as 'a mode I framework into which mode III modules could fit' became the work of a Modular Curriculum Working Group – an invited body consisting of more than twenty senior members of staff (mainly deputy heads) from the authority's secondary schools and further education colleges. In electing to develop a framework, i.e. a kind of 'template' to which all modules should conform, the scheme's originators probably made a very sound decision: it is essentially the conformity of all modules, regardless of their subject bias, to the framework that makes possible their comparability, and provides the basis for building up a certificated programme of study from such diverse modules as *business case study*, *investigating polymers* and *motor vehicle servicing*.

Fundamental Principles

At an early stage in the scheme's development there was a conscious decision to avoid the fragmentary approach of modularizing existing subject content. There now exist examples of modular syllabuses that appear to have been designed on the chopping-board – traditional two-year courses that have been split up into smaller units of study, some resulting in a predominantly linear progression through the subject, with little choice for the student. By contrast, the Curriculum Studies Working Group attempted to facilitate cross-curricular links and the emergence of new curriculum units by avoiding traditional preconceptions of subject titles. It was considered important that the value of each individual module should be recognized and the degree of choice that students have in selecting their personalized routes through the pool of available modules should be central to the development.

To facilitate maximum flexibility it was decided that all modules should require a broadly similar length of study time (or be multiples of this unit), and that each module should be assessed internally and separately from any other module – i.e. there should be no examination at the end of the 'course of study'. However, when it came to defining the optimum length for a module it was rather like answering the question, 'How long is a piece of string?' Comparable schemes seemed to vary from less than 10 to more than 40 hours per module. Just how long should a short course last?

In the end the working group recommended a 20-hour minimum study time for all modules. This was argued on the basis that any less would create a situation in which assessment would interfere with learning, while at above 30 hours modules would lose the motivation effect of short-term goals. In turn this led to the decision that five modules should constitute a programme for GCSE qualification.

It was also recognized that the length of study time was not something that ought to be specified too precisely. Accreditation should be determined primarily by the achievement of outcomes, and the attainment of these outcomes might not take the same period of study for a class of fourth-year students, compared with an adult evening class, or a one-year sixth-form group – the implications being that different organizational constraints and teaching/learning approaches might require a degree of flexibility in the total study-time provision.

Any form of assessment based on specific descriptions of attainment has the advantage of being less age-related than comparable norm-referenced schemes. Nevertheless, there was a view expressed within the working group that the framework should take account of the increasing maturity of students as they progressed to their later modules, and there was some concern that assessment of a student's first module might be completed within the first term of the fourth year. One possibility was to weight modules taken towards the end of the 'course of study' more heavily than earlier modules, but this was eventually rejected on the grounds that it would be a major constraint on the flexibility of the framework. Whether maturation was a significant issue or not, differential weighting was not considered to be the solution to the problem.

The question of whether any account should be taken of age at the point of assessment was further complicated by an emerging vision of students accumulating modular credits over a number of years, even after leaving full-time education. As already stated, the differential weighting of modules was rejected, and the eventual means of taking account of possible maturation effects did not emerge until the issue of aggregation was tackled – but this was after the working group had completed the framework and disbanded.

There were other issues that could not be resolved until later in the development process. Moderation procedures were a matter of speculation at this stage, since the newly-formed examining groups were still finding their modular feet and had as yet published no guidelines. It was equally uncertain what rules of combination might be required to limit the overlap of subject content between modules, or what certification titles might be awarded to a student's programme of five modules. The GCSE was still evolving at this time (i.e. the school year 1984–5), so questions like these had to be answered after the framework had been written and submitted to the examining group.

The Key Features of the Framework

Regardless of these obstacles, the working group eventually succeeded in producing a unique framework for GCSE submission – representing the collective attitudes and experience of teachers across the Leicestershire Education Authority. In addition to encompassing the resolutions and recommendations outlined so far, the framework included two key elements. The first of these was a set of assessment objectives common to all modules, and the other was a carefully constructed grid describing specific levels of achievement for each of these assessment objectives (see Figure 3.1.). It is principally through the application of these objectives and attainment descriptors across all modules that this extensive scheme was able to maintain its uniformity and cohesion.

A REVIEW OF THE
LEICESTERSHIRE MODULAR FRAMEWORK
Approaches to Learning

The framework includes in its introduction a description of the approaches to learning it aims to facilitate. This section also points out the cross-curricular possibilities offered by such a framework, designed to act as a 'template' for individual modules:

> The Modular Studies syllabus seeks to facilitate an approach to learning which is experiential, practical, and related to life in the community and wider world. The syllabus is also based on the premise that schools will wish to allow students considerable flexibility to negotiate with teachers and tutors the modules they study and how they study them.
>
> It is envisaged that students will be engaged in a variety of enquiries, tasks and applications which take them across traditional subject boundaries and which involve a variety of different learning pathways. It is further envisaged that students will pursue a variety of approaches to learning in topics drawn from within traditional subject boundaries. Accordingly, the syllabus has been devised in order to provide a vehicle for the assessment of courses which have such characteristics.
>
> An important feature of the syllabus is that it will facilitate curriculum developments which have a cross-curricular emphasis. Such developments include courses that have arisen out of T.V.E.I.
>
> In order to incorporate the needs of courses which emphasise cross-curricular and experiential approaches to learning, the syllabus offers a general framework which is designed to act as a template for the individual modules. (Midland Examining Group, 1986)

The success or otherwise of any scheme in facilitating active, experiential learning cannot be guaranteed simply because such approaches have been written into the syllabus. In this case responsibility has passed in turn from the originators of the framework to the writers of the individual modules, and on to the classroom practitioner. These approaches are potentially both challenging and exciting. It is to be hoped that teachers (and students) will be able to meet the challenge through the ways in which the syllabus is interpreted.

Assessment objectives	Attainment descriptors			
	Mark range			
	1 *2* *3*	*4* *5*	*6* *7*	*8*
A: *Recognition*	Can decide on a way to proceed	Can identify a number of alternative ways of proceeding	Can choose and develop an overall plan	Can develop an effective plan working through a range of alternatives anticipating outcomes
B: *Location*	Can identify appropriate information	Can select appropriate information, concepts, processes or skills	Can compare different concepts, processes and skills	Can gather and synthesize a selection of concepts, processes and skills
C: *Application*	Can use straight-forward information	Can apply appropriate information, concepts, processes or skills	Can apply in a co-ordinated way a range concepts, processes and skills	Can synthesize a range of concepts, processes and skills with purpose and precision
D: *Communication*	Can produce a recognizable outcome	Can demonstrate purpose in the outcome	Can communicate the outcome of learning	Can communicate the structure, purpose and outcome of learning
E: *Evaluation*	Can describe the task and the way it was *done*	Can describe the task and the way it was *done*; and can draw conclusions from content	Can identify the strengths and weaknesses of the methods used in the task and draw conclusions from content	Can evaluate alternative methodologies applicable to the task and draw inferences from content

Figure 3.1   Grid describing levels of attainment appropriate to each skill area

Aims

The following aims are included in the framework, as being applicable to all individual modules and groups of modules:

> To enable a course of study to be constructed which matches the individual needs, interests and most effective learning processes of students through self-contained units.
>
> To promote the cognitive, manipulative and affective growth of students through a wide range of learning experiences.
>
> To provide the opportunity for students to participate in the construction of their own learning pathways and to reflect on their learning needs.
>
> To enable students to acquire a broad range of skills as a basis for further study and to enhance adaptability in a changing society. (Midland Examining Group, 1986)

Clearly the student's needs are seen as paramount and students are recognized as having an important part to play in choosing and evaluting their own modular pathways.

In addition to these common aims each individual module has its own set of aims related to the field of study and the process skills with which it deals. An example of these has been included below, and is taken from the section entitled 'General Aims, Content and Nature of the Module' for the module, *Environmental Pollution*:

> This module aims to encourage students to develop a knowledge and understanding of the relationships between people and their environment, and the ways in which these relationships can be affected by human activities. It also aims to foster an awareness of the effects of pollution on the quality of life and to encourage a personal concern for the quality of local and distant environments and how these can be improved or conserved for future use.

Assessment Objectives

The framework identifies five skill areas to be assessed in all modules. Equal weighting is given in every module to each of these abilities, thus ensuring a common assessment scheme for any programme of modules.

Students should demonstrate the ability to 'recognise a problem and respond to it; . . . locate or recall appropriate information, concepts, processes and skills; . . . apply appropriate information, concepts, processes and skills; . . . communicate the outcome of their learning; . . . evaluate and reflect upon their learning'.

These objectives are each elaborated as a set of 'can do' statements written in terms relating to the specific context of a particular module. The example chosen is taken from the module, *The British Economy*:

A recognise a problem and respond to it;
- can recognise the economic aspects within a problem, issue or topic of study
- can specify appropriate objectives and boundaries in planning an economic inquiry
- can conduct a systematic investigation of specific features of the British economy

B locate or recall appropriate information, concepts, processes and skills;
- can identify, select and organise material from reference sources relevant to the study of economic activity
- can identify and interpret economic data located in a variety of original forms e.g. statistical, graphical or literary forms
- can recall relevant factual information and economic concepts to describe and explain characteristic features of the British economy

C apply appropriate information, concepts, processes and skills;
- can use basic economic terminology to describe and analyse economic activity in Britain e.g. primary industry, private sector, capital intensive
- can employ simple quantitative techniques as an aid to describing and analysing economic activity in Britain e.g. measuring the rate of inflation or growth, comparing regional unemployment statistics
- can apply economic concepts in describing and analysing economic activity in Britain e.g. G.N.P., demand elasticity, scale economies, cyclical unemployment

D communicate the outcome of their learning;
- can keep accurate and systematic records of information collected and assignments undertaken
- can communicate economic information and ideas in a variety of appropriate forms e.g. oral, literary, statistical, graphical
- can present explanations of issues relating to the British economy
- can maintain and justify a point of view in a reasoned argument

E evaluate and reflect upon their learning;
- can critically evaluate assignments undertaken during study of the module
- can appreciate the interrelated nature of economic topics encountered
- can predict the likely effects of events and policy decisions on economic activity in Britain

Scheme of Assessment

The framework syllabus does not specify the mode or modes of assessment to be used within the scheme – it only requires that they are described for each module, together with the relative weighting to be given to each mode of assessment for each of the five assessment objectives. This allows individual modules to use those methods that are most appropriate for measuring their specific learning objectives. Consequently, the modes of assessment vary considerably from one module to another. All modules encompass an element of course-work assessment, as required by the general criteria for GCSE. Additionally, modules might include practical or written assignments, oral assessment, a planning examination or a written, end-of-module examination. For a summary and definition of the modes of assessment used within the scheme, see Figure 3.2.

In selecting the forms of assessment, a number of principles were considered. One of these was whether they were appropriate in terms of the skills being assessed – for instance, whether it was more important to assess the end product of the work or the processes that went into its production. Another consideration had to be their ease of application, bearing in mind the potential conflict between assessment and learning within the limited time scale of a 20–30-hour module.

It should be noted that the variance in mode of assessment from one module to another did create a problem for the originators of the scheme. When it was submitted to the examining group for GCSE approval, it was debated whether modules assessed in such different ways could be considered as comparable. However, it was accepted that a sufficient degree of comparability was established by the sharing of a common set of assessment objectives across all modules. It was the levels of attainment demonstrated in these skills and processes that should constitute the common thread for assessment purposes, rather than the imposition of any arbitrary standardization of modes of assessment.

The Grid of Attainment Descriptors

Having transferred from an examination system based on norm-referenced assessment to the criterion referenced GCSE examination, there is now a requirement for all syllabuses to contain a clear statement of the intended outcomes at each level of performance. In the case of the Leicestershire modular framework this is represented in the form of a grid, giving four levels of attainment descriptors for each of the five assessment objectives – corresponding to an eight-point scale. The grid was the product of extensive debate held in the light of comparable assessment criteria from other schemes. It is hoped that it represents a clear and meaningful description of outcomes, a tool through which differentiation may be achieved and the comparability of modular assessments may be maintained (see Figure 3.1).

THE SEARCH FOR GCSE APPROVAL

The scheme was finally submitted to MEG in December 1985, as a framework syllabus together with 17 sample modules (and including a list of

Component term	Definition
Written examination	Written test taken under examination conditions at the end of the module
Practical examination	Test of practical skills taken under examination conditions at the end of the module
Planning examination	Test of design and planning skills normally taken during the module
Course-work tests	Short tests which are taken under examination conditions at specified times during the module
Practical assignments	Tests of practical skills taken under examination conditions during the course
Field work	Work which students do as a result of assignments or projects out of the classroom, 'in the field'
Oral examination	Test of oral skills under examination conditions, normally at the end of the module
Oral assessment	Assessment of oral skills as demonstrated during the module
Written assignment/project	Work undertaken during the course in response to specific instructions from the teacher
Course-work folio	A collection of pieces of course-work, the number and nature of which are specified in the assessment objectives of the module
Practical course-work	Assessment of practical skills within course-work or projects, but not under controlled conditions
Project	Assessment of an extensive task with a specific focus. Not a collection of written or practical assignments
Case-study report	Similar in nature to a project, but specifically related to a case-study investigation

Figure 3.2   Modes of assessment with their descriptions

more than 100 other titles under development). MEG had indicated their willingness to receive TVEI schemes for certification and, although the framework has not been developed specifically for TVEI purposes, there was a great deal of commitment to the scheme from the TVEI pilot programme in Leicestershire. In fact, the first batch of modules were written with guidance from the county's TVEI advisory team. The framework was, therefore, submitted to MEG under two headings – first, as a TVEI scheme for joint CSE/O-level certification for 1987, and second, as a Leicestershire mode III GCSE scheme for first certification in 1988. In both cases care had been taken to ensure that the syllabus conformed to the examining group's guidelines on mode II and III preparation (MEG, 1985b), and their working paper on the modular curriculum (MEG, 1985a), as well as the GCSE general criteria established by SEC.

The Appointment of a Modular Curriculum Co-ordinator

At the same time as the scheme was submitted, Leicestershire seconded a team of five experienced teachers to act as its GCSE Support Group to advise the authority's schools and colleges on the management, assessment and teaching issues that accompanied the introduction of GCSE examinations. Since one of the team's first tasks was to support the preparation of mode III syllabuses, it was decided that one member of the team should become the modular curriculum co-ordinator. At the time this appeared to be the only instance of an education authority employing a full-time modular curriculum co-ordinator. It was to have a valuable enabling effect for the continued development of the scheme, making it possible to stimulate and co-ordinate the involvement of a large number of module writers and potential users, even during the depths of the 1985–6 teachers' dispute.

The role of modular co-ordination operated at two levels. On the one hand there was the task of attempting to ensure that the scheme eventually met with MEG approval, preferably without the need to compromise any of its major principles. On the other it entailed continuing support for the development of individual modules, encouraging a sharing of ideas whenever possible, as well as ensuring that all modules eventually conformed to the framework.

In many respects the two functions overlapped. A clear instance of school/college representatives being involved in the development of policy was the Modular Curriculum Convention held at the authority's INSET centre in February 1986. This event was planned to include group discussions on the aggregation of module assessments, certificate titles and moderation procedures – each of them contentious or unresolved issues. In each case proposals had to be made in the absence of specific guidelines by the examining group, and therefore the outcome of these discussions at the convention were not only incorporated into the proposals for the scheme but were also sent as a set of general recommendations (GCSE Support Group, 1986) to the MEG Examinations Committee for their consideration.

Negotiations with the Examining Group

Throughout the academic year 1985–6 examining groups were receiving proposed mode III GCSE syllabuses, as well as having to produce their own mode I schemes in all subjects for which a need existed. It is hardly surprising that they were not quick in responding to new initiatives – particularly when these challenged some of the preconceptions of those involved in the validation of examination syllabuses. MEG had to establish a Modular Working Party with responsibility for the formulation of policy on modular issues, and a Multi-disciplinary Sub-Committee, whose duty it was to receive modular and other cross-curricular or innovatory GCSE sylla-buses, with a view to recommending their approval to the group's Examina-tions Committee.

When the Leicestershire scheme eventually came before the Multi-disciplinary Sub-Committee it posed a few problems. In the first place it was not neatly packaged under subject headings – it was a cross-curricular scheme designed to allow any potential combination of modules towards a GCSE qualification. Second, each module had its own unique scheme of assessment. Finally, the modules had been described predominantly in terms of processes and skills. Their content was defined as a set of organizing ideas and contexts for the development of those processes and skills. There was little to be found by way of traditional subject content.

Both parties to the validation process were engaged in a new learning situation, and any initial resistance was soon overcome as the interests of each became more clearly evident to the other. Those representing the scheme learned to value the principles of reliability, validity and compara-bility, while the board respresentatives came to accept that cross-curriculum learning could play a valuable role in balancing the curriculum for each individual student, and that groups of modules could show an alternative form of coherence – not in terms of subject content, but via common assessment objectives and a consistent approach to learning.

Aggregation through Profiling

One of the most significant developments to emerge from the approval meetings at the board was a solution to the problem of aggregating the marks awarded for each module towards an overall grade. It was proposed that the common assessment objectives provided the means by which an overview could be taken of the student's development across the five modules. The set of marks awarded for each assessment objective would provide a profile of the student's performance on that particular skill, and it was accepted that the aggregation process should involve identifying the highest level of achievement in each of the skill areas, within agreed rules of consistency. This proposal overcame the concerns of those who believed that any form of aggregation by averaging would tend to prevent the attainment of the highest grades, by forcing all marks towards the mid range. In finding a solution to this problem the concerns expressed earlier over the maturation of students were also alleviated.

Pilot Project Arrangements

The Leicestershire modular framework syllabus was eventually approved in June 1986, with the proposal that it would become a MEG pilot project in the first instance. This was to allow assessment procedures to be evaluated and adjusted without compromising the interest of candidates, and permit a greater degree of interaction between the examining group and those involved in the scheme than would otherwise be possible. The pilot project commenced in September 1986, involving a total of 23 schools and 2 colleges of further education (20 from within Leicestershire and 5 from outside of the authority), a pool of 120 modules and several thousand students seeking GCSE certification for their modular studies in 1988.

SUPPORT AND CO-ORDINATION
Writing the Modules

The development of such an extensive pool of modules relied heavily upon the energy, co-operation and inspiration of many teachers. It also depended upon the continued support and co-ordination provided by the Leicestershire Education Authority. The 120 modules that formed the pilot project represented most areas of the secondary curriculum (mathematics and languages being notable exceptions). However, modules were not commissioned – they developed according to the interests and experience of their authors, and the needs of the schools these teachers represented. Co-ordination of these activities was, therefore, necessary to ensure that unnecessary duplication of ideas or overlap of modular content was avoided. It was also considered important that modules should be written in a way that permitted flexibility of use and differences in interpretation from one centre to another.

Many of the individual authors had little experience of syllabus preparation, and so the first line of support was in helping them to interpret their intended learning experiences in terms of the framework and the assessment requirements for GCSE. A series of booklets produced by the authority's TVEI advisory team on the theme *Designing the Modular Curriculum* (Turner, 1986), gave practical advice to teachers on the design and assessment requirements of modules. The first of these provided a step-by-step account of how to write a module, including such basic, but essential advice as 'keep it simple' and 'do not over-assess'.

Assessment by Levels of Outcome

Another area in which support was given was in the development of suitably differentiated course-work tasks, assignments and examination papers. It became apparent that the assessment of student outcomes using the grid of attainment descriptors would need some form of a 'levels marking' scheme. Each assignment or examination question required an analysis of expected outcomes in terms of the five assessment objectives, together with the levels on the grid to which they would be examinable, i.e. the marking of student work was tied directly to the eight-point scale of the grid.

The job of keeping the modular developments ticking over and of steering the scheme to the GCSE starting line for September 1986, was not made any easier by the period of industrial action and the reluctance of many teachers to engage in GCSE preparation. However, commitment to the concept of the modular framework was deep rooted, and modules continued to be developed for the pool.

Timetabling the Modules

At the same time, schools were having to make their choice of GCSE syllabuses, and for many there were additional decisions to make concerning the place of modules within their timetable structures. It soon became apparent that schools were adopting a variety of different approaches. The most common was to timetable modules in one or more option columns, either alongside or instead of more traditional two-year courses – providing a means of incorporating new bodies of knowledge and experiences into the curriculum without requiring the replacement of existing subjects. In many respects this is how TVEI programmes had been built into the timetable, and certainly the Leicestershire TVEI scheme had become firmly committed to the use of the modular framework.

Offering modules within option columns was seen by many to be a safe approach in the first instance, yet a minority of schools had already envisaged modules as an important element of their core curriculum. For some, modules were to replace an existing core experience, for example, science, while other schools saw in them a means of constructing a new core experience, such as expressive arts. A further alternative was to use modules to complement an integrated course, such as integrated humanities, as a set of enrichment options.

As well as offering motivational advantages and flexibility of use, modules promise to be a valuable facility for curriculum change. A number of different instances of such developmental applications became apparent during these conversations with the schools. Modules could form the basis of a continuity of curriculum experience across years 14–18, with students picking up modular credits throughout this period of their schooling. They might also provide a welcome bridge between the secondary and further education curricula. There was the proposal that modules might be time-tabled for vertical groups of students. With assessment being based on specific criteria, why should fourth-year and sixth-year students not take the same unit together? Perhaps most significantly, in terms of the nature of the framework syllabus, modules were viewed as a means of providing cross-curricular experiences that might blur the edges of traditional subject content.

CONCLUSION

With the formation of a Syllabus Sub-Committee the scheme became self-governing and established a structure through which communication with the examining group would continue during the pilot period.

The success of any innovatory scheme only emerges with time, and in this case will depend to a large extent on the degree to which the principles embodied in the framework are respected or ignored. Nevertheless, the Leicestershire modular framework represents an example of the coherence that may be achieved through the development of a framework syllabus, and points the way towards the need for unit accreditation and the certification of individual modules. It also demonstrates what can be achieved through local authority support and co-ordination, particularly when this is allied to a working partnership with an examining body.

REFERENCES

Burke, A.C. and D'Hooghe, D. (1985) *Modular Curriculum Development: a Possible Framework*, report of Leicestershire Education Authority, Leicester.

GCSE Support Group (1986) *GCSE Modular Curriculum Convention: A Report*, Leicestershire Education Authority, Leicester.

Midland Examining Group (1985a) *A Modular Curriculum: Guidelines for Development*, Working Paper No. 1, Nottingham.

Midland Examining Group (1985b) *Regulations Governing the Submission of Mode II and Mode III Syllabuses for GCSE Certification*, Nottingham.

Midland Examining Group (1986) *Leicestershire Modular Framework, Mode III GCSE Syllabus*, Nottingham.

Turner, J. (1986) *Designing the Modular Curriculum*, Parts 1, 2 and 3, Leicestershire TVEI Advisory Team, Leicester.

NOTES AND ILLUSTRATIONS

PROPOSED TITLES FOR MODULAR
STUDIES CERTIFICATION

1. The following proposal considers titles for certification of the Leicestershire Modular Framework syllabus within a structure that reflects the curriculum developments that modules have responded to and help foster.
2. The structure is one in which titles relate to three levels of specificity.
   (a) where a student's programme of modules is interdisciplinary and does not relate to a more specific title, then the certificate title "Modular Studies" should be awarded.
   (b) where a student's programme of modules has sufficient coherence it should lead to the award of one of the eight family titles listed below. These modules will have a common theme and will have links in terms of skills and context. The family titles each cover a broad range of modules.
   BUSINESS AND INFORMATION STUDIES
   INDIVIDUAL, SOCIETY AND ENVIRONMENT
   SERVICES TO PEOPLE
   COMMUNICATION STUDIES
   TECHNOLOGY
   CREATIVE DESIGN
   EXPRESSIVE ARTS
   SCIENCE
   (c) a limited number of more specific titles are proposed. These modules will have a tighter coherence and a more specific theme. There will need to be tighter rules of combination for these titles to introduce the concept of balance within a very clearly linked context e.g. the "Enterprise Skills" title will need to include "Enterprise Experience" as a core module plus elements of Marketing and Finance with other closely related modules.

   The list of specific titles below has been drawn up on the basis of the minimum number of titles required to award the likely programmes of study within the pilot cohort 1986–88. Further titles of a specific nature are likely to be sought as the total pool of modules increases.
   TECHNICAL SERVICES
   COMPUTER APPLICATIONS
   PHYSICAL SCIENCE
   FOOD AND CATERING STUDIES
   PERSONAL PRESENTATION
   INFORMATION TECHNOLOGY
   UNDERSTANDING BRITISH INDUSTRY
   CONTROL TECHNOLOGY
   SCIENCE 2
   ENVIRONMENTAL SCIENCE
   CARING SKILLS
   OFFICE TECHNOLOGY
   ENTERPRISE SKILLS

3. The pools of modules relating to each of the proposed titles are attached. Some modules relate to more than one title pool. Equally the diagram does not imply that each title pool from the outer ring is a strict subset of the broader "family" title for that segment of the diagram.

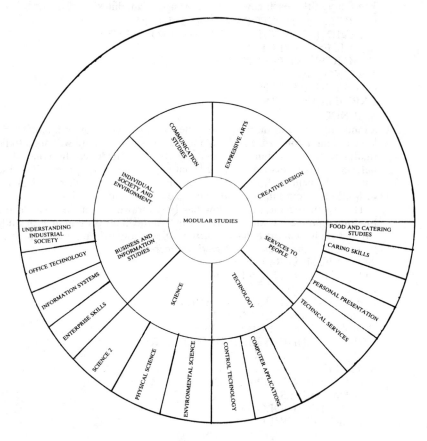

Module Pools

TITLES – MODULES FOR 1988 CERTIFICATION (partial list)

		A	B	C	D	E	F	G	H
1.	Business Case Study		B						
2.	Consumer Affairs		B	C				G	
3.	Enterprise Experience		B						
4.	Economic Awareness		B						
5.	I.T. Business Applications		B						H
6.	Personal Finance		B	C					
7.	Keyboarding (1)		B		D				
8.	Business Environment		B						
9.	Clerical Skills		B						
10.	Business Organisation		B						
11.	Britain in the International Economy		B	C					
12.	The British Economy		B	C					
13.	Business Calculations and Accounts		B						
14.	Office Organisation		B						
15.	Marketing and Distribution		B					G	
16.	Economic Concepts		B						
17.	Industrial Studies		B	C					
18.	Wordprocessing		B		D				H
19.	Wordprocessing (2)		B		D				H
21.	Information Systems: Information Retrieval		B		D				H
22.	Information Systems: Videotex		B		D				H
23.	Information Systems: Computer Graphics		B		D	E	F		H
24.	Information Systems: Foundation		B		D				H
25.	Informaton Systems: Computer		B		D				H
34.	Computer Aided Drafting and Design				D		F		H
41.	Graphic Communication				D		F		
42.	Microprocessor Control								H
43.	Electronics								H
44.	Digital Electronics								H
45.	Control Technology Project						F		H
46.	Structural/Mechanical Systems						F		H
47.	Electrical Control								H
49.	Pneumatic Control								H
50.	Electronic Systems								H
52.	Technology and Society			C					H
53.	Control Technology Design						F		H
54.	Home Electrics						F	G	H
55.	Plumbing for the Home						F	G	H
56.	Brickwork for the Home						F	G	H
57.	Painting and Decorating for the Home						F	G	
58.	Carpentry for the Home						F	G	
59.	Motor Vehicle Servicing							G	H
60.	Technology: Problem Solving						F		H
62.	Media Studies: Introductory				D	E			
80.	Photography				D	E	F		
81.	Science: Ecology	A							

82. Science: Elements	A		
83. Science: Chemicals in the Environment	A	C	
84. Science: Forces and Motion	A		
85. Science: Electricity and Magnetism	A		
86. Science: Energy and Waves	A		
87. Science: Chemicals at Work	A		
88. Science: Responding to Change	A		
89. Science: Exchange with the Environment	A	C	
90. Science: Earth Resources	A	C	
91. Environmental Pollution	A	C	
92. Field Study	A	C	
93. Diseases and how we prevent them	A	C	G
94. Energy in the Home	A		G
95. Investigating Polymers	A		
96. Water and the Living World	A		
97. Science: Inheritance and Evolution	A	C	
98. Science Techniques	A		

KEY

A Science
B Business and Information Studies
C Individual, Society and Environment
D Communication Studies
E Expressive Arts
F Creative Design
G Services to People
H Technology

TITLES: MODULE COMBINATIONS

Food and Catering Studies
– any five modules from
111 Catering
112 Pastry Work
121 International Cuisine
133 Design Food
134 Catering for Profit
135 Healthy Eating
136 Cookery on a Budget

Caring Skills
228 Care Case Study
229 The Needs of Young Children
230 Childbirth and the Family
231 Childcare
166 Design and Make an Article for a Young Child

Personal Presentation
234   Haircare
235   Hairstyle Techniques
236   Beauty and Manicure
237   Design – Hairstyles
161   Fashion Design

Computer Applications
– any five modules from
 42   Microprocessor Control
 34   Computer Aided Drafting and Design
201   Production Engineering
202   Computer Aided Manufacture
204   Robotics
205   Robotic Applications
214   Microcomputer Control

Control Technology
– any five modules from
 42   Microprocessor Control
 43   Electronics
 44   Digital Electronics
 45   Control Technology Project
 47   Electrical Control
 49   Pneumatic Control
 50   Electronic Systems
 53   Control Technology Design
214   Microcomputer Control

Technical Services
– any five modules from
 54   Home Electrics
 55   Plumbing for the Home
 56   Brickwork for the Home
 57   Painting and Decorating for the Home
 58   Carpentry for the Home
 59   Motor Vehicle Servicing
209   Motor Vehicle Engines and Transmissions
210   Motor Vehicle Bodywork and Electrics

SAMPLE MODULES
MIDLAND EXAMINING GROUP

G.C.S.E. (Mode 3) MODULAR STUDIES
MODULE 62 MEDIA STUDIES: INTRODUCTORY

GENERAL AIM, CONTENT AND NATURE OF THE MODULE

Aims to give an overview of Media Studies, with a particular emphasis on "visual literacy". As such this module will provide a valid experience of various approaches to Media Studies. It may also be used as the basis for more detailed study of specific aspects of the media within a modular programme.

The module will include consideration of the key concepts of Media Studies (construction; convention; mediation; representation and stereotyping; institution – see Notes, below) and experience of at least two of the following media: television, film, radio, photography and the press. Students will be encouraged to think not only about how meanings are produced in particular media but also about the context of their production – which organisations are involved, who is addressed and to what ends?

Wherever possible, "hands on" practical experience of aspects of media production, such as compiling a newspaper page or producing a "pre-credit sequence" on video, will be included. Some of this work may be best approached through simulation exercises. Such practical experience will be combined with the analysis of professional material in order to bring out both the similarities and differences between the processes involved.

STATEMENT OF SPECIFIC LEARNING OBJECTIVES

Students should be able to demonstrate the ability to:

A. recognise a problem and respond to it;

- can identify the nature of media products in terms of their generic characteristics and production contexts (origin, aims and audience)
- can demonstrate an awareness of media production processes
- can plan the production of their own media artefact
- can select appropriate techniques to achieve a desired media outcome

B. locate or recall appropriate information, concepts, processes and skills;
- can identify the range of media and their various styles and genres.
- can locate technical information relating to production techniques and equipment
- can locate source material relevant to the production of audio-visual outcomes

C. apply appropriate information, concepts, processes and skills;

- can critically analyse a media product in relation to the conventions employed and the context of production

- can operate selected items of audio-visual equipment in order to produce meaningful results
- can employ appropriate techniques and conventions to achieve a desired outcome

D. communicate the outcomes of their learning;

- can explain how meanings are produced in media products
- can produce a media artefact which displays both a knowledge of appropriate conventions and an ability to manipulate available techniques

E. evaluate and reflect upon their learning;

- can relate experience of practical work and critical analysis to everyday encounters with the media and media products
- can assess the significance of media products for different audiences
- can assess the extent to which a piece of practical work has achieved its initial aims
- can analyse difficulties experienced in the realisation of practical tasks and suggest ways in which these might have been avoided

SCHEME OF ASSESSMENT
Assessment will involve two components:

- course work folio
- practical coursework

Differentiation will be by outcome and by teachers taking care to set coursework tasks and practical assignments appropriate to each individual student's level of ability.

SPECIFICATION GRID
The weighting given to each assessment objective in each component of the scheme of assessment is indicated by the distribution of the total marks available in the following specification grid:

OBJECTIVES	A	B	C	D	E	Total
Coursework folio	4	4	4	4	8	24
Practical C/work	4	4	4	4	0	16
Total	8	8	8	8	8	40

CRITERIA FOR ASSESSMENT
The criteria for awarding marks to candidates work correspond to the attainment descriptors listed in paragaph 6.2 of this syllabus. Teachers will award up to eight raw marks for each of the objectives assessed by each of the methods of assessment employed. Every raw mark will reflect the level of attainment demonstrated by the

candidate in relation to the criterion referenced continuum of attainment descriptors for each assessment objective, as set out in paragraph 6.2. These raw marks will be scaled down to recognize the weighting attached to each assessment objective in the specification grid, before aggregation to obtain the final total mark for the module.

SPECIMEN ASSESSMENT RECORD SHEET

The following specimen assessment record sheet shows how teachers raw marks will be recorded for each assessment component, scaled down and aggregated to reach a final total mark for the module.

ASSESSMENT OBJECTIVE		A	B	C	D	E	TOTAL
COURSE WORK FOLIO	RAW MARK	/8	/8	/8	/8	/8	
	SCALE TO	/4	/4	/4	/4	/8	/24
PRACTICAL COURSE WORK	RAW MARK	/8	/8	/8	/8	/0	
	SCALE TO	/4	/4	/4	/4	/0	/16

						FINAL TOTAL	/40

NOTES
(Extract from Leics. Mode III GCSE Media Studies)

The following five key concepts are fundamental throughout the syllabus:

(i) the *construction* of meaning: its production through the selection and combination of elements. E.g., in a newspaper front page, meaning is *constructed* through the use of headlines and sub-headings, text, photographs and captions – each of these in itself a construction – and through layout.

(ii) *convention*: the role of traditional, usually unspoken, rules in the construction of meanings – seen, e.g., in film in the use of the "dissolve" between shots to indicate the passing of time; or in radio drama in the marking of scene changes by the fading of sound.

(iii) *mediation*: the involvement of individuals, organisations and technological processes in the transformation of reality into its fictional or non-fictional representations, e.g., in the translation of contemporary issues of law and order into TV crime series; or in coverage of major international conflicts as "human interest" stories.

(iv) *representation and stereotyping*: the relationship between media images and the social groups they portray; the existence of stereotypes; the process of stereotyping. E.g., the relationship between images of teenagers produced by television and the Press and school students themselves; carefree, fashion-conscious young people in television pop-music programmes, hooligans and victims of adult exploitation in the daily papers.

(v) *institution*: established but continually developing systems of production and distribution in the media, incorporating both conventions of meaning and patterns of media consumption. E.g., in cinema, the structures and pressures which shape a project from initial treatment, through script, casting of appropriate stars, and production to marketing, distribution and exhibition.

MIDLAND EXAMINING GROUP

G.C.S.E. (Mode 3) MODULAR STUDIES
MODULE (117) THE GROWTH AND DEVELOPMENT OF THE LOCAL
AREA

GENERAL AIM, CONTENT AND NATURE OF THE MODULE

This module aims to show students that development is not something that only happens in the Third World, but that it occurs locally and is an ongoing process. Photographic evidence will be used as well as direct observation in an attempt to develop skills in interpreting/analysing visual stimuli and in order to build up a "picture" of the selected urban area in the past as well as in the present. Areas of interest might include:

1) Education: the variety and development of educational provision.
2) Local Economy: including local shops/markets.
3) Urban redevelopment.
4) Leisure facilities.
5) Religion, including a study of the multi-ethnicity of the chosen urban area.

STATEMENT OF SPECIFIC LEARNING OBJECTIVES

Students should be able to demonstrate the ability to:

A. Recognise a problem and respond to it:

1) Can recognise issues relating to the development of the chosen urban area.
2) Can plan alternative lines of enquiry.
3) Can recognise that change need not necessarily represent progress.
4) Can determine appropriate methods for seeking information relating to the selected issue.

B. Locate or recall appropriate information, concepts, processes and skills:

1) Can locate appropriate sources of information on the selected issue – such as local newspapers, books, photographs and people.
2) Can select information appropriate for use in the enquiry.
3) Can recall and classify knowledge concerning particular areas of development, for instance, the growth of the chosen urban area, the provision of leisure facilities.

C. Apply appropriate information, concepts, processes and skills:

1) Can interrogate a photograph to obtain information and evidence.
2) Can apply various research skills to the location and selection of information.
3) Can take or select photographs with a sense of historical perspective.

D. Communicate the outcome of their learning:

1) Can organise and present material in a coherent and appropriate form.
2) Can compile a photographic representation of the selected urban area.
3) Can describe and explain their enquiry to others.

E. Evaluate and reflect upon their learning:

1) Can evaluate critically the usefulness of photographs as a communication medium.
2) Can appreciate that development is something that continues on a local, national, and international level.
3) Can evaluate evidence and draw a reasoned conclusion.

SCHEME OF ASSESSMENT
The scheme of assessment will involve two components:

Project: to be assembled after extensive research into an aspect of development occurring within the local area.
Oral examination: An oral assessment of objectives C, D and E related to the finished project (10 mins)

DIFFERENTIATION
Differentiation will be by outcome and by teachers taking care to set project tasks appropriate to each individual student's level of ability.

SPECIFICATION GRID
The weighting given to each assessment objective in each component of the scheme of assessment is indicated by the distribution of the total marks available in the following specification grid:

Objectives	A	B	C	D	E	Totals
Project	8	8	6	4	4	30
Oral examination	0	0	2	4	4	10
Total	8	8	8	8	8	40

CRITERIA FOR ASSESSMENT
The criteria for awarding marks to candidates' work correspond to the attainment descriptors listed in paragraph 6.2 of this syllabus. Teachers will award up to eight raw marks for each of the objectives assessed by each of the methods of assessment employed. Every raw mark will reflect the level of attainment demonstrated by the candidate in relation to the criterion referenced continuum of attainment descriptors for each assessment objective. These raw marks will be scaled down to recognise the weighting attached to each assessment objective in the specification grid, before aggregation to obtain the final total mark for the module.

SPECIMEN ASSESSMENT RECORD SHEET
The following specimen assessment record sheet shows how teachers' raw marks will be recorded for each assessment component, scaled down and aggregated to reach a final total mark for the module.

Assessment objective	A	B	C	D	E	Totals
Project: Raw mark	8	8	8	8	8	40
Scale to	8	8	6	4	4	30
Oral examination						
Raw mark	8	8	8	8	8	40
Scale to:			2	4	4	10
						/40

MIDLAND EXAMINING GROUP

G.C.S.E.   (Mode 3)   MODULAR STUDIES
MODULE 136   COOKERY ON A BUDGET

GENERAL AIM, CONTENT AND NATURE OF THE MODULE
This module aims to enable students to make informed choices in the management of time, money and equipment through cooking on a limited budget. Students will be expected to plan and produce palatable and aesthetically pleasing food, while showing an awareness of current nutritional thinking.

STATEMENT OF SPECIFIC ASSESSMENT OBJECTIVES
Students should be able to demonstrate the ability to:

A recognise a problem and respond to it;

1. Can identify priorities of the topic being studied.
2. Can plan a menu using these priorities.
3. Can identify ingredients and use the most suitable method of cooking.

B locate or recall appropriate concepts, processes and skills;

1. Can seek out information on food, methods of production and cooking from various sources.
2. Can select ingredients suitable for the task in hand.

C apply appropriate concepts, processes and skills;

1. Can make effective use of facilities available.
2. Can prepare a well-balanced meal on a budget relevant to the situation being studied.

D communicate the outcomes of their learning;

1. Can present a prepared dish in an attractive way within the constraints of time, money and equipment.

2. Can explain reasons for choice of a given dish using the priorities previously identified.

E evaluate and reflect upon their learning;

1. Can assess the alternative courses of action in food preparation in terms of money, time and equipment.
2. Can evaluate different approaches to food preparation.

SCHEME OF ASSESSMENT
Assessment will involve 2 components:

Written Asignment   – Assessment of student activities in producing a 'preparation sheet' based on the principles within the coursework.

Practical Assignment – Assessment of the practical skills demonstrated in producing dishes based on a 'preparation sheet'.

DIFFERENTIATION Differentiation will be by outcome and by Teachers taking care to set Written/Practical Assignments appropriate to each individual student's level of ability.

SPECIFICATION GRID
The weighting given to each assessment objective in each component of the scheme of assessment is indicated by the distribution of the total marks available in the following specification grid.

Objective	A	B	C	D	E	Total
Practical Assignments	4	4	6	8	2	24
Written Assignments	4	4	2	0	6	16
Total	8	8	8	8	8	40

CRITERIA FOR ASSESSMENT
The criteria for awarding marks to candidates' work correspond to the attainment descriptors listed in paragraph 6.2 of this syllabus. Teachers will award up to eight raw marks for each of the objectives assessed by each of the methods of assessment employed. Every raw mark will reflect the level of attainment demonstrated by the candidate in relation to the criterion-referenced continuum of attainment descriptors for each assessment objective. These raw marks will be scaled down to recognise the weighting attached to each assessment objective in the specification grid, before aggregation to obtain the final total mark for the module.

Specimen Assessment Record Sheet

The following specimen assessment record sheet shows how teachers' raw marks will be recorded for each assessment component, scaled down and aggregated to reach a final total mark for the module.

ASSESSMENT OBJECTIVE		A	B	C	D	E	TOTAL
Practical	RAW MARK	8	8	8	8	8	
Assignment	SCALE TO	4	4	6	6	2	22
Written	RAW MARK	8	8	8	8	8	
Assignment	SCALE TO	4	4	2	2	6	18

FINAL TOTAL   40

MIDLAND EXAMINING GROUP

G.C.S.E.   (Mode 3)   MODULAR STUDIES
MODULE 173   DRAWING

GENERAL AIM, CONTENT AND NATURE OF THE MODULE

In this module students will be encouraged to develop an understanding of drawing. By practical work it is hoped to foster an appreciation and enjoyment of a variety of drawing skills including, drawing in proportion, use of tone, texture and colour.

It is envisaged that at least one finished piece of work will be produced together with the relevant research and experiment.

During the course it is hoped to foster a feeling of enjoyment in the student to give them a sense of achievement and give them the opportunity to become confident and visually literate in terms of drawing.

STATEMENT OF SPECIFIC LEARNING OBJECTIVES

Students should be able to demonstrate the ability to:

A recognise a problem and respond to it;

- can show they are aware of different methods of drawing
- can select a drawing type appropriate to the problem set

B locate or recall appropriate information, concepts, processes and skills;

- can use the information available to progress into research in the chosen method(s) of drawing in relation to the problem

C apply appropriate information, concepts, processes and skills;

- can show an understanding of various methods of drawing
- can produce a completed drawing in answer to the problem set
- can apply appropriate drawing techniques to produce results that are high in quality and relevant to the problem set

D communicate the outcomes of their learning;

- can show work produced in the process of achieving the final result

E evaluate and reflect upon their learning;

- can show a critical awareness of their drawings

- can suggest ways of improving their drawings
- can suggest developments of the technique used and the skills learned

SCHEME OF ASSESSMENT
Assessment will involve 1 component;

- Coursework Folio – To include evidence of all practical work completed in preparation for the final outcome. The Folio will also include the final outcome(s) which will be achieved in terms of use of skills and techniques.

Differentiation will be achieved by outcome and by teachers taking care to set coursework tasks appropriate to each individual student's level of ability.

SPECIFICATION GRID
The weighting given to each assessment objective in each component of the scheme of assessment is indicated by the distribution of the total marks available in the following specification grid.

Objectives	A	B	C	D	E	Total
Coursework Folio	8	8	8	8	8	40
Total	8	8	8	8	8	40

CRITERIA FOR ASSESSMENT
The criteria for awarding marks to candidates work correspond to the attainment descriptors listed in paragraph 6.2 of this syllabus. Teachers will award up to eight raw marks for each of the objectives assessed by each of the methods of assessment employed. Every raw mark will reflect the level of attainment demonstrated by the candidate in relation to the criterion referenced continuum of attainment descriptors for each assessment objective, as set out in paragraph 6.2. These raw marks will be scaled down to recognise the weighting attached to each assessment objective in the specification grid, before aggregation to obtain the final total mark for the module.

SPECIMEN ASSESSMENT RECORD SHEET
The following specimen assessment record sheet shows how teachers raw marks will be recorded for each assessment component, scaled down and aggregated to reach a final total mark for the module.

ASSESSMENT OBJECTIVE		A	B	C	D	E	TOTAL
COURSEWORK FOLIO	RAW MARK	/8	/8	/8	/8	/8	
	SCALE TO	/8	/8	/8	/8	/8	/40
					FINAL TOTAL		/40

4

THE MODULAR INITIATIVE: SHEFFIELD
Bob Gregory

INTRODUCTION

In setting out to describe the experience in Sheffield it is essential to point
out that the views contained in each of the following paragraphs represent a
personal perspective of the initiative, shared by many teacher and adviser
colleagues, but not yet sufficiently distilled to represent a corporate view
ready to be enshrined in LEA policy. Moreover, the existence of prescrip-
tive curriculum policies would be entirely inconsistent with a period of
exciting and revolutionary activity that surrounds the first tentative steps
towards the development of a fully modular curriculum. Even at this early
stage in the process, there are many clear indications that traditional
classroom practice is being rigorously examined, and that many of our
traditional and mystical perceptions of the educational world are being
challenged – the roles of advisers and administrators, the responsibilities of
headteachers and teachers in general, the relationships between teachers
and students and the identity of corporate bodies such as curriculum
development groups, the advisory service and the LEA itself. There is, in
addition, a growing awareness of pressures arising from a new degree of
'public accountability' and, of course, the need for change resulting from the
realization that 'to stand still is to fall further behind' in a rapidly changing
world that reveals technical change and new social and economic factors day
by day.

The present move towards a complete re-appraisal and reform of the
curriculum in Sheffield's secondary schools stems inevitably on the part of
teachers with a considerable feeling of dissatisfaction with the status quo,
coupled with an enthusiasm and commitment for change and innovation on
a scale and in a style that is difficult to match. Perhaps one of the most
striking features that should be revealed in any adequate case study of the

current initiative is the desire of all the participants to succeed – a somewhat obvious prerequisite for ultimate success. At best the curriculum changes could give students a complete education entirely appropriate to the next century, and at worst could give individuals glimpses of what the future must surely hold. In short, the development of a fully modular curriculum is seen as a way of providing a broader and more flexible curriculum structure, with more opportunity for student choice and personal 'negotiation' (or perhaps periodical renegotiation) of individual learning programmes and curriculum pathways. It also gives us the opportunity of addressing educational issues in a way that has never been possible before.

In this context, TVEI becomes 'an opportunity for change, a means to an end and not just an end in itself' (City of Sheffield Education Dept, 1986), with much wider concerns than might be conveyed by its title. The initiative is not seen in Sheffield as a way of enhancing the technical and vocational education of young people in schools from the age of 14, but it is recognized as a spearhead for curriculum change within the overall framework of an authority-wide programme for change. This is a far cry from the potential divisiveness and resource-led approach that characterized some of the earlier schemes: lasting change must surely not be confused with short-sighted propositions such as the installation of CNC lathes.

If a major tenet for TVEI is, therefore, that it provides a unique opportunity for curriculum change as part of a substantial authority-wide initiative as well as forming a programme for change in its own right, it must surely be concerned with curriculum innovation in terms of strategies for teaching, learning, achievement and assessment within a new framework to satisfy the needs of young people in contemporary society. The approach should clearly take note of the various emerging sets of criteria for the curriculum, such as the national criteria for GCSE and the aims of TVEI as published by the MSC, and a plethora of other publications ranging from information and discussion documents from the old Schools Council and HMI to the various white papers and policy statements of the DES. Perhaps of even greater importance, however, is the realization that it is the collective experience of our teachers that constitutes the greatest resource, and the effective management of change must proceed through a process that builds on grass-roots experience and provides opportunities for 'participative management' through the active involvement of teachers in curriculum development. Staff development is, therefore, an integral part of effective curriculum development that gives rise to a host of inter-related questions such as, 'How can this type of approach be managed? How can teachers work effectively together? Should so-called experts exert an over-riding influence on developments? How can the work be disseminated?'

As a further consideration at the start of the initiative, it was unfortunate that many teachers had mixed feelings about the involvement of the MSC in curriculum change in a way that appears to bypass the DES. Clearly, teachers are concerned about the selective use of resources and the political and long-term consequences of such an approach. The overall aims of the TVEI scheme, however, are acceptable to the vast majority of teachers as they are clearly founded on educational and pedagogical principles that constitute the 'new curriculum' thinking. How much better, therefore, to reflect on a curriculum initiative that offers opportunity for change without any form of discrimination, and without the traditional constraints of woefully inadequate resources and the usual demands of mode I examination syllabuses. The Sheffield scheme has never been associated with a shift in the balance between education and training in the pre-16 curriculum in a way that would favour training, and from its inception the scheme has set out to avoid a sharp distinction between academic and vocational studies for students of different abilities in the 14–16 age range. The possibility of more differentiated routes for students in the 16–18 age range remains, however, and the 'negotiation' of individual learning programmes, as stated earlier, is seen as a key feature of the scheme as a whole for all students within the complete 14–18 age range.

The development of a fully modular curriculum would enable individual schools with differences in philosophy and priority to implement changes to meet their own requirements within their own structural and organizational frameworks in order to satisfy, to a greater or lesser extent, the various DES and TVEI criteria. In such a development, care is obviously needed to avoid a proliferation of module titles and the possible overlap of content in two or more modular units of work in an attempt to accommodate differences between schools. It is also obvious, of course, that a joint and collaborative approach involving a wide range of different institutions is a major factor for the success of the scheme as a whole.

STARTING OUT

The current dynamism for disciplined curriculum change within the authority as a whole would appear to have been sparked off in no uncertain way by a letter from the Chief Education Officer to schools in December 1985 that was headed 'The Future of Sheffield's Secondary Schools' – a letter that marks a watershed in the authority's approach to curriculum development. The letter introduced the idea of a school-focused secondment programme (SFS), in which structured partnership of school, LEA and higher education staff would assist seconded teachers to tackle identified curriculum development tasks as part of an overall, composite and coherent strategy for authority-wide curriculum reform. In this connection, the TVEI scheme itself has made considerable headway and using the structured partnership principle has made enormous progress in curriculum development terms in a relatively short space of time. It has, however, always been a major concern that the rapid pace of change would make it difficult to share the experience with colleagues who had been less involved at the beginning. This, in pragmatic terms, could be reflected in the difficulty of forming working relationships between seconded teachers and school-based teachers, developers and implementers and the staffs of schools already involved in externally funded curriculum initiatives such as TVEI and those from schools about to join the authority's SFS programme.

Clearly, the notion of TVEI being a spearhead for the SFS programme while also constituting a programme of staff and curriculum development in its own right has enormous implications. The aim of the secondment programme must surely be to give as many staff as possible the opportunity to experience at first hand the important processes of curriculum change and *not* the creation of a wide range of curriculum packages that have been prepared for all on a 'take-it-or-leave-it' basis. It is this development experience – with its emphasis on process – that the secondees can most usefully share with others. A consideration of the number of secondary projects that have 'disappeared without trace' supports the view that effective change in the classroom is much more likely to come about as a result of this 'hearts and minds' approach than from the dissemination of curriculum materials associated with new teaching, learning and assessment strategies.

Returning to the modular curriculum itself, a common vision of what could be created, initially through the spearhead project but then more substantially through the SFS programme as a whole, was quickly established at a conference of representatives of the structured partnership. The vision can be conveniently described using the familiar rhetoric. The mechanism of 'modularization' was described in terms such as 'free-standing and sequenced units of work', 'module stacks' and 'modular pathways'. The form of the assessment and certification was described in terms such as 'assessment objectives', 'criterion referenced assessment' and 'unit credits'. 'Equal opportunities' and 'student-centred', 'negotiated' and 'experiential learning' were considered to be important themes and linking threads in the reformed curriculum. But, as with all terminology (or perhaps jargon), it was important to achieve some degree of common understanding of the words and phrases. It was imperative to establish that 'equal opportunities' meant more than just giving students an awareness of the relevant issues, and 'experiential learning' meant more than a style of learning that was not constrained by the chapter headings in a textbook. Clearly, a wide variety of crucial educational issues were debated at this time.

The drafting of a revised TVEI submission to the MSC following this period of debate had the effect of reinforcing the Chief Education Officer's letter to schools, especially in relation to 'a modular approach in all areas of the curriculum' (City of Sheffield Education Dept, 1985). It was argued that there was a need for 'extensive curriculum development in terms of unified areas of work within modules, pedagogy and assessment strategies' (Sheffield City Council, 1986, p. 16). The submission also emphasized a 'bottom-up' approach to curriculum development based on a process of building from the first principles – identifying the ground to be covered, the skills and abilities that have to be acquired and the essential experiences that students should undergo. This was seen in sharp contrast to a 'top-down' approach that is often associated with 'centre-periphery' and so-called 'teacher-proof' developments.

Certainly, the authors of the revised submission took the utmost care to produce a document that would serve as a framework to direct those first tentative steps towards the modular curriculum without the risk of constraining future developments through a misguided ambition to be the sole architects of the scheme. It is also significant to note that the development of a modular curriculum in itself could easily become an example of 'innovation without change' unless the learning and assessment experiences of young people were really going to be subject to a radical re-appraisal and reform.

THE FIRST STEPS

Few accounts of curriculum development reflect on the experimental nature of the process and the need for an ongoing and supple approach based on the collective and changing perceptions of all those involved. In this respect, the first few steps were crucial to the enterprise, involving all the participants in the structured partnership in both developmental *and* management issues. The fundamental question at this stage became 'How could the change be achieved?' rather than 'What change could be achieved?' A strategy was clearly necessary that would build on the enthusiasm and commitment of teachers in order to promote the two fundamental concepts of 'ownership' and 'participative management'. The management of change in these terms steps outside the certainty of pre-conceived schemes associated with interventionist strategies and the use of a large, skilful and central team of experts that can result in rapid, but perhaps superficial progress. 'Ownership', of course, can only be achieved through active teacher participation with an opportunity to be closely involved in decision making.

The organization and co-ordination of development teams of teachers and advisers from all the institutions involved, together with co-ordinating and planning groups, has presented a real challenge that, on the one hand, has resulted in periods of outstanding progress, but on the other has resulted in periods of great uncertainty. No one could deny this type of experience from the spearhead project has provided an invaluable foretaste of the tasks that must be faced within the authority-wide SFS initiative as a whole, or in any other major curriculum initiative.

Looking back, therefore, there have been many salutary lessons for all concerned. First, there is the growing realization among leaders and advisers that from the inception of any work there are no experts, but only facilitators, and there is no single correct view or policy, but only a desire to find an agreed solution or strategy that can stand on its own right. Furthermore, the notion that participants are working towards a consensus view has been rejected as the final solution could lack the distinctive features of any of the initial proposals. It is true, however, that the participants need to be aware of all factors that could influence the success of the development – organizational possibilities and constraints, assessment requirements and work in progress elsewhere could influence the likelihood of successful implementation.

Second, the composition of development teams is known to be critical with the need to incorporate particular strengths while avoiding a narrow subject-based approach. In addition, other factors are extremely important including plenary and working-group size, status factors and the need to review the composition of development teams to facilitate progress. The recognition that student guidance, learning and assessment strategies form an essential and integral component of work in all areas of the curriculum has also had a bearing on team composition.

Lastly, the importance of the 'bottom-up' approach must never be undervalued, even if this type of development leads to some duplication of work, or perhaps in extreme cases a complete re-invention of the wheel. It would be wrong to assume, however, that the development teams have not undertaken any 'reconnaisance' and were naïvely 'glorifying the uniqueness' of their situation. At this stage it would be more appropriate to say that the teams have been searching for the various 'building blocks' of the reformed curriculum that can then be adapted and assembled in new ways to meet the needs, interests and aspirations of all young people in the various schools within a fully modular curriculum.

The pressures on the development teams have been enormous and individual participants have encountered both negative and positive learning experiences. 'Fright' and 'enlightenment' have been two underlying and alternating sensations for all involved in the development work. What LEA, co-ordinator or headteacher could really expect new modular courses to be devised in the space of three or four weeks? Team-building exercises to achieve effective group relationships and identities have been clear priorities for the cross-curricular, inter-institutional development teams that were assembled in order to take the first steps towards a fully modular curriculum. Certainly, the start of any secondment programme is bound to be 'fraught with uncertainty', but in this particular case the tasks appeared to be 'daunting in both their size and complexity' (Nixon, 1987, p. 78).

MAPS AND MODULES

Although it is difficult to recall the individual standpoints of all the participants at the start of the development, a clear rationale in favour of the modular approach has emerged as part of a comprehensive reform of the secondary curriculum. Indeed, the experience to date has significantly contributed to the initial progress made in moving towards a holistic authority-wide policy that will eventually be aimed at producing uniformity of approach within the SFS curriculum development initiative as a whole, and reducing the risk of TVEI being considered as a separate 'enclave of activity'. The rationale stems from an underlying concern that the traditional curriculum has become ossified and that student under-achievement can be related, in the words of the Hargreaves Report (1984, p. 74), to 'a vague two year educational journey towards nebulous and distant goals'. The advantages of the modular approach are not, therefore, simply thought to lie in the flexibility in module combinations with more opportunity for student choice, but also in terms of the relatively small syllabus content of modules, 'negotiated' methodology between teachers and students to achieve clearly defined goals and clear, tangible methods of assessment.

But what are the characteristics of a modular curriculum in Sheffield, and how can a module be defined? Clear definitions are important if the 'bottom-up' approach is to give rise to a comprehensive, uniform and coherent approach. Moreover, the characteristics of a modular curriculum had to be established before mounting a considerable programme of in-service training in order to give teachers from all areas of the curriculum first-hand experience in constructing specimen modules for the purpose of understanding the processes involved – processes that have given rise to modules such as *Allez en Vacances*, *Worlds Apart* and *Banking on It*.

In the Sheffield scheme, a module is considered to be a component part of an educational programme that can be assessed and accredited in its own right giving a unit of accreditation. A module can be defined, therefore, as an area of knowledge, concepts, skills and attitudes that

1. has its own integral unity and coherence such that it is worth learning in its own right;
2. is suitable for learning by the average student in a prescribed time (say 15–20 hours);
3. provides a set of learning objectives against which achievement can be measured; and
4. can be linked with other modules, both in its own curriculum area and in other areas.

A close inspection of the modules reveals several other important features. First, it should be noted that individual modules are sufficiently open-ended to be appropriate for girls and boys across the complete ability range – and may serve a number of different aims within the curriculum – with differentiation of student performance by outcome according to clearly stated assessment criteria. Second, all modules emphasize active learning strategies and student-centred approaches, which are considered to be crucial elements for effective learning, particularly within the shorter time scales introduced through the modular approach. In fact, a considerable shift has been achieved away from the traditional content-laden curriculum towards a more process orientated approach. Third, care has been taken to devise a system of 'equal esteem' modules in order to reduce the distinction between 'vocational' and 'academic' courses. From the outset it was realized that modules of a so-called 'vocational' nature could be mainly concerned with continuing general education through a number of pre-vocational focuses, and that modules of a so-called 'academic' nature would become more applied, activity-based and related to the world of work. Students would, therefore, be able to 'mix and match' modules, with appropriate guidance, to give coherent courses and individual educational programmes in order to meet their individual needs. Indeed, this complete notion of more choice, open-ended work, experiential learning and 'negotiated' curricula has started to become a reality, with all modules being suitable for inclusion in one or more GCSE courses.

In using the 'bottom-up' approach there has been a significant move towards the development of a more broadly-based curriculum. Conventional two-year syllabuses within existing subject domains are being challenged as new modular courses have started to extend cross-curricular thinking by breaking down inter-subject barriers and interfaces, many of which appear to be arbitrary and traditional with little relevance to real-life situations. The integration of generic skills and other learning objectives has been encouraged in all modules, together with an integration of curriculum areas traditionally associated with separate subjects. This is thought to be very important in offsetting the risk of producing a highly fragmented modular curriculum and can be illustrated by the following two examples. Information technology modules have been designed so that they fit naturally into many different modular courses across the curriculum as well as forming a coherent course in their own right. Integrated design modules have been formulated to incorporate two inter-related strands – practical problem-solving using a wide range of durable materials to promote the idea of fitness for purpose; and the development of personal skills and ideas, the expression of understandings and feelings in appropriate media and the appreciation of beauty. The integrated design modular course, therefore, has roots in CDT–design and realization, CDT–technology, CDT–design and communication, home economics and art and design.

The difficulties in planning a complete modular map are clearly formidable, although a map of this type would ensure that modules were developed in a co-ordinated way so that overlaps and gaps between modules would be avoided and a complete curriculum model would be built up. Indeed, a well-defined curriculum policy is considered to be a necessary precursor for the development of a modular curriculum. A more pragmatic approach was, therefore, adopted at the start of the scheme in which identified modules were classified under various curricular headings to give a catalogue of modules that was continually being augmented and reviewed. Cross-curricular modules would, of course, appear under several curricular headings and would be developed by appropriate cross-curricular teams of teachers.

There is increasing evidence to suggest that the time is right for the development teams to return to the question of the modular map. Whole 'tracts of territory' are becoming clear in the light of current experience. The development of modular business studies courses, for example, are seen to encompass modules in information technology and human and social studies as well as business studies in its own right. Strong linking threads between these modules, including integrated business themes and links with the 'real world' of business and commerce, will give rise to a number of coherent and recognizable courses rather than a series of narrowly focused 'taster' modules in a range of relevant learning areas. In similar vein, the development of modular science courses will encompass modules from a number of traditionally separate curriculum areas including science, technology, home economics and integrated design. A reduction in the content of these courses, with more emphasis on the processes of science and problem-solving activities as linking threads between the modules, is seen as a key issue for the development team. In addition, cross-curricular themes such as economic awareness, information technology and environmental studies have the potential of unifying the curriculum into a meaningful learning experience for students. Although the effectiveness of this strategy remains to be seen, it certainly helps to allay concern that a fully modular curriculum might be even more fragmented than the conventional curriculum with its subject-based approach.

The structural unification of the curriculum as a whole, rather like the reversal of continental drift to give an ancient supercontinent, depends on a more complete understanding of the modular map in its entirety. The development teams are aware that many issues require further clarification in order to ensure that all modules 'fit snugly together'. The place of foreign languages, typically a 'sore thumb' in the curriculum, either within language arts, human and social studies or both areas illustrates the type of dilemma that requires considerable debate.

PATHWAYS AND GOALS

The simple goal of linking modules together to achieve GCSE certification, both in one area of the curriculum and across the curriculum as a whole, is fundamental to the scheme. Each modular course would constitute a particular pathway through the modular map and would be expected to

1. correspond approximately to the usual time demands of a conventional two-year course of study (say seven 15–20 hour modules); and
2. form a coherent and recognizable course of study that meets the requirements of the national criteria for GCSE.

Although rules of module combination would make explicit how different course titles would be derived from different combinations of modules, and what selections of modules would be required to achieve particular course titles, an additional important principle has been established – that students would not be required to offer work from all the modules in a course for final assessment and accreditation.

A rationale for this so-called 'discard' principle is firmly based on the belief that there is a tendency in moving towards the modular curriculum to over-assess students' work in comparison with conventional two-year courses, and that all the assessment objectives of the chosen modules would adequately reflect the assessment objectives of the course as a whole. In practical terms, however, the 'discard' principle helps to overcome some inherent difficulties of the modular approach. This includes factors such as the effect of student maturity on levels of achievement and the risk of performance within the shorter time scale of a module being adversely affected by illness or other factors outside the direct control of students. A further important consideration stems from the possibility of using certain modules within a course to accredit student achievement in a particular area of learning that is cross-curricular in nature – a type of 'horizontal' rather than 'vertical stacking' of modules.

Although for the purpose of GCSE certification students will obtain an overall grade for each course as a whole, it is also argued that they should be notified of their levels of achievement within individual modules. This would clearly give students the opportunity for improving grades by

1. repeating certain modules (or particular elements of the assessment);
2. completing alternative modules; or
3. 'negotiating' new curriculum pathways and learning programmes.

Each module would, therefore, be assessed in its own right and as a discrete part of a whole course. In making modules synonymous with units of accreditation, it is stressed that the type of assessment used in any module would not constitute a 'hurdle' test. The nature of the assessment used would, therefore, be open-ended in order to ensure that students can demonstrate what they have achieved in a positive sense without the expectation of failure.

It is also recognized that smaller units will allow students to have experience in new areas of the curriculum that could otherwise be in danger of becoming overcrowded and unbalanced. Many of these new units will, of course, put more emphasis on process-based approaches, such as problem-solving, with a reduction in the amount of subject content frequently found in more conventional approaches. This will almost certainly require new methods of assessment, with more emphasis on practical rather than theoretical achievement, oral rather than written work, personal and group skills and student attitudes. Clearly, these issues are closely linked with the development of records of achievement and the hope that teachers and moderators will play more imaginative roles in the assessment and recording processes, with teachers assuming more responsibility for assessment and moderators assuming more responsibility for the validation of modular courses and assessment procedures.

THE WAY AHEAD

Thus far, the intention has been to describe in outline the main features of the fully modular curriculum at its present stage of development in Sheffield, and to give some indication about the exciting – and somewhat revolutionary – activity that surrounds the first tentative steps towards the creation of this 'new' curriculum. Clearly, the processes of 'modularization' in the present context are mainly concerned with the building up of a complete modular map from first principles to provide a series of coherent educational programmes to meet individual needs, rather than the breaking down of conventional subject areas into a series of discrete learning experiences.

Undoubtedly, the 'new' curriculum will be created through the endeavours of the structured partnership of school, LEA and higher education staff, but the success of the scheme will always be dependent on the enthusiasm and commitment of individual teachers to implement the proposals in the classroom with the flair and panache that can help to motivate students. In this respect it is recognized that classroom teachers must be free to adopt a flexible approach in devising teaching schemes and in 'fleshing out' the modular syllabuses. Such an approach extends the degree of 'grass-root' involvement and gives all teachers the opportunity to acquire a sense of 'ownership' of the curriculum change in a way that could encourage initiative, enthusiasm and the 'negotiation' of methodology between teachers and students to achieve clearly defined goals. It is also hoped that this approach will encourage teachers to become more involved in the evaluation of their own work with the effect that the traditional gulfs between development, implementation and evaluation will be reduced.

Although much further development work remains to be done to give coherence, continuity and progression for all students, there have already been considerable changes in learning and assessment strategies. Further change is thought to be essential, however, particularly in promoting and recognizing students' personal skills such as self-confidence, initiative, enterprise and creativity – qualities that have not been assessed within the more 'academic' curriculum. In general, therefore, a more rational approach to assessment and the recording of achievement within the modular structure is required, in a way that would be more meaningful to both students and the users of the final certification alike.

The 'new' curriculum must inevitably give rise to new course titles that reflect the changed nature of the educational experiences certificated. Modular awards in media studies, performing and expressive arts, physical and biological science, world studies, social studies and local studies – to name a few – are expected to become more commonplace, but these awards must be afforded the same degree of currency as the largely subject-orientated conventional GCSE awards. This important issue can only be resolved by widening the structured partnership to include parents, the local community and local industry. In short, an important aim for the initiative as a whole must involve the building of better links between education, parents and employers.

Undoubtedly, since its inception, the TVEI scheme in Sheffield has been extremely valuable both as a 'catalyst for initiating change', and as a spearhead project for an authority-wide process of curriculum re-appraisal and reform. In this context, the 'modularization' of the curriculum as a whole is proving to be a remarkably effective 'vehicle' for curriculum and staff development in a way that will have a lasting effect on the processes and management of curriculum change. Perhaps it could be concluded that, in breaking the mould, the newly emerging creative and participative processes will ensure that things will never be the same again.

REFERENCES

City of Sheffield Education Department (1985) *The Future of Sheffield Secondary Schools: A Letter From the Chief Education Officer*, Sheffield MDC.

City of Sheffield Education Department (TRIST) (1986) *TVEI Senior Management Conference: A Brief Report*, Jon Nixon.

Hargreaves, D.H. (1984) *Improving Secondary Schools*, ILEA, London.

Nixon, J. (ed.) (1987) *Curriculum Change: The Sheffield Experience*, USDE paper, University of Sheffield.

Sheffield City Council (1986) *TVEI in Sheffield: A Submission to the Manpower Services Commission*.

NOTES AND ILLUSTRATIONS

THE SHEFFIELD MODULAR HUMANITIES PROPOSAL

Robert Gregory, April 1987. Outline of a proposal for GCSE certification.

Perhaps the modular mode III GCSE humanities proposal represents one of the most comprehensive and innovatory modular developments to have emerged from the Sheffield initiative to date. Although it has been created by drawing on the concepts, skills, values and attitudes conventionally found in separate subject areas such as economics, geography, history and RE, the new modular combinations and styles of learning have been produced in a way that emphasizes the common ground that exists across the various subject domains. In outline, the scheme is based on a package of 24 modules that can be 'mixed and matched' to give a number of distinct courses. Each of these courses would lead to a GCSE award and can be identified as leaning towards either a more integrated, subject orientated or cross-curricular type of approach within the learning experience.

A closer examination of the 24 modules reveals that 7 modules are of an integrated nature while the remaining 17 modules are more subject orientated. This is shown in detail in Tables 1 and 2. The modules are not, of course, fixed for all time and it is anticipated that further modules would be added in order to increase the degree of curriculum flexibility and reflect the major technological, social, environmental and cultural changes taking place in contemporary society. It is also important to note that the modules are entirely 'free-standing' and that the individual module reference codes do not imply any sequencing within the various courses.

In addition, the importance of an integrated core of modules is stressed within each course, together with the possibility of forming links with other areas of the curriculum as the modular approach expands through the initiative as a whole. In each module, students' work would be assessed according to a set of common assessment criteria, and the outcomes from 5 modules from the 7 comprising a particular course would be required for final assessment and accreditation. Ten distinct modular courses have been identified at the present time and the permitted module combinations for each GCSE award are shown in Table 3 using the various module reference codes given in Tables 1 and 2.

Integrated module titles			
Life is for Living (I1)	Power (I2)	Change (I3)	Variety is the Spice of Life (I4)
People and Places (I5)	Work, Wealth and Welfare (I6)	Conflict and Co-operation (I7)	

Table 1   Modular humanities: integrated module titles

Subject orientated module titles

Economics	Geography	History	Religious studies	People and politics
World Economic Issues	Development Gap	Twentieth-Century History	Contemporary Religious and Moral Issues	Participation and Representation
(E1)	(G1)	(H1)	(R1)	(P1)
Government, Economy and People	Cities and People	The Individual and Society	Life in the City	
(E2)	(G2)	(H2)	(R2)	
The Structure of Industry	Using the Countryside	Living and Working	Religion, the Community and the Individual	
(E3)	(G3)	(H3)	(R3)	
Economics and the Environment	People and the Natural Environment	History Around Us	Religion, Responsibility and Changes	
(E4)	(G4)	(H4)	(R4)	

Table 2   Modular humanities: subject orientated module titles

Course	Nature of course	Module combinations
Humanities	Integrated	I1, I2, I3, I4, I5, I6, I7
Economics	Subject orientated	Three from I2, I3, I6, I7 combined with E1, E2, E3, E4
Geography	Subject orientated	Three from I1, I2, I5, I6, I7 combined with G1, G2, G3, G4
History	Subject orientated	Three from I1, I2, I3, I7 combined with H1, H2, H3, H4

Religious studies	Subject orientated	Three from I1, I4, I5, I7 combined with R1, R2, R3, R4
World issues	Cross-curricular	Three from I2, I3, I4, I7 combined with E1, G1, H1, R1
Urban and industrial studies	Cross-curricular	Three from I3, I4, I5, I7 combined with four from E3, G2, H3, H4, R2
People and society	Cross-curricular	Three from I2, I3, I6, I7 combined with E2, G2, H2, R2
Environmental studies	Cross-curricular	Three from I2, I3, I5, I7 combined with four from E4, G3, G4, H4, R4
People and politics	Cross-curricular	Three from I2, I3, I4, I7 combined with four from E2, G2, H1, R4, P1

Table 3   Possible module combinations for GCSE awards

Acknowledgement

The writer would like to thank the members of the development team for their work in formulating the above proposals and the LEA for permission to describe the outline scheme in this chapter. Inevitably changes are likely as the scheme evolves. The information should be considered as being mainly illustrative at the present stage of development. The potential of such a scheme has, however, been widely recognized.

5

MODULAR DEVELOPMENTS IN CLWYD AND COVENTRY
Gareth Newman

INTRODUCTION

Some of the important steps towards establishing modular courses inside schools were taken in the most unlikely places. Nowhere less likely was Ysgol Emrys ap Iwan, Abergele that, since the school was established, had delivered a traditional nine-subject curriculum. By contrast, in the West Midlands borough of Coventry, such developments were entirely predictable – indeed a modular system based upon a process of credit accumulation was a curriculum target for which Coventry's comprehensives could aim.

A stimulus to both models being translated into action was the MSC's TVEI. For Abergele and Clwyd this occurred in September 1983 and for Coventry in Septembr 1984, but Coventry also devoted other resources towards the achievement of this goal.

CLWYD

This part of the chapter attempts to catalogue the processes that enabled modules to gain respectability during the past four years when the germs of the ideas originated exclusively within the school. The model's origins lay in a sixth-form general studies programme that operated on an eight-week rotational basis. This idea was translated into the fourth-year curriculum as a response to needs concerning motivational factors that were not unique to Abergele but that were evident within the school.

Modules were originally offered as an opportunity for youngsters to pursue real alternatives – not to *what* they learned but to *how* they would learn. The modules offered the pupils chances to learn in an active experimental way as opposed to being taught in a traditional didactic fashion. The choices that were available led many to suspect that those who were the least able would respond to the modular option with its new ideas, while the bulk would opt for the proven and tested traditional modes. The response, of course, was the most single important factor in ensuring that this small curriculum adventure in this relatively unknown corner of Wales would not die. Of the 242 students presented with the choice, 206 decided that modules were for them and that over 30 per cent of their 14–16 options would be delivered in modular form.

The responsibility such a large cohort of students placed upon the management was probably the major factor in consolidating the development. Important issues needed to be addressed, and one of the most crucial was accreditation. While it was quite acceptable for students to pursue, over a two-year period, modules that would, in context terms, be equal to a GCE/CSE syllabus when combined together (e.g. drama, electronics, computing, etc.) there was a host of modules offered that had either no accreditation or had no traditional accreditation, for example, CGLI, Pitmans, RSA, etc. No opportunity then existed for modules to be combined in a more flexible manner than the traditional mode I syllabuses allowed.

The school decided that the way forward was to open negotiations with the Welsh Joint Education Committee (WJEC) to secure a set of rules that would allow modules to be combined in different ways in order to secure a variety of Mode III GCE/CSE qualifications. This urgency was not because the school was failing to meet any of the obligations it had offered the students but more because it was increasingly recognized that students would be given greater negotiating power and have more responsibility and control over their modular choices if there were a variety of possible uses for each module studied.

The WJEC were, at first, cool about the proposals. GCSE was on the horizon and GCE/CSE mode III submissions were being actively discouraged. Other factors, however, were also at play. CPVE was shortly to be introduced and the CGLI 365 course was taking a strong hold in many Welsh comprehensives. These newer courses were not directly controlled by the WJEC and they had, furthermore, been frustrated in their efforts to gain control over 'a Welsh CPVE'. It is suspected that there was real anxiety at WJEC headquarters over the potential loss of income that would result from these new qualifications. These pressures played some part in persuading the WJEC to yield to the Abergele overtures and the consequence was that the school was able to establish excellent relationships with two WJEC officers, Peter Davies and Gareth Pierce. Both officers were able to provide an advisory support service to the school that guided it through a complex labyrinth of committees, which finally resulted in approval for the school's modular schemes.

The role of the curriculum development officers, particularly that of Peter Davies, was crucial in the move towards accreditation, but the important features of the WJEC initiative were that it did not attempt to neutralize the school's teaching/learning strategies, it supported the assessment procedures being developed by the school and it made massive changes in examination board roles and responsibilities in order to accommodate these new curriculum ideas. The modular initiatives seemed to be just what the WJEC needed and it responded admirably. The product of all the negotiation and debate was a document entitled *14–18 Curriculum – The Challenge and the Changes Needed* (WJEC, 1983). The major features of the document are given in points 1 to 10 below, and despite all the wonderful qualities that were embodied in the Abergele modular curriculum, it was the relationship with the WJEC and the accreditation that resulted which caused the education world to wake up.

From that moment onwards the school was inundated with visits from all parts of the education world: professors, directors, headteachers, advisers, politicians and others came to marvel at this 'new' approach to teaching. The mould was on the way to being broken and the next year all students were offered a range of modular choices. The demand for the traditional type of course was so weak as to be non-viable.

The Curriculum and Assessment 14–18

1. The curriculum should be considered as being made up of cross-curricular activities and disciplines as well as the traditional subject.
2. The curriculum should be couched in terms of skills as well as content.
3. Syllabuses/courses could be considered as consisting of modules, each self-contained but – as a group – capable of forming a unit.
4. A flexible curriculum structure or framework is not compatible with a largely terminal examination programme of assessment.
5. There should be the development of pre-vocational and vocational syllabuses and courses, at the ages 14–16 and at 17 plus.
6. The local initiative or special scheme (mode II and mode III) could be a base for curriculum innovation.
7. Provision will have to be made for the opportunity to participate in, and be evaluated in, planned work experience.
8. The extension and enrichment of the curriculum necessitates a

modification in the role of the WJEC as an assessing–moderating instrument.

9. The curriculum and assessment changes demand a more comprehensive form of reporting pupil progress and attainment.

10. The 14–18 age group will have to be seen in terms of a complete curriculum–assessment grouping.

COVENTRY

The Coventry moves towards modularity were of an entirely different pedigree. The model does not appear to have originated from a grass-roots response to need but more to an attractive philosophical idea translated into practicality. Certainly the Coventry model owes much to the insight of its now retired Chief Officer, Robert Aitken, who was impressed by the Canadian method of unit credits and who expounded its virtues in the Coventry LEA document (1982) *Comprehensive Education for Life*.

The Coventry modular curriculum did not emerge as a result of TVEI. It was the Low Achieving Pupils Project (LAPP) – which in Coventry was referred to as the DES project – that gave birth to the modules in the 14–16 curriculum. At the Edgwick centre (one of the famous Coventry Top-shops)[1] the LAPP pupils were offered a series of vocational experiences for one day a week in an environment that resembled more an industrial setting than a school.

The centre was created in the vacated factory premises of a well-known industrial engineering company that had collapsed when the present recession first hit Coventry. It had originally provided for post-16 youngsters under MSC schemes but the LEA, impressed by the impact the centre had upon the youngsters, felt that such opportunities could be successfully exploited for 14-year-olds – and so they were.

A team of teachers working with a team of craftsmen and women (mostly made redundant at the onset of the depression) delivered the modules for one day a week over a ten-week period. The youngsters were encouraged to explore a range of different modules varying from office practice to brickwork, food preparation to motor-vehicle repair, and hairdressing to home maintenance.

The Edgwick modules carried no specific accreditation. However, they did carry certain essential ingredients. They encouraged students towards self-assessment. They were organized so as to ensure that students learned by doing (all day at the same module). They allowed youngsters the opportunity to negotiate their programmes within the modules as well as between them. They helped the young persons to relate their learning to life (particularly helpful in this were the relationships established between the students and the craftsmen and women). At all times the centre delivered its modules to all students irrespective of gender, race or physical/mental handicap.

The Edgwick initiative did not mature in the same fashion as the Abergele experiment and the centre's staff paid little attention to the need to seek for traditional GCE/CSE mode III accreditation. The nature of the clientele caused the staff to concentrate more upon the learning processes than accreditation – effective learning was the clear priority. The latest development, however, have seen the Edgwick centre modules being submitted to the Midland Examination Group for GCSE accreditation in combination with other modules that may be delivered at the centre, at the student's school, at the local further education college or at a neighbouring school. Furthermore, the centre is, through its own YTS and its involvement in the city-wide CPVE programme, ensuring that progression from pre-16 to these schemes is addressed through a series of hierarchical modules.

The TVEI developments were far more active in the promotion of the modular curriculum. The modules were delivered mostly in schools or in the local college at Henley. From the outset the accreditation was a major factor and negotiations with the local examination boards, and later with the Midland Examination Group, was a major consideration in the marketing of TVEI in the pilot schools.

The modules that were offered bore a striking resemblance to the Abergele modules. This was probably due to two factors. First, the MSC made no secret of its desire to promote 'new technology' related subjects in the curriculum and second, the Coventry team visited Abergele and other centres prior to its implementation of TVEI in phase 2. Whatever the motivation the Coventry team expended great energy, through a series of curricular groups, in the preparation and accreditation of modules.

Outside TVEI and LAPP the Coventry Advisory Service has maintained a keen interest in the promotion of a modular curriculum. The most notable development has been in the humanities project. Under the leadership of David Maund, the humanities teachers have developed a series of modules that can, by a series of rules of combination, be used to create a GCSE qualification in humanities. Students can, by studying additional modules, gain qualifications in GCSE History, Geography and Business Studies. Similar schemes are currently being developed in science and mathematics and the modern linguists have begun the preparation of a series of modules for introduction later while RE teachers are embarking upon the preparation of a range of non-accredited modules.

It is clear that Coventry's intention is to modularize the whole of the curriculum with an extended core being offered in a series of negotiated modules that can, depending upon the aptitudes, inclinations and interests of the students, be added to or supplemented in a variety of ways. All of the combinations are currently linked to a variety of GCSE outcomes and the next stage is to secure free-standing credits for the modules. Such a development is precisely what is required for the furtherance of community education – another Coventry speciality.

CONCLUSION

The Abergele and Coventry schemes represent different approaches to the promotion of the modular curriculum. In simple terms the former would fit the 'bottom-up' model while the latter represents a 'top-down' approach. There are those who would argue that the most effective method is when teachers at the chalk face are involved in the creation of the model and the idea. It is dearly liked to believe that this is the case and yet by far the greatest progress towards a wholly modular curriculum has taken place in Coventry, where positive direction from the top has helped to guide the city's teachers along the direction in which it wishes them to go.

REFERENCES

WJEC (1983) *14–18 Curriculum: The Challenge and the Changes Needed*, Cardiff.
Coventry LEA (1982) *Comprehensive Education for Life*, Coventry Education Committee.

NOTES AND ILLUSTRATIONS

[1]Coventry Topshops were developed by Coventry Education Committee as vocational training centres and later, under the LAP Project, were extended to provide pre-vocational education to the 14–16-year-olds in all of Coventry's comprehensive schools.

COVENTRY MODULAR HUMANITIES COURSES

Humanities in the Curriculum 14–16

In most schools children are required to choose a humanities subject chosen from a list in one of the options columns, and to follow this for two years. The basis of the option system seems to be twofold. Firstly, to offer choice which relates to the relevance which the child sees in terms of their future need (and through this give motivation); secondly, to bring about a balanced curriculum. Thus a simple curriculum might be (*see Figure 1*).

CORE			
Eng	Maths	PE/ Games	Tutor/ Careers
3	3	2	2

OPTION				
1	2	3	4	5
Sci.	Hums.	Design/ H. Ec.	Lang.	Other
2	2	2	2	2

Figure 1

From Option 2 a child may choose, say, History. In doing this all those ideas and experiences contained in Geography or Economics or Social Studies are forgone in favour of perhaps an examination of the Social and Political History of 19th Century England.

There are obvious problems in this case – a balanced curriculum assumes that History is a substitute for Geography or Physics for Biology. In fact any balance is a spurious one since under this system ideas important to the development of children may be entirely omitted through 'choice'. Some attempts to redress this is made through the fifth option block where it is possible to do a second humanities or second science. However, despite this, there are whole areas of experience which may be, and frequently are, omitted altogether. For example, this is the entire thrust of the issue surrounding the lack of provision for political and economic education. To include these under the present structure of curriculum would either mean the removal of something already there or further dilution of the concept of balance. So the achievement of balance seems to indicate expansion of the core and a reduction in the amount of time given to each element.

One other feature of the present system is worth mentioning as a significant characteristic. Some subjects are considered too 'difficult' for some children so in the option block in which they occur there frequently appears an 'easy' option. As an extreme example, the following may result from the option system outlined above:

Child A: Core +   Chemistry, Economics, Design, French, Physics
Child B: Core +   Gen Sci., Environ. St. Home Econ., Childcare, Commerce

This clearly has strong implications for the concept of balance, and worse may disadvantage one child despite them both having to contend with the same world and having, in a comprehensive system, equal rights to access to education.

In suggesting solutions to these problems, a number of assumptions are made which it would be useful to make clear. They stem in the main from the view that there are certain ideas about the world which all children have a right to be acquainted with, and without which they are severely disadvantaged as citizens. Thus there are a range of social, political and economic processes which we all need to be aware of if we are to operate as adequate human beings. The same is probably true of various processes which we think of as scientific and technical. This is not to deny that there are other ideas of a specialist nature or which are only of partial interest which should be optional.

Further, it must be acknowledged that these 'core' ideas are not easy to identify and can probably only be done over a period of time and as a result of emerging consensus. But to facilitate the process our pre-conception about the present curriculum and its structure needs to be challenged.

Probably the major obstacle to structural change is the adherence to the notion that a subject's worth must take two years. This in a way means that if you wish to have some of the ideas offered by a subject then you must take the lot or nothing. The only significant attempts to get round this has been through some form of integration. These attempts have generally foundered for a number of inter-related reasons. It is very difficult to construct an adequate conceptual framework and resort is made to skills which are frequently trivial, unrelated and because of the lack of a conceptual framework, not transferable. Teachers too, are frequently unenthusiastic about integration, maintaining that they teach their own subject best. Finally there is the problem of wider credibility with parents, employers and higher education.

Ideas about a modular curriculum brings a whole new dimension to the problem. In the context of humanities, and probably other areas as well, notably Science and Design, it offers freedom from present constraints whilst keeping many of the strengths.

The scheme described below was designed locally and is accepted by MEG as a joint certification. At the moment it consists of seven modules of which the children must do five (*see Figure 2*).

At the moment this is a modular course rather than a modular curriculum. It is intended for the core and therefore occupies one 'subject's worth' of the timetable. Its main features are:

1. It enables a balanced curriculum from a wide range of subjects.
2. All children are in contact with a wide range of ideas.
3. 'New' experiences can be introduced.
4. The subject expertise of teachers is retained.

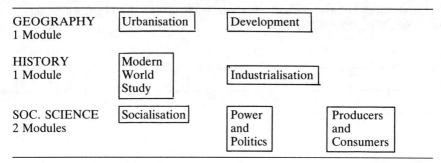

and any ONE other module.

Figure 2

5. Schools can introduce it without major re-organisation of either staffing or timetable.
6. Since each module has its own integrity it enables, through the continuous assessment system, the setting of short-term goals, and therefore quick feedback on attainment.

Allied to this development for the core has been the construction of a number of modular option courses (*see Figure 3*).

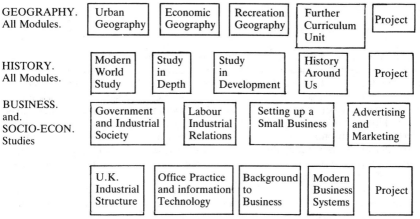

Figure 3

Each of these modules has its own coherence, assessed by course work, and modular examination during the teaching of the module. There is now a deal of evidence to suggest that this form of delivery and assessment benefits all children.

The two schemes which make up the core and options, in addition to having modules of similar length and structure, also have common assessment objectives. This would enable the two schemes to be brought together into one matrix of modules. Thus a column (a) would give a humanities core, a row (b) would give a subject option, and a carefully chosen cluster of modules (x) would give a particularly desired theme (*see Figure 4*).

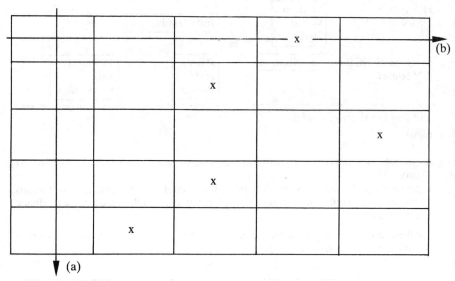

Figure 4

This is therefore a modular curriculum and has a number of obvious advantages over the traditional curriculum. Perhaps most radically it enables modular accreditation. This means that a student could take modules spaced over a long period of time, return to education after leaving school to complete or even start a cluster. There is also opportunity for schools to develop their own modules adapted to their own needs. There is no need for pupils to be taught in year groups or ability groups. There is no reason why mixed ages and abilities should not be timetabled. Indeed the scheme also offers opportunity for distance learning – a sort of post 14-Open University! If there were similar matrices in other subject areas, there would be the opportunity for genuine multi-disciplinary examination of issues.

This development begins to open up our thinking on the whole curriculum, to offer more flexible courses with the pupil's need at the centre – a genuine option system with balance produced as a result of genuine counselling.

What is Modular Humanities?

How many times in the past few years has reference been made by our illustrious peers to the amount of 'clutter' that exists in the secondary school curriculum? How often has the problem of planning a curriculum module for History, Geography or Social Studies been complicated by the need to take into account the fact that some pupils will not follow the subject beyond the age of fourteen?.

It was questions such as these that led teachers from the broad areas of the Humanities and Social Sciences to look for innovatory structures. It is not the purpose of this article to describe the process by which a solution was devised, but to concentrate on the end result. The reference group established to review the 'problem' under the direction of a seconded Coventry teacher, Roy Little, constructed a modular curriculum based on discrete subject areas. Why 'modular'? Two lines of reasoning influenced thinking. Firstly, the experience of Geography teachers, and more recently, historians had fostered a belief that by 'banking' achievements motivation and results were likely to improve. Secondly, national thinking in terms of the total curriculum package on offer to 14–16 year olds at present, led the group to believe that a modular structure would capitalise on the strengths of existing experience and move towards a curriculum structure that may allow pupils a much greater say in determining their own learning experience. In the pilot stage, seven modules were identified as forming, what the reference group regarded as essential elements of experience which would help Coventry pupils make sense of the world.

- Urbanisation
- Development
- Modern World Study
- Industrialisation
- Socialisation
- Power and Politics
- Producers and Consumers

The course is a 16+, at present jointly certificated through MEG. In order to assess progress, an assessment structure was devised based on experience from existing courses. Each module was to include two elements of assessment; an examination to be completed at the end of the module and one detailed piece of coursework, which may be substituted by two shorter pieces. Each module is required to test pre-specified assessment objectives, based on the Bloom Taxonomy in proportions that are consistent with discrete courses in History, Geography and other curriculum projects such as the Authority's TVEI scheme.

In September 1984, four pilot schools, Barrs Hill, Coundon Court, Lyng Hall and Woodway Park began the course. Each school determined the five modules they would teach, although the eventual intention is to allow pupils as wide an element of choice as possible. The course is intended to occupy the normal time allocation of one subject in the 14–16 curriculum. As each specialist area was expected to identify its 'core' content the reference group decided that the structure of the course meant the only valid place for such a course was in the core. Schools admitted into the scheme were required to accept this philosophy.

The implications for the management of departments and facilities is far reaching. The pilot phase is continually raising questions and issues for teaching strategies, assessment (both formative and summative) and the professional development of colleagues. The course also opens up opportunities; notably the chance to develop a planned curriculum model over a five years period ie. 11–16. As more modules are developed (R.E. and Business Studies already have modules in outline), the opportunity arises to present pupils with a real choice regarding the selection of modules they wish to study. The implementation of such a vision requires the specific inclusion of counselling within the course structure if we are to avoid a fragmentary experience for our pupils. The fact that the structure operates as a Mode III means that those involved are in a real position to react to feedback from participants. The course should be accepted for the start of GCSE next year.

The structure of modular Humanities capitalises on subject specialisms and has a potential for future development as part of a modular curriculum.

To the teacher grappling for the first time with the application of Bloom's Taxonomy in setting coursework assignments and modular tests there may be little comfort in the opening paragraphs of this article. Neither will their confidence have been enhanced by the difficulties imposed by the lack of support caused by industrial action. Despite all the constraints, however, it is quite remarkable what has been achieved over the first term of the course. Every teacher in the scheme (and there are twenty six of them) has produced a coursework assignment and a modular test, frequently after several attempts, and the quality of the items augers well for future developments.

In all this there is an essential need for a supportive structure and there are several strands in this. The city course co-ordinator plays a vital role, but the role of the school co-ordinators in their own schools and through a central reference group is even more vital. Also the use of seconded teachers, working on the ground with and crossfertilising ideas from one teacher to another and from one school to another, may prove an added strength. There is also a crucial need for a detailed in-service programme of active support for all teachers in the scheme, a policy at present largely thwarted by the dispute.

All this has to be placed against the context of the new GCSE proposals from the DES. Their model, at first sight appears to revolve largely round assessment procedures. (Concern has been shown by teachers that current proposals for GCSE training of Heads of Departments do not take account of what has happened in local curriculum development over the years.)

We need to demand an alternative model such as we have expounded over the past decade in certain subject areas. The development of philosophies and skills must be school and intra-school based, ideas must be generated 'upwards' and the 'manual' must be a working document to be modified and amended in the light of experience.

In conclusion, the previous views are precisely expressed in an article by Harry Torrance (*Forum* V.27 No.3) in which he says:

Whatever the focus, it also seems that in-service provision for school based examining would have to be a continuous activity, feeding off and feeding into the actual marking of work in schools. It seems clear that such follow-through would be most effective if it were part of the examining and *moderating* process itself. Rather than opting for postal sampling and statistical manipulation of grades which the logistics of GCSE might suggest is inevitable, leading to school based grades being changed without teachers knowing how or why, if the Examining Groups chose instead to liaise with LEA's over in-service training and establish a network of visiting moderators who would maintain control with schools during GCSE courses curriculum, pedagogy and comparative standards could ensue.

With goodwill and commitment in the Modular Humanities course in Coventry that argument could well be unassailable by the time GCSE is instituted.

A Modular History Course

Some History teachers in Coventry since 1978 have adopted the Schools' Council

Project: History 13–16 and experience of this has led to the view that some form of modular assessment is appropriate. This would enable the development of a flexible system of short-term units of work which might increase motivation by setting targets more precisely and rewarding success more regularly. It would allow greater opportunity to develop new topics and allow for change without disrupting the overall course. In any case, to quote one American writer, albeit out of context(!) ' – the good things in history are usually of short duration . . . but afterwards have a decisive influence over what happens over long periods of time'. (Hannah Arendt).

In 1983 therefore, some Heads of History agreed to devise a modular course which could also be put forward for Joint Certification. This was finally accepted by the Midland Examination Group in the summer of 1984 and piloted by Barrs Hill, Tile Hill Wood and Whitley Abbey Schools. Six other schools joined the scheme in September 1985.

As in Schools' Council History, the Coventry scheme is composed of four modules which can be undertaken in any order over a two year period. The modules together represent the nature of history and the methodology of the historian and should help students to understand the way in which historians use evidence to reconstruct and understand the past and present world in which they find themselves.

Each module is assessed by a combination of examination and coursework. Towards the end of the course an 'Historical Method' paper is given to all candidates in which they are presented with a range of previously unseen evidence on a topic they have not studied in the course.

The four modules are weighted as follows (*see Figure 5*).

MODULES	COURSE ASSIGN.	END OF MODULE EXAM	TOTAL
Study in Development	15	10	25
Modern World Study	10	10	20
Depth Study	15	10	25
History Around Us	20	–	20
Historical Method	–	10	10
Total	60	40	100

Figure 5

The aims and assessment of the Coventry scheme emphasise the importance of pupils developing an understanding of historical concepts. The syllabus and teaching materials deal with historical information, underlying which are specific key ideas.

It is early days to make a real evaluation of the course but one immediate problem emerging from the pilot schools is the amount of assessment that is required.

In response to this, changes have been proposed to reduce the amount of compulsory assessed work. Also the weighting of marks will be adjusted to make all the modules equal (*see Figure 6*).

MODULES	COURSE ASSIGN.	END OF MODULE EXAM	TOTAL
Study in Development	5	15	20
Modern World Study	20	–	20
Depth Study	10	10	20
History Around Us	20	–	20
Historical Method/Enquiry	–	20*	20
Total	55	45	100

Figure 6

*The skills and abilities tested by the 'Historical Method' examination could equally well be assessed by a course assignment based on 'Historical Enquiry'. Such an enquiry would aim at promoting intellectual curiosity and the development of pupils' research skills. It would enhance the role of history as a problem solving discipline, enabling pupils to develop the skills and understanding necessary for engagement in any historical enquiry.

The Coventry scheme is obviously still in a developmental stage and owes much to the work of the teachers involved. There are many possibilities for the future – the introduction of new modules and mixed age groups with content relating to attainment rather than age. It might even be possible for students to follow just one or two modules in the VI form or even for others to repeat modules where their performance was poor. As with all new schemes, problems will emerge and its success will depend ultimately on the dedication and enthusiasm of its teachers. So far, despite the present climate, the signs are promising.

6
THE SCOTTISH
ACTION PLAN EXPERIENCE
John Hart

INTRODUCTION

In January 1983 the Scottish Education Department (SED) published a document entitled *16–18s in Scotland: an Action Plan*. What this proposed was a framework of new courses, based on modules, that would lead to a new National Certificate. It was an answer to current worries about provision in schools and colleges during the first two years of post-compulsory education. It offered new courses of a less academic nature to those who stayed on in the secondary schools and it set out to replace the profusion of courses and certificates below the level of advanced certificates that were being offered by the further education sector.

Although the publication of this document took most educational institutions by surprise, it had been in the writing since the mid-1970s. Its begetters were the HMI for Scotland – a smaller, and possibly more powerful group of mandarins than their English counterparts. Much of the immediate reaction was due to the fact that the Scottish educational establishment had become used (over the previous decade or so) to a less direct, more devolved approach to educational reform. But as far as those who were aware of the development of HMI thinking on 16–18 provision were concerned, the surprises were still to come – for those who grasped the implications of the proposals did not, by and large, believe that they could be implemented.

Among both groups – those who accepted reluctantly and those who did not accept – the title of the new framework for post-compulsory non-advanced education in Scotland was quickly familiarized to the *Action Plan* and it is under this title that, in the words of the SED (1986a, p. 1) 'a quiet revolution has been taking place in Scottish education' over the last three and a half years.

THE CONTEXT

The *Action Plan* was developed in response to problems that were being experienced on both sides of the border. It also fed on national attempts to meet these difficulties. Some of the problems had been longstanding, such as how to induce more young people to participate in post-compulsory education and training. Some were more recent, such as how to disentangle the complex system of certificates being offered by bodies such as SCOTBEC, SCOTEC and CGLI. Some were recent and crucial, such as the sudden loss of employment opportunities for young people, and some were concerned with the forecast future, such as the foreseen need to enable people to change and develop their skills in response to rapid technological change.

The theoretical success of the *Action Plan* (it has not yet come fully into operation) can be measured by the international interest it has aroused. Enquiries have come to the SED from Europe, from the Commonwealth and from America, and at least two of the larger vocational agencies in the USA have already decided to adopt its principles. So there is evidence that the *Action Plan* philosophy is applicable to a wide range of educational circumstances. What is not so easily measured is the extent to which its development is due to the specific conditions in which it emerged – in other (plainer) words, why it was Scotland that produced the *Action Plan*.

It is tempting to see the *Action Plan* as a culmination of time-honoured Scottish attitudes to education. In particular the much-vaunted twin traditions of 'the lad o' pairts' and 'the democratic intellect' might seem relevant. In recent years, however, scholars have cast doubt on the validity of these traditions and there have been times when Scots' pride in the national education system has been somewhat undermined. Nonetheless, the belief that we offer – and should offer – a broad education on an open basis at all levels is firmly established in the Scottish educational psyche and, as such, may be deemed to be influential. Certainly breadth of curriculum and openness of access are two of the main features of official thinking on the *Action Plan*. The breadth may be indicated by the fact that the National Catalogue contains more than 2,000 modules which will make up the basic curriculum. More than 20 per cent of these come into the category of interdisciplinary studies. The openness of access may be indicated by considering the variety of client groups for which the *Action Plan* is now setting out to cater. These include school pupils following academic and non-academic courses, full-time and day-release college students following both fully vocational and general courses, youngsters on YTS placements and unemployed school-leavers making use of the DHSS 21-hour ruling to pursue vocational, general interest or leisure-related educational aims. In addition, in spite of its original 16–18 target, the *Action Plan* is now seen as relevant both to 14–16-year-olds on TVEI programmes and to adults seeking to acquire new skills or to enhance their employment or promotion prospects. And so it goes on – the limitations appear to be only the practical ones.

It has already been suggested that the structure of the Scottish educational administration may have been an important factor in the production of such a radical system as the *Action Plan*.The SED is one of five departments within the Scottish Office and the cabinet minister responsible for the running of the Scottish Office is the Secretary of State for Scotland. This individual has considerable power, and in discussions about educational reform in Scotland the influence of the current holder of the office – for good or ill – generally has to be taken into account. Within the Education Department are somewhat more than 100 inspectors, headed by a Senior Chief Inspector. With such a relatively small establishment, the opportunity for the individual to have an effective national role is enhanced and, in fact, the inspectorate uses a system of 'national specialists' in their organization. The influence of Senior Chief Inspectors is also widely recognized.[1]

It may be appropriate here to cite as an example the work for which one of these men, J.S. Brunton, is best remembered. Coming as it were, between the Education (Scotland) Act 1945 and ROSLA in 1972, the report *From School to Further Education* of 1963 – *The Brunton Report* – recommended broadly vocational interdisciplinary courses for 14–15-year-olds, followed by extended courses in schools and colleges to follow on from these. His recognition of 'the vocational impulse' as a key to motivation is given a reference in the first *Action Plan* document (SED, 1983a, sect. 2.5, p. 6), although it is recognized that for the 1980s and beyond a sophisticated interpretation of the phrase is required.

If we are considering the context in which the *Action Plan* emerged, however, the degree of devolved responsibility within the Scottish system must also be taken into account. Unlike the *Action Plan*, the reforms that preceded it, pertaining to the 14–16 age group, had been brought about by professional groups appointed by the Secretary of State. This arrangement, which has been fully formed for ten years, is headed by the Consultative Committee on the Curriculum, composed mainly of headteachers, principals of colleges and LEA officials. Its function is to keep the school curriculum under review, to initiate development work where this proves necessary, and to issue guidance to schools on curricular matters, and so on. To help it do this there are about two-dozen standing committess – on aspects of primary education, on secondary subject areas and on special projects. Membership of these committees tends to be at the level of school head of department or senior college lecturer. There is also a Curriculum Development Service, whose work is carried out by a combination of permanent officers and seconded teachers.

Complementary to this curriculum review structure are the bodies that examine and certificate. The main institution in this field is the Scottish Examination Board (SEB), a statutory body established in 1963 to take over from the SED (and the HMI) the job of conducting examinations and awarding certificates relating to secondary education. As part of its structure, SEB appoints a series of subject panels that draw their members mainly from schools, colleges and universities. These panels are charged with the review of syllabuses and examination arrangements and with the maintenance of standards. As far as further education was concerned before the *Action Plan*, the important bodies were SCOTBEC and SCOTEC, which carried out similar functions to their counterparts in England and Wales.

From the 1960s there were three levels of national award to pupils in Scottish schools. These awards were made on the Scottish Certificate of Education. Pupils in Scotland start their secondary education at 12 plus, and at the age of 15 plus (during their fourth year) just over 80 per cent of the cohort have been sitting Ordinary Grade examinations in anything from one to ten subjects. Almost a quarter of these candidates would attempt seven O-grades. In general, the courses for this award appear to aim at a level of difficulty that was something between CSE and O-level in England, although obviously there are differences that make comparison difficult in some subject areas.

By the 1980s slightly less that 60 per cent of these pupils were continuing their education into the first non-compulsory year (their fifth year). For just over 85 per cent of those who did continue this meant following anything from one to seven courses at the Higher Grade. Many were likely to be repeating O-grade courses or taking new 'crash' O-grades, so that four or five Higher courses were most likely. The standard of these H-grades lay somewhere between O-level and A-level and one of the aims of the fifth year is to continue a broad education, even for the more academically inclined. Another special feature of the system is the 16 plus 'exit point' for pupils going on to higher education. Traditionally, both ordinary and honours degree courses start with one or two years of general education: the ordinary course lasts three years and the honours lasts four.

For those who successfully complete a programme of H-grades, the second non-compulsory year (the sixth year) offers the Certificate of Sixth Year Studies (CSYS). Relative to the English system, they may come between A- and S-level. Certainly they are more specialized in their nature than the other, lower, awards. Also, the courses leading to the CSYS have tended to be very forward looking in their methods, allowing pupils to become independent learners at last. In spite of, or because of, these features they have not been notably successful in establishing themselves. They have proved popular with teachers, who welcome the chance to take on some more academic work, but the take-up in most schools is low, with most of the likely pupils preferring to take new H-grades or repeat old ones looking for improved grades. They tend to be a low timetabling priority in schools and the universities have not generally given them such credence.

Over the years, there have been occasional moves to adopt parts of the English system of awards. The lack of a national certificate for the new fourth-year pupils created by the raising of the school leaving age pushed a number of schools in the direction of CSE, particularly mode III, an adaptation they found satisfactory. In contrast, dissatisfaction with CSYS has caused certain schools to offer A-level courses. The latter change has tended to happen in isolated cases, whereas the introduction of CSE has been more concerted.

Indeed, more people seem to have been aware of a need for reform at the 14–16 level of the curriculum than were aware of 16–18 problems. Although 16–18 reform has been more radical and far-reaching it has received considerably less public attention or media coverage than the changes at 14–16, which preceded it. A conspiracy theory might suggest that the latter had been used as a stalking horse for the former, but it seems more likely that events – including the teachers' industrial action, which began in the autumn of 1984 – overtook both sets of change, altering their relationship to each other.

Reform of the educational provision for 14–16-year-olds in Scotland was set in motion by the Secretary of State for Scotland when he established, in the mid-1970s, two committees: the first, known after its chairman as the Munn Committee, was to consider the structure of the curriculum and to make recommendations that would ensure 'that all pupils receive a balanced education suitable to their needs and abilities' (SED, 1977b, sect. 1.1, p. 9); while the second, the Dunning Committee, was 'to identify the aims and purposes of assessment and certification' and 'to consider what form or forms of examination or assessment would be most likely to meet the needs of . . . pupils of varying academic ability' in the age group (SED, 1977a, p. 5).

The recommendations of these committees were largely accepted by the Secretary of State and in 1982, in a publication entitled *Framework for Decision*, the SED published their proposals for the implementation of a new curricular and assessment structure for the last two years of compulsory education. The broad curricular changes have already been made, although the programme of change was amended in response to the teachers' action.

The Munn Committee identified four sets of aims that should lead the curriculum: these were concerned with knowledge and understanding of the self and the environment; with skills of all kinds; with affective develop-ment; and with the demands of society. They also identified eight 'modes of activity, which constitute for us distinctive ways of knowing and interpreting experience' (SED, 1977b, sect. 4.9, p. 27). These are linguistic and literary, mathematical, scientific, social studies, creative and aesthetic, physical, religious and moral. These form the basis of the Munn curriculum and schools are expected to ensure that each pupil should have substantial experience in each mode.

In spite of this modal approach, however, the Munn Committee declined to condemn the subject-based approach to the curriculum that Scottish schools, almost without exception, take. As long as steps were taken to ensure that timetabling was flexible enough to ensure that the curriculum did not become excessively fragmented, that teaching methods were not narrowly didactic, and that attention was being paid to the inter-relationships that exist, the individual subject was to remain the basic unit of study.

Building on this fairly conservative foundation, the Consultative Commit-tee on the Curriculum recommended that courses should be of three types: subject-based and multi-disciplinary courses, of national design, lasting two academic years; clusters of short courses, of national design, lasting about 40 hours each but capable of aggregation over two academic years; and free-standing short courses, either school-based or taken from the national clusters. Awards arising from all these courses would be recorded on a single national certificate (SED, 1982, sects. 4.3, 4.4). The government generally endorsed these proposals, which can now be seen as foreshadowing a number of features of the *Action Plan*.

The Dunning Report proved considerably more controversial, although a number of its debated recommendations were shared with Munn. It also recommmended a new National Certificate that should be available to all pupils. Certificated subjects should be taught and examined at three over-lapping levels and minimum lengths for courses were laid down. Assessment was to be partly internal and was to take place across both years of teaching. Having taken into account the comments of the Scottish Examination Board, the government again found itself broadly in favour of the changes.

Perhaps the most significant statement in the report of the Dunning Committee is that which heads their list of 36 recommendations (SED, 1982): 'Assessment should make a positive contribution to the teaching and learning processes for all pupils'. The implications of that simple, and apparently unremarkable, proposition are still being explored at all levels – and it represents an important aspect of the *Action Plan*.

The result of the Munn and Dunning Reports was the drafting of an eight-year plan to introduce an entirely new system of curriculum and assessment for 14–16-year-olds. This was to be called Standard Grade. It would start with pilot work in two subjects, English and mathematics, that would later be introduced at three levels (to be called Foundation, General and Credit), and in two multi-disciplinary courses, science and social and vocational skills, which would later be introduced at two levels only (Foundation and General).

The Dunning Committee also wondered aloud about the advisability of a system in which curriculum and assessment responsibilities were lodged with separate institutions. No formal steps were taken in this regard, but the devising of syllabus guidelines was carried out in the first place by joint working parties whose membership was drawn from the national curriculum committees and from the examination board's subject panels. Ultimate responsibility for these guidelines, however, rested with the examination board that, for the first time, had to make arrangements for the moderation and validation of syllabuses. Previous board responsibility had gone no further than providing sets of *Conditions and Arrangements* for each paper. In this way, and others, the preparation for Standard Grade broke new ground in most schools and paved the way for important aspects of the *Action Plan*.

The guidelines for Standard Grade also opened up questions of assessment and forced teachers to consider these where they had not had to do so before. The differences between, and roles of, formative, summative, diagnostic and evaluative assessment became everyday issues, as did the meaning of continuous assessment. Linked to these were important questions of method, such as ways of ensuring choice and risk in pupils' work, finding places for the reworking of ideas and the transfer of skills, introducing 'real' sources and situations into the classroom, and securing an active role for pupils in the programme. In other words, Standard Grade was moving Scottish secondary education from a concern with content to a concern with process, and although there may be no direct connection, the *Action Plan* will now continue that push.

The main debate the earliest work on Standard Grade courses started, however, did have a direct influence on the *Action Plan*. This was the debate over a move towards criterion referenced assessment. To those who advocated criterion referencing, Standard Grade was not going far enough; to those who wished to retain norm referencing, traditional standards were at stake. The debate crystallized around an SED device – grade related criteria. These emerged during the early feasability studies that were carried out by pilot schools under the auspices of the HMI. They exist in two forms. Summary grade related criteria describe, briefly – for pupils, parents and other users – the attainments of those who have been given an award in a specific subject at a specific level. They exist for each assessable element of each subject. In English these elements were to be listening, talking, reading and writing. Maths and science shared elements such as handling information and problem-solving – they also had specific elements such as selecting strategies and practical skills. In each case the elements were simplified in line with proposals made by an SED Review Group (SED, 1986b). Extended grade related criteria were to be set out for each grade point. It was felt that they would be useful in syllabus construction and assessment design. 'They would have to be specified in sufficient detail to avoid meaningless generalities but at the same time they should not be too complex' (SED, 1982, sect. 3.10, p. 21). They could express current norms of attainment or could be arrived at through field trials; they could be accompanied by exemplars; they would have to be set alongside statements of aims, objectives and assessment procedures. They were felt by many to be neither fish, flesh nor fowl, and in 1984 an SED committee was set up that has recommended a number of changes in their form and use. The development of the *Action Plan* assessment, while it has flirted with similar complexities in its development, has eschewed them and has espoused a simpler approach to the description of attainment.

THE *ACTION PLAN*

The basic administrative unit of the *Action Plan* is the 40-hour module. Modules were defined as 'curriculum components . . . which are sufficiently flexible to be built into individual's programmes in a large variety of ways, and be a process of negotiation' (SED, 1983a, sect. 4.8, p. 31). The length of 40 hours – which had already appeared in the Munn recommendations and had some basis in limited areas of college practice – was deemed suitable for both full-time and part-time students. The former would tackle about twenty modules a year, the latter about six.

It is interesting at this point to consider the images that were used initially to explain the concept of modularization. The modules were explained as bricks, or Lego pieces or sections of mosaic – delimited and inorganic images that carried no sense of interactivity between teacher, learner and materials. Indeed, of the three images cited, only the third gives any notion of the differences between modules and the role of the learner in selecting or negotiating a programme. This is not the fault of the *Action Plan* that, from the beginning, gave clear warning that such freedom was part of its philosophy. As will be seen, the nature of the modules is such that the implications of this modularized education for 16–18-year-olds are still being discovered.

These 'curriculum components', then, were to be available to a wide range of clients in such a way that they could be fitted into programmes of study that met vocational or other needs, could be used as part of a recognized qualification, or to top up existing qualifications or to satisfy an interest. In order to achieve this, modules would be of two – or three – kinds: there would be general modules that would be appropriate to many purposes and would serve a range of different disciplines; there would be specialist modules whose application would be more restricted and that would vary in the degree of their speciality; and there would be integrative modules, seen as a sub-set of the specialist category, which would call on the student to apply the skills and knowledge gained in other modules in a new context. Integration was initially seen in vocational terms, such as a module in office practice employing skills from a number of modules in clerical and secretarial skills. The existence of this category, or sub-category, of modules was decided upon to meet the danger of modularization leading to fragmentation or disintegration of the curriculum. A modular approach must not appear to give the learner permission to forget at the end of each module.

It is said that, in the early stages of discussion, the *Action Plan* was thought of in terms of a small number of units, possibly as few as 200. The figure now talked about is more like 2,000, but the plan got under way in 1985 with about 1,300 modules and a programme of revision and development has been in operation since. Half of the students, however, studied in common only about 5 per cent of these modules, while each of the participating colleges offered about 400 modules.

The modules are presented in the *National Catalogue* (published by SCOTVEC) in nine categories: Interdisciplinary Studies; Business and Administration; Distribution Studies, Food Services and Personal Services; Engineering; Built Environment; Caring; Industrial Processing; Land and Sea-Based Industries; and Pure and Applied Sciences. In all categories there are both general and specialist modules. There are also half modules (lasting 20 hours), double modules (lasting 80 hours) and aggregates of modules. These aggregates normally last for 120 to 200 hours, each module building on its predecessor – for example, a modern language can be studied in three single modules and one double general module, tractor operation can be studied in one general and two specialist modules, and mining legislation can be studied in four specialist modules, although there is also a general introductory module on the topic. Interdisciplinary studies include communications, mathematics, computing and a variety of aesthetic, physical, behavioural and social studies. This category obviously contains more general modules than the others, but almost half of its over 400 modules are specialist. In the future, new areas of study such as crime prevention and skills for the hearing impaired will be considered for module development in the interdisciplinary category.

In future also, it is assumed that presenting centres will submit locally devised modules for inclusion in the *National Catalogue*. The motive is expected to be some perceived local need, as expressed by students, employers or planners. In this practical way the *Action Plan* will be able to meet its broad aim of changing with society. The devisers of the *Action Plan* see the modularized curriculum as being capable of a kind of evolutionary change that neither the present SEB courses nor the old non-advanced SCOTBEC and SCOTEC courses could match. In the case of SEB, syllabus change is a major process that is estimated to take at least five years (SED, 1983b, sect. 3.26, p. 18ff). In the case of the non-advanced courses change was likely to mean the introduction of new courses, which might well overlap with existing courses, but without the possibility of the transfer of credits in awards.

The body that has been established to manage the new structure is the Scottish Vocational Education Council, known as SCOTVEC. This institution was brought into being by the Secretary of State for Scotland in 1985, replacing both SCOTBEC and SCOTEC. It is responsible for the development, administration and assessment of the new National Certificate and also for continuing and refining the system of advanced courses previously offered by its predecessor bodies. In the course of the debate that preceded the formation of SCOTVEC, consideration was given to the establishment of a single examination board for all academic and vocational awards in Scotland. Such a body would be charged with the assessment and certification of pupils and students from 14 onwards, using a single certificate that could be amended as the individual progressed or diversified. As a corollary, the work of the Consultative Committee on the Curriculum would be extended into further education, where no equivalent body exists at present. In the event the argument that the change was too huge and that the single certificate would be too unwieldy seems to have prevailed and there is no timetabled plan for a merger between SCOTVEC and SEB. It seems unlikely, however, that this situation will continue indefinitely.

The structure of the individual modules within the modular curriculum is important to an understanding of the *Action Plan* and its implication. A definition from the introduction to discussion papers commissioned by the Scottish Council for Research in Education provides a good starting point for a consideration of this matter. Modules, says the author drawing on the *Action Plan*, are 'structure units . . . each designed to develop both knowledge of content and skills and containing a specification of objectives, criteria of achievement and suggestions about methodology' (Spencer, 1984, p. 1). All of this is contained in the format known as a module descriptor in which all the necessary information about the module is presented under seven standard headings.

First come the title, the type and purpose, and the preferred entry level. 'Type' refers to the categorization, general or specialist. 'Purpose' is expressed in a brief statement that will indicate the broad aims of the module and the likely clientele –this may be expressed in terms of other modules with which this one may be profitably linked. The level of achievement that is advised for those wishing to undertake the module is expressed in terms of a Standard Grade award in a particular subject, or in terms of related modules that ought to be completed before embarking on the module under consideration. In the case of some general modules no formal qualifications are listed, and in the case of certain interdisciplinary modules it is made clear that previous experience is an important factor. In any case the SED has made it clear that 'entry levels should not be interpreted too rigidly' since 'achievement depends on motivation as well as on aptitude, and attitudes to learning can change over time' (SED, 1984b, sect. 4.1, p. 12).

Arguably, the most important heading is the fourth – that dealing with 'learning outcomes'. These are related to Standard Grade GRC (grade related criteria) in two ways: first, they express the 'assessable elements' of the modules, just as the GRC are based on the assessable elements of the courses in which they operate; second, it is through the GRC of Standard Grade courses and the learning outcomes of the *Action Plan* modules that subject continuity is ensured. Similarly, of course, continuity or articulation between modules to ensure compatability or sequence is brought about by a careful statement of learning outcomes.

Unlike Standard Grade GRC, however, the learning outcomes of the modules are not expressed in terms of levels of achievement. It might be said that they embody a purer form of criterion referencing (SED, 1984a, Introduction, *passim*). It is unequivocally the case that students must attain all the stated learning outcomes specified in a given module if a pass is to be awarded – and all must be met at the appropriate degree of confidence. Investigations were carried out to ascertain whether it would be possible to write modules that could lead to different levels of award – say, distinction levels. However, it was found that what was created was a new module and this led to the creation of the aggregates of modules seen here.

Like Standard Grade GRC, the learning outcomes are public statements of achievement, available both to the student considering the course and to the employer considering the student's achievements. They form the course and they ensure that the aims of the *Action Plan* are met. These aims are said to exist in three 'clusters' (SED, 1983a, sects. 2.7–2.12, pp. 7–10) concerned with knowledge, skills and attitudes. In terms of practice they are expressed as revealing the capacity to apply knowledge, employing skills, and demonstrating the acquisition of values by certain behaviours. An example of a module in which the learning outcomes are stated in a manner that conforms to this analysis is the specialist half-module, *Negotiating Skills*. On completion of this module the student should

1. know the range of circumstances in which negotiation skills can be used;
2. prepare a case for a negotiation with clear and realistic objectives, 'fall-back' position, main arguments and counter-arguments; and
3. present a case using appropriate techniques of negotiation and conduct – the negotiation in an effective and realistic manner.

Normally, the learning outcomes, which will be three or four in number, do not follow this pattern, although they will cover all aspects of the aims.

In fact, the aims of the *Action Plan* may well be seen as over-inclusive. The education of 16–18-year-olds is to be concerned with the development and understanding of oneself, one's community and one's environment; it is to foster self-confidence, self-reliance and a sense of responsibility; it is to develop the ability to work fruitfully with others; it is to ensure basic literacy and numeracy; it is to include life skills, physical skills and practical skills; it is to nurture concern, compassion, tolerance and justice; it is to teach respect for democratic authority, for evidence and for truth. In sum, it is to prepare young people for 'active, participating citizenship and involvement in the democratic process' (SED, 1983a, sect. 2.10, p. 9). The devisers of the *Action Plan* could not be accused of narrowness in their conception.

What they have done, it might be said, is to attempt to bring the hidden curriculum into the curriculum for, by making the objectives of the modules so comprehensive and so public, they have put the teachers and lecturers into a new relationship with the courses, the students and the public. The relationship exists to a lesser extent with Standard Grade, but the word 'new' can be justified in that neither the profession nor the public had really had the time to adjust to that. As long as the learning outcomes are served – and they may be demanding masters – the teacher is left free to find the best way to bring his students to success. The three remaining module headings – content/context; learning and teaching approaches; and assessment procedures – become advisory to a greater or lesser extent depending on the topic, the resources available and the rule of best practice. In order to assist with development in this respect, the Scottish Office set up the Curriculum Advice and Support Team (16 plus) – CAST (16 plus) – that would, during the first two years of the *Action Plan*, assist teachers and lecturers with implementation. This has been done mainly through specialist working parties, through in-service training and through the production and dissemination of materials. Together with SCOTVEC, the CAST(16 plus) team have produced sets of exemplars, or graded examples of pupils' work, to assist teachers in the assessment of their students in certain areas of the curriculum.

But the aspect of modularization that has probably caused most worry among teachers and lecturers – if the educational press is any guide – is the freedom it gives the student: the introduction of the 'negotiated curriculum'. This is not intended to suggest that the Scottish teaching profession is particularly reactionary or jealous of its power, for there were a number of legitimate worries associated with the concept. For a start, the *Action Plan* was officially sanctioning a student-centred approach into an area where content had tended to dominate. Certainly in schools the inspectorate had recently reported that a generally high rate of success in achieving objectives with pupils in the post-compulsory years was maintained 'largely by surrendering opportunities to enjoy the best approaches recommended for modern teaching and to practice techniques of learning and study essential for continuing education' (SED, 1983b, sect. 6.1, p. 37). A later SED publication, however, expressed the view that effective implementation of the *Action Plan* as far as teaching methods were concerned 'may involve changes of emphasis and a greater variety of approach rather than extensive innovation' (SED, 1985, sect. 1, p. 1).

The changes in method that were being talked about were overtly connected with another underlying aim of the *Action Plan*, and that was the distinction between education and training. An earlier consultative paper had raised this issue, together with the possibility of new forms of organization or institution for 16–18-year-olds. The profession had been largely in favour of the maintenance of a school population and a college population, insisting that there were values in each type of community. This did not mean that pedagogic differences could not be eliminated. If schools were too academic and colleges too job-specific in what they offered, the *Action Plan* would mean that both lecturers and teachers would have to change, 'to develop new relationships with their teaching groups so that students will be encouraged to make choices about which modules to take, which methods of study to use . . . and about the best place for their learning' (SED, 1984c, p. 6).

A formal system of guidance has existed in Scottish secondary schools since 1971 when promoted guidance posts were introduced and in most – if not all – cases this includes vocational and academic counselling for post-compulsory students. The provision in colleges has been less sure. But, as the *Times Educational Supplement* (Scotland) pointed out in 1984, lack of understanding of the age group was not confined to one sector. Schools, said the writer, 'can be socially over-protective of senior pupils, while at the same time expecting them to tackle a formidable series of exams which will shape their lives'. Colleges paid only patchy attention to guidance in spite of the fact that 'the students on college courses are often less mature than their friends still at school'. What was needed was a guidance system geared to the age group (*Times Educational Supplement*, 1984). Not long after this, the SED and SCOTVEC set up a three-year action research project, which recently reported a need for extended guidance within the *Action Plan*. (Hart, Roger and Mulvie, 1987)

The consideration of guidance and choice raises a number of the issues already touched on. There is the matter of the fundamental aims of the educational system – and in Scotland, as we have seen, one of these is to ensure that every young person continues a broad education as long as possible. There is the matter of motivation, and in this case that means allowing the student's own perceived purposes – interests, needs – to lead the learning. There are the needs of society, and here the education system has a duty to satisfy not only present, vocational needs, but also to anticipate as far as can be done. There is the need for learning to be a maturing experience, and that means tackling real issues and taking real risks.

A survey of 218 lecturers involved in the *Action Plan* (by two lecturers at the School of Further Education, Jordanhill, Glasgow) showed that, although their general attitude to the plan became more positive over the first year of operation, 'the intention that the Action Plan would allow improved progression and more freedom of movement within the education system is seen as increasingly unlikely' (Dougall and Halliday, 1985, p.16). They also felt that their own freedom of action, particularly regarding the choice of procedures for assessing whether students have achieved the modules' learning outcomes, was being restricted. Here and elsewhere the suggestion is that pressure from outside agencies is making the plan too rigid in operation. Since there have also been publicly expressed worries about the maintenance of standards and the currency of modules among employers it would not be too much of a leap to suggest that the restrictions are a function of this uncertainty. The question remains whether an increase in confidence, if brought about by restriction, would allow an increase in freedom.

In one respect, investigations into the modules has suggested that one set of guidelines may be relaxed. An early statement, concerned obviously with the need to ensure that the 'vocational impulse' did not reduce the modularized curriculum to a series of narrow training units, put it this way: 'it is important that all modular programmes of study . . . should include a broad coverage of fundamental components such as: Problem Solving, Interpretation and Communication, Planning, Processing Data (including Number Skills), Manipulative Skills, Social Skills and Personal Development' (SED, 1984b, sect. 2.3, p. 5). In this way, both the broad aims of the *Action Plan* and the core elements of YTS would be covered. It seems likely that a different view may be taken of this in the future.

If this change comes about, it will arise out of investigations into generic skills and personal effectiveness – two of the four YTS core elements. Originally it had been felt that integrative modules might be required in which generic skills and personal effectiveness could be examined, but recent reviews of the modules have suggested that, in an important sense, a large proportion of the modules are 'integrative'. One implication would appear to be that any programme of modules could meet the broad aims of the *Action Plan*. What remains is to find a way of recording the performance of the student in terms of generic skills and personal effectiveness – and the ability to transfer, a third YTS outcome – and to set up modules that would allow students who were failing in these respects to improve themselves. Increaing attention has been given to the role of communication and personal and social development modules in this respect. Some revision has taken place and further research commissioned into the role of these groups of modules in the students' programmes.

CONCLUSION

At the start it was observed that the *Action Plan* was intended to meet current worries about educational provision for 16–18-year-olds, but the course of the chapter has increasingly tried to reveal the vision that is believed to be real spirit of the plan. However, as it has been pointed out, a number of difficulties and real doubts already exist about the practicability of the vision. If there is one central idea that can link everyday worries and ideal ends it must be the idea of motivation. The *Action Plan* offers a structure in which all the elements can come together to motivate young people, if they can be motivated at all. Concepts ranging from the 'vocational impulse' to 'active citizenship' have emerged in the discussion, but perhaps a broader, more homely, idea will serve to express the value found in the *Action Plan* and that is the notion of self-improvement. More importantly, the plan can offer self-judged self-improvement. The openness that is suggested by the arrangements of the plan, and in particular the stress on public learning outcomes, surely means that the most thorough moderation of the system will be carried out by the students themselves, who will choose the modules that suit their own aims and will not want to waste time on failure. Well-designed modules and good teaching can then ensure that, in the course of this, society's needs are also being met.

REFERENCES

Dougall, D. and Halliday, J. (1985) 'Conflicts in the making', *Times Educational Supplement* (Scotland) 6 December.

Scottish Education Department (1977a) *Assessment for All: Report of the Committee to Review Assessment in the Third and Fourth Years of Secondary Education in Scotland*, HMSO, Edinburgh.

Scottish Education Department (1977b) *The Structure of the Curriculum in the Third and Fourth Years of the Scottish Secondary School*, HMSO, Edinburgh.

Scottish Education Department (1982) *The Munn and Dunning Reports: Framework for Decision*, SED, Edinburgh.

Scottish Education Department (1983a) *16–18's in Scotland, An Action Plan*, SED, Edinburgh.

Scottish Education Department (1983b) *Teaching and Learning in the Senior Stages of the Scottish Secondary School, A Report by HM Inspectors of Schools*, HMSO, Edinburgh.

Scottish Education Department (1984a) *16–18's in Scotland, An Action Plan: Guidelines on Assessment*, SED, Edinburgh.

Scottish Education Department (1984b) *16–18's in Scotland, An Action Plan: Guidelines on Curriculum and Assessment*, SED, Edinburgh.

Scottish Education Department (1984c) *16–18's in Scotland, An Action Plan: Guide to Teaching Staff*, SED, Edinburgh.

Scottish Education Department (1985) *16+ Development Programme, Guidelines on Teaching and Learning Approaches*, SED, Edinburgh.

Scottish Education Department (1986a) *16+ in Scotland, The National Certificate: Guide to Parents and Students*, SED, Edinburgh.

Scottish Education Department (1986b) *Assessment in Standard Grade Courses: Proposals for Simplification*, SED, Edinburgh.

Spencer, E. (ed.) (1984) *Modules for All? Discussion Papers on New Proposals for the Education of 16–18's,* Scottish Council for Research in Education, Edinburgh.

Hart, J., Roger, A., Mulvie, A., Munn, P. (1987) Managing Modules: Guidance and choice in further education colleges, Scottish Council for Research in Education, Edinburgh.

Times Educational Supplement (Scotland) (1984) Editorial, 23 March.

NOTES AND ILLUSTRATIONS

[1]The hierarchy within the Scottish Inspectorate is as follows: Inspectors, Chief Inspectors, Depute Senior Chief Inspectors (2) and a Senior Chief Inspector.

MODULE DESCRIPTOR GUIDELINES

SCOTTISH EDUCATION DEPARTMENT
New St. Andrew's House Edinburgh EP1 3SY

16–18 MODULE DESCRIPTOR – GUIDELINES

Ref No./Date	1.9.83

Title	

Type and Purpose	[General or Specialist] [A brief statement indicating the broad aims of the module and the probable target audience]
Preferred Entry level	[Expressed in terms of achievement, for example, F, G, C, or previous modules]
Learning Outcomes	The student should: – [knowledge:– know and use the key ideas, principles, language structure, processes . . . etc.] – [skills:– communicate clearly, plan, design, solve problems, manipulate data, order ideas, diagnose, rectify, assemble, dismantle, manipulate a keyboard, align, measure . . . etc.] – [behaviours:– work safely, hygienically, co-operatively, diligently . . . etc.]
Content/ Context	[Content will be expressed according to the nature of particular subject areas. In some cases use and want and industrial expectation will influence the form of presentation and the degree of specificity required; in other cases the material selected in relation to learning outcomes and the special needs of the student group will be relatively free of these constraints. Overloading should be avoided; learners should be provided with opportunities for reflecting and reinforcement.]
Learning and Teaching Approaches	[Appropriate to achieving the learning outcomes, selected from among the following:

Learning and Teaching Approaches *continued*	Working alone Working in pairs Working in groups Group discussion Debates Exposition Demonstration Team teaching Visitors Surveys Questionnaires Interviews	Practical work Case studies Projects Assignments Simulations Individualised learning Computer Assisted learning Programmed learning Work experience Residential experience Field studies Visits etc]
Assessment Procedures	[Appropriate to the learning outcomes and the selected learning approaches – and indicating what are considered to be satisfactory performances for each learning outcome:	

	Objective test (eg multiple choice)
	Short Answer
	Essay
	Log book
	Folio
	Questionnaire
	Self-profile
		Observations of performance *in*:
		    Practical, case studies, projects etc
		Reports (oral/written/graphic) resulting *from*:
		    Practical, case studies, projects etc
		Finished produce
		Orals]

EXAMPLES FROM THE NATIONAL CATALOGUE

01 INTERDISCIPLINARY STUDIES

61109 Computer Networks (G)
61110 Computer Graphics (G)
71111 Introduction to Computer Programming – BASIC (G)
71112 Introduction to Computer Programming – COBOL (G)
71113 Introduction to Computer Programming – COMAL (G)
71114 Introduction to Computer Programming – FORTRAN (G)
71115 Introduction to Computer Programming – PASCAL (G)
61116 Business Systems Analysis and Design 2 – (Project) (S)
71117 Introduction to Computer Control Systems (G)
71119 Computer System Software (S)
71121 Computer Programming (Project) – BASIC (S)
71122 Computer Programming (Project) – COBOL (S)
71123 Computer Programming (Project) – COMAL (S)
71124 Computer Programming (Project) – FORTRAN (S)

71125 Computer Programming (Project) – PASCAL (S)

INDUSTRIAL AND BEHAVIOURAL STUDIES
61131 Industrial Relations in the Workplace (G)
61132 British Industrial Relations (S)
61133 Introduction to Behavioural Science (G)
61134 Leadership and Motivation at Work (S)
61136 Personnel Services (S)
61137 Supervision and Management (S)
61138 Economics of Industrial Relations (S)
71139 Supervisory Management 1 (S)
71140 Supervisory Management 2 (S)
61144 Industrial Studies 1 (G)
61145 Industrial Studies 2 (G)
61149 Training Skills ($\times$1/2) (S)
61151 Introduction to Work Study ($\times$1/2) (G)
61152 Work Study 1 ($\times$1/2) (G)
61153 Work Study 2 (S)
61154 Organisation and Methods (S)
61158 Staff Management and Development (S)
61159 Labour in a Small Business (S)
61161 Quality Assurance 1($\times$1/2) (G)
61162 Quality Assurance 2($\times$1/2) (G)
61163 Quality Assurance 3 (G)
61164 Quality Assurance Procedures (G)

PERSONAL AND SOCIAL DEVELOPMENT
61171 Personal and Social Development: Life and Work ($\times$1/2) (G)
61172 Personal and Social Development: Community Welfare (G)
61173 Personal and Social Development: Managing Your Money (G)
61174 Personal and Social Development: Environmental Studies in the Local Area (G)
61175 Personal and Social Development: Recreation and Leisure (G)
61176 Personal and Social Development: A Residential Experience (G)
61177 Personal and Social Development: Community Involvement (G)
61178 Personal and Social Development: Health and Fitness (G)
61179 Personal and Social Development: Accident Prevention and First Aid ($\times$1/2) (G)
61180 Personal and Social Development: Coping with Unemployment, and Job Seeking Skills ($\times$1/2) (G)
61181 Personal and Social Development: Consumer Skills ($\times$1/2) (G)
61182 Personal and Social Development: Local Decision Making (G)
61183 Personal and Social Development: History in the Local Area (G)
61184 Personal and Social Development: Contemporary Issues ($\times$1/2) (G)
61186 Personal and Social Development: Understanding Roles and Behaviour ($\times$1/2) (G)
61187 Personal and Social Development: Work Experience (G)
61188 Personal and Social Development: Induction ($\times$1/2) (G)
61189 Personal and Social Development: Parentcraft (G)
61190 Personal and Social Development: Cultural Studies in the Local Community (G)

61191 Personal and Social Development: Living Skills (G)
61192 Personal and Social Development: Enterprise Skills (G)
61193 Personal and Social Development: Linking On-The-Job Experiences With Off-The-Job Education and Training (G)

HEARING IMPAIRED
61215 Introduction to Signs and Fingerspelling (S)
61216 Communication using Signs and Fingerspelling (×2) (S)
61217 Production Skills Related to Speech (×3) (S)
61218 Lip-Reading Skills (×2) (S)

DRAMA
61250 Drama Theory and Practice (×3) (S)
61251 Production 1: A Revue (×2 1/2) (S)
61252 Production 2: A Published Play (×2 1/2) (S)
61253 Production 3: A New Play (×2 1/2) (S)
61254 Production 4: Touring/Theatre in Education (×2 1/2) (S)
61255 Community Drama: Basic Skills (S)
61256 Community Drama: Drama/Games Sessions (S)
61257 Community Drama: Production 5 (×2 1/2) (S)
61258 Video Production Techniques (×3) (S)
61259 Stage Make-Up (S)
61260 Acting (×2) (S)
61261 Voice (S)
61262 Theatre Skills (S)
61263 Stage Carpentry (×2) (S)
61264 Movement and Dance (×2) (S)
61284 Theatre Arts (G)
61285 Creative Drama 1 (G)
61286 Studio Production (G)
61287 Theatre for the Community (G)
61288 Creative Drama 2 (G)
61289 History of Theatre (G)
61291 Play and Theatre Appreciation (G)

YOUTH WORK
71480 Introduction to Youth Work (G)

MUSIC
71310 Music and the Young Child 0–8 years (×3) (S)

MUSICAL ELECTRONICS
61315 Music Production and Sound Engineering 1 (G)
61316 Music Production and Sound Engineering 2(×2) (G)
61320 Synthesisers 1 (S)
61321 Synthesisers 2 (S)
61322 Synthesisers 3 (S)
61325 Computers in Music 1 (S)
61326 Computers in Music 2 (S)

MUSIC IN MOVEMENT
61335 Music in Movement Activities 1 (G)

61336 Music in Movement Activities 2 (S)
61337 Music in Movement Activities: Scottish Dance (G)
61338 Music in Movement Activities: Folk/Ethnic Dance (G)

MUSICAL INVENTION
61350 Musical Invention: Basic (G)
61351 Musical Invention: Arranging (S)
61352 Musical Invention: Composition (S)
61353 Musical Invention: Improvisation (S)

MUSIC THEATRE
61354 Music Theatre 1 (G)
61355 Music Theatre 2 (S)

LISTENING TO MUSIC
61356 Listening to Music: An Introduction (G)
61357 Listening to Music: Instrumental (Modern) (G)
61358 Listening to Music: Instrumental (Romantic) (G)

TWO COMPLETED MODULE DESCRIPTORS

SCOTTISH VOCATIONAL EDUCATION COUNCIL

38 Queen Street
Glasgow G1 3DY
Tel: 041 248 7900

22 Great King Street
Edinburgh EH3 6QH
Tel: 031 557 4555

NATIONAL CERTIFICATE MODULE DESCRIPTOR	
Ref No. 61192	Session 1986–87

Title	PERSONAL AND SOCIAL DEVELOPMENT: ENTERPRISE SKILLS
Type and Purpose	A *General* Module – one of a range which provide breadth and balance in programmes of learning. The discriptor should be read in conjunction with the Guidelines in Personal and Social Development.

The modules which focus on personal and social development share common educational aims:–

– the development of ways of thinking, feeling and behaving;
– growth in self-confidence and independence;
– the development of communication and inter-personal skills and the capacity for co-operative action;
– the development of planning and decision-making skills.

Type and Purpose *continued*	These aims have vocational as much as personal and social relevance.

The particular purpose of this module is to provide the opportunity for students to develop enterprise skills in relation to an area of interest which they have previously identified.

Students will be encouraged to identify the technical, managerial and entrepreneural skills relevant to their own area of interest, and to plan and undertake experiences designed to enhance these skills. They will be responsible for setting their own goals, initiating their own learning experiences and maintaining a record of their progress.

The module provides an introduction to activities which can be developed more fully in 02206 Starting and Running a Small Business.

Preferred Entry Level

Personal and Social Development modules are designed to be both accessible to and place demands on a wide range of students.

An individual's previous experience should be considered when selecting a PSD module: some will wish to pursue previous interests and studies, perhaps in a different way, through PSD modules; others will prefer to extend their interests and experiences in new areas through PSD modules.

This module is suitable for students who have previous experience of organising and taking part in activities in areas which are suitable for the application of enterprise skills, e.g. 01177 Community Involvement; 01187 Work Experience; Standard Grade Social and Vocational Skills; O Grade or Standard Grade Home Economics.

Previous experience of taking responsibility for one's own learning and working cooperatively with others is desirable.

Standard Grade in English at 4, 01002 Communication 2 or equivalent is desirable.

Learning Outcomes

The student should:

1. identify the enterprise skills relevant to a project based on his/her own interests;

2. evaluate his/her personal characteristics in relation to Learning Outcome 1;

3. plan and undertake a range of activities designed to develop his/her strengths and compensate for weaknesses identified in Learning Outcome 2;

4. produce a revised plan for the project based on the experience gained.

Content/
Context

Corresponding to Learning Outcomes 1–4:

1 & 2 Since the module is intended for those students who have clearly identified an area within which they wish to further develop their enterprise skills, it is likely that a wide diversity of projects will be undertaken.

The project undertaken may be based on an idea for a small business which the student wishes to develop and plan within a supportive environment before setting up commercially. On the other hand, the project may be envisaged as a community venture or a cooperative activity. All of these would be legitimate vehicles for the application of enterprise skills.

There can be no absolute definition of enterprise skills, and students may already have identified some of the characteristics and skills which they wish to develop.

Certain features of enterprise have, however, been identified, and factors such as the following should be taken into account in the student's planning:

– Motivational factors: have I thought clearly enough about whether I genuinely want to to this?
: do I have the necessary self-confidence to cope with set-backs?
: how much work am I prepared to put into this?
: can I obtain the cooperation of others when necessary?

– Abilities & skills : can I solve problems and make decisions quickly and accurately?
: am I flexible enough to undertake the range of tasks which this will require?
: can I work with others and take a leadership role when necessary?
: can I contribute accurately and effectively to discussions?
: do I have the necessary skills to keep accounts and records accurately?
: can I make plans and be systematic enough to keep them?
: can I respond positively to advice?

Content/   – Recources &   : will anyone use the goods or
Context   information   services I am offering?
continued   : how does what I am offering differ
                                        from what is already available?
                                      : do I know where to get help if
                                        necessary with – legal matters
                                                       – financial
                                                         matters
                                                       – any other areas
                                                         of difficulty
                                                         which I have
                                                         identified?

3 & 4 The activities undertaken should be clearly based on the
       learning from outcomes 1 & 2 above.

       Depending on the student's needs, it may be more
       appropriate that the student undertakes one relatively
       large scale project, or a series of shorter ones, each
       designed to deal with an aspect or aspects of his identified
       needs.

       Since the most effective demonstration of enterprise is
       often achieved through the ability to recognise and
       capitalise on the complementary skills of the group, it
       should not be assumed that the project must be undertaken
       on an individual basis.

The student may undertake the project alone, or as the leader of a
team, but it is equally possible that the project will be run as a
cooperative, either in conjunction with other students or with
existing enterprises.

The final revised plan should clearly identify the areas where there
has been a revision of the original concept, and should state the
reasons for such revisions.

Suggested   Involving students in the decisions which affect them is valuable
Learning and   for personal development as well as a powerful motivating factor.
Teaching
Approaches   It should not be assumed that enterprise skills have to be taught,
                 since many students will already be competent in this area through
                 their own previous experience. The approach adopted in the
                 module should therefore not be of formal teaching, but rather of
                 enabling and encouraging the student to widen his/her experience
                 in relevant areas, and of encouraging reflection on the learning
                 which has taken place.

                 The advantages of role modelling in developing enterprise skills
                 should be recognised, and in this respect the involvement of those
                 already engaged in enterprises relevant to the student's interests
                 should be encouraged. This offers scope for negotiation between
                 tutor and student in deciding on a suitable community contact

Suggested
Learning and
Teaching
Approaches
continued

person, and between the contact person and the tutor in refining the original idea. Such contact might be either in the form of a consultancy or through a work placement.

Since the module is based on the individual interests of the student, it is inevitable that a wide variety of projects will be undertaken. Nevertheless, there are advantages in encouraging a regular interchange of ideas in small groups, as many of the enterprise skills identified will be common across a range of contexts. The role of the tutor is thus one of identifying areas of common interest, and stimulating supportive discussion on an individual or group basis.

The development of enterprise is likely to require an element of risk-taking by the student. It is therefore essential not only that the tutor encourages this, but is able to create a supportive atmosphere during discussion so that effective learning can take place.

Depending on the nature of the student's identified needs, it may be appropriate to include one or more short case studies of existing enterprises which provide relevant learning experiences.

Assessment
Procedures

Formative assessment should operate as an integral part of learning and teaching in the module. It may include self-assessment, assessment by peers and assessment by the tutor.

Each student should keep a folio of work undertaken during the module. These folios, together with any products of groupwork (tape/slide presentations, posters etc.) should be available to a subject assessor.

It is recommended that each student is issued with a record sheet at the outset of the module and that its various purposes are explained.

The record sheet:
– informs the student of the minimum which is to be taught and learned,
– provides a continuous record of attainment and should help both the student and the tutor to keep a track of learning and teaching,
– could be used by the student to inform a third party (e.g. a potential employer) of what he/she has learned.

The Performance Criteria which follow provide the tutor and the student with a statement of the minimum performance which is judged to be acceptable in the key aspects of each Learning Outcome. Many students, given the opportunity and encouragement, will go well beyond the minimum performance. A decision on whether or not a student has achieved the criteria should, where appropriate, only be taken after he/she has had the benefit of additional teaching support in areas of weakness and the

Assessment
Procedures
continued

opportunity to revise, redraft or rework unsatisfactory efforts.

Where appropriate, hearing impaired students may use signs and fingerspelling and visually impaired students may use braille.

LO   Learning Outcome
AP   Assessment Procedure
PC   Performance Criteria

LO1, AP   project folio

      PC   The student:

           1. clearly explains the proposed project;
           2. identifies the range of enterprise skills which the proposed project requires and produces a short written report on these.

LO2, AP   project folio

      PC   The student:
           1. completes a profile of his/her personal characteristics in relation to LO1;
           2. sets personal targets, identifying his/her own strengths and/or weaknesses.

LO3, AP   project folio, observation of project activity and, where appropriate, report from community contact person

      PC   The student:

           1. plans a project or series of activities related to his/her personal needs identified in LO2;
           2. monitors his/her project continuously in relation to its stated aims and records his/her observations in a logbook;
           3. works without close supervision;
           4. seeks appropriate help when necessary.

LO4, AP   project folio

      PC   The student:
           1. identifies what he/she has learned;
           2. identifies what he/she still requires to learn or to experience related to the project;
           3. produces a revised plan which clearly identifies modifications from the original;
           4. produces a written report on proposed future action to further develop his/her enterprise skills.

NATIONAL CERTIFICATE RECORD SHEET

Ref No: 61192   Title: ENTERPRISE SKILLS   Student: Group: Centre:

Learning Outcomes	Performance Criteria	Tutor's Signature and Date
1. Identify the enterprise skills relevant to a project based on his/her own interests	1. Clearly explains the proposed project.	
	2. Identifies the range of enterprise skills which the proposed project requires and produces a short written report on these.	
2. Evaluate his/her personal characteristics in relation to Learning Outcome 1.	1. Completes a profile of his/her personal characteristics in relation to Learning Outcome 1.	
	2. Sets personal targets, identifying his/her own strengths or weaknesses.	
3. Plan and undertake a range of activities designed to develop his/her strengths and compensate for weaknesses identified in Learning Outcome 2.	1. Plans a project or series of activities related to his/her personal needs identified in Learning Outcome 2.	
	2. Monitors his/her project continuously in relation to its stated aims and records his/her observations in a logbook.	
	3. Works without close supervision.	
	4. Seeks appropriate help where necessary.	
4. Produce a revised plan for the project based on the experience gained.	1. Identifies what he/she has learned.	
	2. Identifies what he/she still requires to learn or to experience related to the project.	
	3. Produces a revised plan which clearly identifies modifications from the original.	
	4. Produces a written report on proposed future action to further develop his/her enterprise skills.	

SCOTTISH VOCATIONAL EDUCATION COUNCIL

22 Great King Street
EDINBURGH EH3 6QH
031-557 4555

38 Queen Street
GLASGOW G1 3DY
041-248 7900

NATIONAL CERTIFICATE MODULE DESCRIPTOR

Ref No.	64411	Session 1986–87

Title	ENGINEERING SYSTEMS 2: PNEUMATICS AND HYDRAULICS

Type and Purpose	A *general* module which enables the student to understand the function and methods of construction of pneumatic and hydraulic circuits and their industrial applications.

Preferred Entry Level	04410 Engineering Systems 1: Machines and Mechanisms.

Learning Outcomes	The student should:

1. interpret pneumatic and hydraulic symbols, circuit diagrams and fluid specifications;

2. sketch pneumatic and/or hydraulic systems and describe the function of the elements;

3. design and build pneumatic and/or hydraulic circuits;

4. locate and rectify design faults, installation faults and developed faults in pneumatic and hydraulic systems;

5. comply with regulations and procedures and use safe working practices specified for equipment and work areas.

Content/ Context	*Pneumatics*

Properties of compressed air; generation and distribution.

BS symbols, conventions and terminology (BS2917).

Elements of pneumatic systems: compressors and service components, motors, cylinders and pistons, valves, seals.

Circuit construction: single and multi-cylinder circuits with pressure, speed and stroke control; automatic cycling.

Electro-pneumatic circuits: use of solenoids, pressure switches and micro-switches (24 volts maximum).

Practical applications to engineering systems: machine tools, portable tools, brake systems, mechanical handling and control systems.

Content/	*Hydraulics*
Context	Principles of hydraulic systems and properties of transmission/
continued	fluids.

BS symbols, conventions and terminology (BS2917).

Elements of hydraulic systems: pumps, motors and service components, cylinders and pistons, valves, seals, accumulators and intensifiers.

Circuit construction: single and multi-cylinder circuits with pressure, speed and stroke control.

Electro-hydraulic circuits: use of solenoids, pressure switches and micro-switches (24 volts maximum).

Practical applications to engineering systems: machine tools, transmission systems, lifting, handling and work holding.

Principles of hydro-pneumatic systems – application to work holding, press tooling.

Fault Finding
Systematic approach to finding design, installation and developed faults.

Common causes of failure: dirt, heat, misapplication, improper fluids, leaks.

Preparation and use of fault finding charts.

Safety precautions applicable to tools, equipment and work areas.

Suggested	A systems approach is recommended, i.e. the operation of the
Learning and	circuits should be explained using system diagrams in which the
Teaching	components are initially represented by block diagrams and
Approaches	replaced by conventional symbols as they are identified and
	examined.

A laboratory equipped with 'didactic' units on which circuit elements can be assembled, connected and demonstrated is strongly recommended. Additionally, sectioned or transparent models and polarised diagrams should be used to establish the operating principles of components which would be difficult to strip and re-assemble.

The students, working in pairs, should assemble pneumatic and/or hydraulic circuits ranging from a simple clamping circuit with one cylinder to sequential circuits having up to three cylinders and including electrical components.

Each student should investigate and report on a minimum of one pneumatic and one hydraulic system. Each report should include a systems diagram, a circuit diagram, a description of the circuit operation and examples of practical applications.

Suggested Learning and Teaching Approaches *continued*	Each student should also complete a project which includes design and construction of a pneumatic or hydraulic circuit to satisfy a brief such as: 'Design and build a prototype system to clamp, stamp and eject a given component'.

Where possible students should be encouraged to discuss and exchange ideas and to assist each other.

Safety and safe working practices, care and use of equipment should be an integral part of all module activities.

Assessment Procedures	All learning outcomes must be validly assessed.

The student must be informed of the tasks which contribute to summative assessment. Any unsatisfactory aspects of performance should, if possible, be discussed with the student as and when they arise.

Acceptable performance in the module will be satisfactory achievement of the performance criteria specified for each learning outcome.

The following abbreviations are used below:

LO   Learned Outcome
IA   Instrument of Assessment
PC   Performance Criteria

LO1 IA   Graphical/written exercise.
&2

PC   The student:

LO1   (a)   correctly interprets circuit symbols, circuits and specifications;

LO2   (b)   satisfactorily sketches simple fluid systems and accurately describes the function of the elements.

LO3 IA   Project.
&4

PC   The student:

LO3 (a)   constructs a practical circuit to satisfy given requirements;

(b)   uses correct components and elements;

(c)   operates the system;

LO4 (d)   locates faults in system using diagnostic techniques;

(e)   rectifies faults and re-designs the system if necessary.

Assessment Procedures *continued*	LO5	IA	Observation checklist (in which the following elements must be included).

PC The student consistently:

(a) wears all necessary safety clothing and equipment;

(b) behaves in a manner appropriate to the working environment;

(c) uses tools and equipment safely.

EXAMPLES OF MODULAR PROGRAMMES IN BUSINESS, SCIENTIFIC AND TECHNICAL STUDIES

1. BUSINESS STUDIES

Modules which are likely to be taken by all students:

61004 Communication 4 (double module)
61053 Mathematics: Business Numeracy (S)
62250 Financial Record Keeping 1 (G)
62251 Financial Record Keeping 2 (S)
62252 Financial Record Keeping 3 (S)
61063 Mathematics: Statistics 1 (G)
62201 Introduction to Economics (S)
62203 Contemporary Economic Issues (S)
62204 Organisation of Industry (G)
62351 The Legal Framework (S)
62353 Law in the Workplace (S)
plus a selection of elective modules from:
61174 Personal and Social Development:Environmental Studies in the Local Area (G)
62253 Accounting 1 (S)
62254 Accounting 2 (S)
62202 Introduction to Financial Services (S)
61092 Computer Hardware (G)
62300 Costing 1 (S)
62301 Costing 2 (S)
62302 Costing 3 (S)
62450 Insurance 1: Nature and Functions (S)
62451 Insurance 2: Principles and Practice (S)
62404 Travel and Tourism Geography 1 (S)
62405 Travel and Tourism Geography 2 (S)
61133 Introduction to Behavioural Science (G)

The above list provides examples of modules which may form the basis of electives, e.g. Environmental Studies in the Local Area is drawn from the Personal and Social Development Area but other modules from that catalogue would be equally suitable. Similarly, other modules may be drawn from Inter-Disciplinary Studies, Business Studies, Science and Technology catalogues.

To gain a qualification under the modular programme equivalent to the former SNC, students must be successful in the modules 61004, 62250, 61063, 62201, 62203 listed above. In addition they must successfully complete at least a further 6 modules drawn in part from the subject areas previously offered in the SNC award.

It is recognised that in some subjects more than 2 modules may be completed successfully. In estimating the equivalence of the modular programme completed vis-a-vis the SNC, however, such subjects (e.g. Financial Record Keeping) can only be credited with 2 modules towards the minimum total of 11 modules required for purposes of equivalence.

2. DISTRIBUTIVE STUDIES
Modules which are likely to be taken by all students:
61004 Communication 4 (double module)
62251 Financial Record Keeping 2 (S)
62252 Financial Record Keeping 3 (S)
62351 The Legal Framework (S)
62354 Consumer Law (S)(½ module)
63100 Introduction to Distribution (G)
63104 Organisation of Distribution (S)
63101 Selling Skills (G)
63107 Stock Control (G)
63108 Buying (S)
63109 Merchandising (S)(double module)
63102 Display 1 (G)
63103 Consumer Studies (G)
plus a selection of elective modules from:
63105 Wholesale Distribution (S)
63106 Warehousing and Transportation (S)
62204 Organisation of Industry (G)
62352 Health and Safety in the Work Environment (S)
61133 Introduction to Behavioural Science (G)
62353 Law in the Workplace (S)
61174 Personal and Social Development: Environmental Studies in the Local Area (G)

The above list provides examples of modules which may form the basis of electives, e.g. Environmental Studies in the Local Area is drawn from the Personal and Social Development Area but other modules from that catalogue would be equally suitable. Similarly, other modules may be drawn from Inter-Disciplinary Studies, Business Studies, Science and Technology catalogues.

To gain a qualification under the modular programme equivalent to the former SNC in Distribution Studies, students must be successful in the modules 61004, 62252, 62351, 62354, 63104 and 63107 listed above. In addition they must successfully complete at least a further 5½ modules drawn in part from the subject areas previously offered in the SNC in Distribution Studies.

3. OFFICE SKILLS (Secretarial Option)
Modules which are likely to be taken by all students:
61002 Communication 2 (G)

61003 Communication 3 (G)
62100 Introduction to the Office and General Office Services (G)
62101 Business Documents and Methods of Payment (G)
62107 Typewriting 1–6 (although time for successful completion of up to 6
–12 modules is provided for in this programme, in pratice the majority of students may only achieve the learning outcomes associated with modules 1–4)
62113 Audio Typewriting 1 (S)
62256 Employment and Payroll (G)
62103 Reception 1 (G)
61053 Mathematics: Business Numeracy (S)
62120 Simulated Office Work 2 (S)(½ or full module)
62121 Simulated Office Work 3 (S) (½ or full module)
62122 Simulated Office Work 4 (S)(½ or full module)
plus a selection of elective modules from:
61174 Personal and Social Development. Environmental Studies in the Local Area (G)
61010 Learning and Study Skills 1 (G)(½ module)
63301 Personal Presentation A (G)(½ module)
63302 Personal Presentation B (G)(½ module)
62255 Cash Handling (G)
62150 Word Processing 1 (S)(½ module)
61091 Introduction to Computers (G)
62200 Local Economy (G)
62500 People and Politics (G)

The above list provides examples of modules which may form the basis of electives, e.g. Environmental Studies in the Local Area is drawn from the Personal and Social Development Area but other modules from that catalogue would be equally suitable. Similarly, other modules may be drawn from Inter-Disciplinary Studies, Business Studies, Science and Technology catalogues.

To gain a qualification under the modular programme equivalent to the former SCOS, students must be successful in the modules 61003, 62100, 62101 and 62107–62110 listed above. In addition they must successfully complete at least a further 6 modules drawn in part from the subject areas previously offered in the SCOS award.

It is recognised that in some subjects more than 2 modules may be completed successfully. In estimating the equivalence of the modular programme completed vis-a-vis the SCOS, however, such subjects Typewriting 1–4 can only be credited with 2 modules towards the minimum total of 13 modules required for purposes of equivalence.

BIOLOGICAL SCIENCES (Animal Technology Option)
No. *Title*
69180 Basic Husbandry Techniques for Small Laboratory Animals (S)(½ module)
69181 Basic Small Laboratory Animal Unit Management (S)(½ module)
69182 The Control of Disease in Laboratory Animals (S)(½ module)
69183 Specialist Techniques Relating to Laboratory Animals (S)(½ module)
69184 Breeding of Laboratory Animals (S)(½ module)
69185 Nutrition of Laboratory Animals (S)(½ module)
PLUS three full modules (or equivalent) selected from:
69071 Human Physiology (G)

69072 Cell Structure and Biochemistry (G)
69073 Metabolic Pathways and Physiological Processes (G)
69074 Microscopy and Histology (G)(½ module)
69076 Homeostasis and Control in Animals (G)
69077 Plant Physiology (G)
69078 Genetic Investigations (G)
69079 Ecology (G)
69080 Microbiology 1 (G)
69081 Microbiology 2 (G)(½ module)
PLUS where appropriate the following modules which are specified as preferred entry requirements for the compulsory modules:
61002 Communication 2 (G)
69062 Chemistry Laboratory Techniques (G)
69071 Human Physiology (G)
69074 Microscopy and Histology (G)(½ module)
69080 Microbiology 1 (G)

7

THE MOVE TO MODULAR
VOCATIONAL CERTIFICATIONS
Peter Seazell

INTRODUCTION

Until the 1970s the pattern of vocational education and training had evolved progressively through the years, with attempts to revise and change it (such as the Industrial Training Act 1964) proving too slow or even unsuccessful. Such training had become stratified between the time-constrained company specific at one end and the almost non-existent at the other. With the steep rise in unemployment, particularly among the school-leaver, and the growing social and economic difficulties in the now rapidly declining industrial heartlands came a new incentive to re-examine the whole process of preparing and training people for a role in a reducing and changing workforce – one fitted to the demands of 'new technology'.

The plea, nationally, was to adopt a flexible approach to work skills and practices – to become mobile, relocating to the areas where industries had survived or the new industries were beginning to evolve and flourish.

Such industrial, demographic and social changes inevitably had an effect on the way the workforce was prepared for its roles. The 'new' industries had no traditional training pattern and the older ones were having to adapt or to abandon theirs because of economic pressures and the demands of process changes.

All these acted as stimuli to the inevitable changes in training needs and began to find a focus through the MSC and its programmes of vocational training and experience. This organization originally provided support for the short-term, mainly young, unemployed, but gradually became the most dominant influence on vocational education and training from its pre-16 TVEI scheme to the field of adult training and re-training.

These new demands and methodologies produced a wider client group for the trainers to manage and began to raise questions about the ways we gave recognition to any training. The tradition methods of national or local qualifications were rigid in their content and in the ways they assessed skills. The range of validating bodies was such that certification was confusing, frequently parochial and often meaningless outside narrow geographic or vocational bands. While the country was coming to terms with the more generally high-profile move to a new system of 'academic' examinations (GCSE) a quiet but no less important change was evolving in the field of vocational qualifications.

DEVELOPMENTS IN THE WEST MIDLANDS

In October 1984 Birmingham Education Authority moved to address a problem that the Careers Service and a consortium of city colleges (acting as a group of managing agents for YTS) were identifying with growing concern. It had become apparent that a significant cohort of young people were leaving training schemes, across both the private and public sector, without employment or a defined route to some form of continued training. The city Council, together with some financial support from the European Social Fund, launched a programme called Beyond YTS (BYTS). The essential objectives of the programme were to mirror the training provided throughout the YTS year with a mixture of city colleges and local employers providing closely monitored work experience and matched 'off-the-job' further education. There was, however, to be one essential difference in this second year: all the trainees were to be provided with the clear target of vocational qualifications (for some, at a second level and for others at a first level).

Once in operation it became obvious very quickly that this declared intention was going to prove very difficult to deliver. There was a vast difference in abilities, backgrounds, experiences and qualifications brought by the participants to the scheme. At one end of the spectrum were those whose training and experience had been very thorough and who had managed to obtain a level-one qualification. In contrast there were significant numbers whose mixture of training and work experience had been poor and who had no accurate records of achievement as vocational qualifications. Because of the comparatively small size of the programme (approximately 1,200 places across the city) and the demographic/geographic spread of those joining the scheme at its variety of locations, there was often a cross section of the whole cohort in any group at any one location. The original expectations of being able to offer a mixture of discrete groups and infilling proved to be inoperable for some groups and in some vocational areas that were less popular.

In an attempt to resolve these difficulties the co-ordinating group leading the BYTS developments approached the West Midlands Advisory Council for Further Education (WMAC), who, through its examination section (the Union of Education Institutions – UEI), offered regionally based and managed vocational qualifications in a wide range of subjects. Clearly, a simple move to a locally delivered examination system from a national provider was not going to resolve some of the more difficult hurdles:

1. While regional examinations are in many cases more flexible in their timing they still require programming at fixed points in the year. This inevitably disfranchises those who join late or fall between examination dates on leaving or are unable to cover the curriculum within the fixed time allowance.
2. There is no provision in traditional examinations to recognize previous knowledge or skills.
3. There is no means for traditional examinations to record successfully or meaningfully anything less than complete success. While some systems utilize mechanisms such as referrals or partial passes they have not been able to illustrate usefully where any short-fall may be.

Discussions between WMAC and the BYTS group then centred on a radical, if not revolutionary, new approach to the certification of achievement, together with the way it was 'measured'. The initial exercise was to take those vocational certificates offered by the UEI and to break them down into smaller, bite-sized modules of both learning and assessment.

It is important at this point to draw a line to separate two important but different issues: that of modules of learning/teaching and that of modules of assessment – they are different in purpose and in design. Breaking down a syllabus into smaller elements or disaggregating the curriculum provides, in effect, only a timetable for the delivery of the programme. To provide a flexible system that is responsive to the new style of non-advanced further education (NAFE) and its rolling programmes, the assessment has to be delivered in a much more responsive and demand-lead fashion.

Shortly after the initial discussions had begun with a recognition of the two needs of moving to disaggregated delivery, the whole issue was influenced by national events:

1. The announcement of Lord Young of a two-year YTS programme, with a declaration that vocational qualifications must be made available to all its trainees.
2. The establishment of a review of vocational qualifications. It was a

concern to many that the number of examining bodies, together with the proliferation of 'qualifications' issuing from them, was at best confusing. Indeed, because of a lack of clarity in the relationship between subjects, levels and titles, a growing number were, effectively, meaningless and failed to provide the keys to the occupational doors that young people so urgently sought.

3. Along side this review came the establishment of the Youth Certification Board, whose purpose is to establish a list of vocational qualifications that are viewed as suitable for use within the YTS scheme.

By April 1986 WMAC had issued an information pack to all managing agents within the geographical area it covered. This set out the concept of a unit scheme of vocational qualifications and invited those who received it to register as potential centres and to outline the training areas for which they wished certification. The general principles of this early document are broadly as follows:

1. The provision of vocational qualifications by means of credit accumulation.
2. A curriculum built upon groups of related competence statements, each set of statements being a unit of both training *and* assessment.
3. A move away from traditional forms of assessment (end-point written or multi-choice) that were seen as falling into the insensitive and the inappropriate, towards a continuous and demonstrative assessment to set minimum performance criteria, with any knowledge associated with practical skills being evaluated in parallel with the practical.
4. A flexible approach to delivery and assessment. Units were not to be time constrained but could be followed at the trainee's pace, with assessment of the outcomes or achievements provided at such a time when both the trainer and trainee were agreed on the likelihood of success. This sort of exercise was in itself unique in any vocational examination (certification) system. The move by SCOTVEC, as part of the Scottish *Action Plan* (see Chapter 6), to modularize the vocational curriculum had included advice that its modules were also blocks to time (a module being 20 hours).
5. Units were so designed that the training *and* the measurement of achievement in the competences could be undertaken in a variety of places and by a variety of methods – though the method and performance criteria were predetermined to promote standardization of ability levels.
6. Candidates would receive recognition of all competences achieved by the precision of statements of achievement, which would relate to the unit in which they were contained but also provide for accumulation (like Greenshield stamps) until an identified combination could be exchanged for a full vocational qualification.

As a by-product to this process, each unit set out[1] core skills in numeracy, literacy and problem-solving, etc., that could be identified as an integral part of any occupational competency. The initial response to the publication of this first document was overwhelming, with centres from outside the West Midlands (who had learnt of it by word of mouth) expressing interest and support for its intentions.

THE UNIT BASED SCHEME

It was with a mixture of relief and satisfaction that, by the time the National Council for Vocational Qualifications (NCVQ) had published its recommendations in *The Structure of Vocational Qualifications* (January 1987), the format of the Unit Based Scheme (UBS) had evolved to a point where such differences as could be identified were minor if not cosmetic. The one missing element from the original proposal was that it had little national dimension. However, in October 1986, the WMAC signed an overall operational agreement with City and Guilds covering the ending of any duality (or competition) of certification by traditional subjects. It also provided for agreed units to be aggregated, enabling the award of a full CGLI certificate.

One of the greatest dangers in providing a responsive and flexible scheme is that of creating an administrative system that becomes horrendously complex and an unacceptable burden on time and resources. For this reason the WMAC set out from the beginning to ensure that, for the operators of its programmes, procedures should be clear, simple and economic. All that is required of the user is the registration of the candidate (with a single fee) and the return to the WMAC of the candidate's record of achievement at such time when accreditation is required.

The first line of assessment is undertaken by members of the training staff, licensed by the WMAC and supported by teams of visiting assessors, to ensure standardization of performance at assessment. This assessment can then be delivered both off-the-job and on-the-job, or in the case of the job training scheme and work-place re-training, entirely within the company (work placement).

The development of the scheme gathered momentum throughout the autumn of 1986, with small teams of curriculum writers – drawn from further education, training interests and industry – consulting with a wide range of industrial interests and industrial training boards in order to create lists of competencies that were thought necessary for those wishing to claim vocational proficiency. The authors then clustered or nested these into logical, related groups (forming units) and added the four other associated areas:

1. The integrated core skills.
2. The context in which the competencies were set, with background knowledge requirements and an indication of any identifiable transferability of the competency both within and without the vocational setting.
3. A suggested learning/teaching approach with an indicator of 'good practice' and useful training aids or methodology.
4. The way in which the competency was to be assessed, together with the minimum performance required of the candidate before accreditation could take place. The method of assessment and performance were evolved in close consultation with the related industries and training boards to ensure from the outset that the standards being set were those required and accepted by industry, and that they did not create any duality with those already laid down and accepted.

Active interest in the UBS continued to grow and it was not long before its applicability to adult training was apparent. However, perhaps one unexpected development was the possibility of its usage in TVEI schemes. Nothing is more frustrating than having to repeat an exercise simply because previous success is not recognized. TVEI schemes set out to provide a platform for entry to vocational training, yet to date little that is achieved in the 14–16 programme is transferable and creditable post-16 into vocational training. The extension of a UBS both downwards and upwards would provide just the coherence and continuum necessary if we are to address the issue of training flexibility. The ability to build upon skills in a structured way, terminating only when the trainee has decided he or she has reached saturation, will encourage movement towards qualifications that were otherwise out of reach by traditional means. Even more importantly, it would promote a workforce who view training and re-training as both desirable and meaningful.

CONCLUSION

What of the future? By opening up access to qualifications to all a great deal may well be done to deliver a greater measure of equality. There is no doubt that to operate a totally open and flexible system will require fundamental changes in the way we deliver training and further education.

A totally open system would have to be based on the following general principles:

1. Movement away from a closed access or guardianship of skills and knowledge, providing for training and the measuring of the success of that training in a much greater number of venues – with continuous

training and assessment being undertaken as part of everyday activities.

2. Further education and technical training establishments moving away from traditional termly or yearly timetabling and providing a matrix of units of training and assessment. Trainees moving in and out of units once the level of achievement had been reached and collections of credits had accumulated for exchange into vocational qualifications.

3. A much closer harmonization of the two major providers, industry and education, with each responding to the needs of the other rather than placing demands that reflect what they want to offer rather than what they have been asked to provide.

4. An acceptance by the examination bodies that they are to provide a vehicle of assessment, standardization and accreditation that is responsive to the industries and not to the providers of the curriculum.

Last, to make the whole process effective, there must be a system of transference of credits – nationally – across the vocational sectors and the 'academic/vocational' divide, giving access to areas and institutions that to date have had artificial barriers between them. Ideally, though ideals are seldom attained, such a scheme should be international, giving recognition at agreed levels to skills achieved anywhere and at any time. It is certain, however, that even though bodies such as the MSC, NCVQ and the examination bodies have developments in hand, progress appears to be slow.

REFERENCES

[1] Published in the FEU/MSC document *Supporting YTS*, a unit (modular) approach.

NOTES AND ILLUSTRATIONS
SELECTIONS FROM ONE MODULE DESCRIPTOR

See Figure 1.

Learning Objectives for this Unit

Upon completion of this Unit, the candidate will be able to:

LO1.	Prepare the working area and equipment safely.
LO2.	Gown and prepare a client in an efficient manner.
LO3.	Complete a hair and scalp analysis, identifying any contra-indications and select an appropriate shampoo.
LO4.	Ensure client comfortable at the basin.
LO5.	Estimate and apply shampoo correctly.
LO6.	Demonstrate correct massage techniques.
LO7.	Perform thorough rinsing procedure.
LO8.	Towel dry client.
LO9.	Transfer a client to a working area.
LO10.	Prepare a client for the next procedure.
LO11.	Clean and prepare a work station ready for the next client.

Context/Content

Corresponding to the Learning and Core Skills Objectives

LO1.	Preparation of gown, towel, shampoos available ready for use. Brushes and combs to be collected from sterilizer.
LO2.	Greet and gown client. Brush and comb hair.
LO3.	Perform hair and scalp analysis to determine whether procedure can commence and select appropriate shampoo. Enquire if client has any preferences. Give information if required.
LO4.	Position client correctly at front or back basin. Test water temperature and flow before applying. Communicate with client to establish comfort.
LO5.	Estimate (or measure) correct quantity of shampoo, and apply from hand.
LO6.	Apply correct massage using rotary, petrissage and effleurage movements to ensure thorough cleansing of hair and scalp with regard to hair type.
LO7.	Rinse hair thoroughly.
LO8.	Use correct manner to wrap hair in towel and bring client to upright position, and towel dry.
LO9.	Transfer client to working area.
LO10.	Prepare hair for next procedure; comb through correctly and supply dry towel, and inform stylist that client is ready for next service.
LO11.	Clean Work Station for next client.

Suggested Learning and Teaching Approaches

Corresponding to the Learning and Core Skills Objectives

LO1–11 Candidate to demonstrate complete shampoo service, talking through

City and Guilds
of London Institute

West Midlands Advisory Council
for Further Education

UNIT DESCRIPTOR

Category: HAIRDRESSING	

Unit Title: THE PRACTICE OF SHAMPOOING

Unit Reference: UBS/033/011	Date: FEBRUARY 1987

Type and
Purpose:
 	
      To give the candidate the skills required to undertake
      Practical Shampooing.

Preferred   UBS/033/001, 002 & 003 Entry Level: (if any)

Success in this Unit will facilitate progression towards the following Vocational Qualification (s)...   City & Guilds 300 Hairdressing   For details of appropriate combinations of Units which merit these awards please refer to the UBS Equivalence Handbook.

Figure 1

the methods and reasons.

LO1.   Candidate to explain importance of thorough preparation with reference to hygiene and Health and Safety practices – particular reference to sterilisation techniques.

LO2.   Demonstration of correct manner and courtesy in greeting a client. Enquiry as to front/back wash and gown correctly. Taking client to basin and seating comfortably. Brush and comb through hair reassuringly and confidently.

LO3.   Invite candidate to perform hair and scalp analysis, and ask client if they have any preferences. Candidate to advise on correct shampoo. Trainer to explain that if candidate feels any contra-indications are present, senior supervisor's advice must be sought.

LO4.   Allow client to position themselves at basin and re-adjust position if necessary. Test water temperature and flow on back of hand. Adjust water temperature until comfortable before applying to the head. Apply water and enquire if temperature is comfortable (adjust if necessary).

LO5.   Demonstrate how to estimate correct quantity of shampoo in palm and apply evenly to whole of head.

LO6.   Demonstrate the three massage movements (rotary, petrissage and effleurage), so that hair does not become tangled, and ensure that the whole scalp and hair is thoroughly cleansed.

LO7.   Demonstrate testing of water temperature, control of flow before applying to head. Demonstrate method of thorough rinsing avoiding entanglement.

It is suggested that at this stage there should be a repeat of steps LO5, LO6, LO7, with the candidate performing a second application of shampoo with guidance from the trainer, inviting comments and questions from group.

LO8.   Demonstrate correct method of wrapping hair in towel and bringing client to upright position and then the drying method.

LO9.   Demonstrate tactful 'leading' of client to working area and seat them comfortably.

LO10.   Demonstrate how to comb through hair, ensuring there are no tangles and correct positioning of dry towel. Enquiry as to client needs. Inform stylist that client is ready for next service.

LO11.   Demonstrate how to tidy round basin and appropriate hygiene practices. Prepare for next client.

Assessment Procedures

Corresponding to the Learning Objectives

The Performance Criteria which follow provide the tutor and candidate with a statement of the minimum performance which is judged to be acceptable in order to achieve each Learning Objective within this Unit. Candidates will receive accreditation in respect of each Learning Objective they achieve, and upon achieving all the Learning Objectives within this Unit, will be deemed to have passed the Unit.

Many candidates may well achieve performance beyond the minimum requirements. A decision on whether or not a candidate has achieved the criteria should only be taken after he/she has had the benefit of additional tutor support in areas of weakness and the opportunity to revise, redraft or rework unsatisfactory efforts.

It is recommended that each candidate should be issued with a copy of the record sheet supplied at the outset of the Unit and that its various purposes should be explained:

- it informs the candidate of the minimum which is to be taught and learned.
- it provides a continuous record of attainment and should aid both the candidate and the tutor to keep track of learning and teaching.
- it could be used by the candidate to apprise a third party (e.g. a potential employer) of work undertaken, in advance of Unit accreditation.

Key to Abbreviations

LO – Learning Objectives
AP – Assessment Procedure
PC – Performance Criteria

AP   A practical assessment sheet is to be used to assess the candidate during a practical session.

PC   The minimum acceptable standard is that set out on the assessment sheet. All boxes should be ticked, or assessment should be repeated completely.

PART 3

ISSUES FOR MODULAR CURRICULUM PLANNING

8
ASSESSMENT IN MODULAR SCHEMES
Henry Macintosh

INTRODUCTION

As other chapters in this book make clear, the current interest in modules or units has come about for a variety of reasons. Basically, however, these emerge from one central issue, namely a desire to manage learning more effectively in the interests of all students. To this problem, which is not confined to any particular age range, there are no universal solutions and hence no correct answers to such questions as 'How long is a module?' The answers will inevitably depend upon the proposed learning outcomes, the purpose or purposes for which the modules have been undertaken and the needs of the students, tempered by such things as the experience and interests of the teachers, the requirements of society, the demands of politicians and the availability of resources.

In order to manage learning to its best advantage one needs to be able to measure progress. How to do this most effectively and realistically constitutes the central question for assessment, whether a large number of smaller learning units is involved or a small number of larger units. Unfortunately, because the public examination system in the UK has to date largely ignored progression as an issue, and because modular developments have been associated in the main with new 14–18 curricular initiatives such as the TVEI, it has been assumed that something new is needed for assessing modules. This is not the case. What is needed is the will to make use of the full range of techniques that already exist – in other words, the basic problem is attitudinal and not technical. In particular, more stress needs to be laid upon the informal at the expense of the formal and upon assessment during the course rather than at its end. Assessment must remain constantly concerned with finding and using the most appropriate evidence with which to match outcomes and to complement teaching/learning strategies.

The continued existence of formal public examinations for most students at the age of 16 has, moreover, caused the two quite distinct issues – assessment and certification – to become entangled. Much of the current debate carrying the label 'modular assessment' is in reality about modular certification, whether this be for GCSE, with its national criteria, or A-level or to meet the requirements of bodies like BTEC, CGLI and the RSA. In order to take a look at the real assessment issues it is necessary initially to disentangle these from certification and this is what happens in this chapter in the context of 14–18 developments since this is where the main thrust of modules is currently coming. If this is not done then the certification tail will wag the assessment dog. In particular the underpinning rationale for modules and their assessment will be ignored or at least sidelined by the obsessive interest in aggregation that certification induces.

There are, of course, precedents for such separation. As tertiary institutions in both the USA and Australia have introduced semester systems of varying kinds, they have increasingly come to issue students with both a certificate (in the form of a degree) and a transcript of results. The former summarizes and evaluates overall performance whilst the latter records performance as it takes place. Separating assessment and certification does not, of course, remove the problem of how ultimately to mesh the two at the completion of a course of study and the issues that this raises will be returned to later. There is currently at least one major example of this approach at the secondary school level in this country in the shape of the Northern Partnership for Records of Achievement (NPRA) unit accreditation scheme (the transcript) and the Northern Examining Authority's (NEA) modular GCSE (the certificate). Both were established to operate independently but steps are currently being taken to try to reconcile them. Success or failure here will be of considerable significance for modular developments within GCSE. On a smaller scale there has also been a great deal of work undertaken by the Associated Examining Board (AEB) and the Somerset LEA TVEI scheme on certification. Reference is made to all three schemes later in this chapter.

MODULAR ASSESSMENT

The starting point, therefore, for a consideration of 'modular assessment' can most usefully lie with the assessment requirements of the 14–18 curriculum. Despite continued government unwillingness to see 14 as a more relevant break point than 16 there is a growing consensus about both the need for and the agenda for a 14–18 curriculum – see, for example, *Future*

Imperative (Secondary Headteachers Association, 1987) and *Action Plan: A Policy 14–18* (National Association of Head Teachers, 1987). The TVEI extension, moreover, provides an ideal framework around which to undertake such a development.

Amongst the items on the 14–18 agenda that have significance for assessment are the following:

1. Emphasis upon skills and concepts at the expense of factual knowledge for its own sake.
2. Stress upon oral and practical work.
3. A widening of the contexts within which learning takes place.
4. Greater autonomy for students in relation to learning.
5. Increased emphasis upon group work.
6. A dimunition in the importance of single subjects.

In addition to the implications of this agenda there are three important general issues to be considered when preparing assessment programmes for the 14–18 age group.

Criterion Referencing

The first is the impact of criterion referencing. In Britain, as in many other countries, there has been a shift towards criterion referencing in recent years. This has been due in large measure to a belief by governments that assessment – and hence curricula – based upon external criteria can provide a more effective basis for raising standards than those that describe performance as between individuals (norm referencing). Too much can be made of the distinction between norm and criterion referencing and the assessment of individuals in practice will continue to remain a mixture of both. It is of course also possible to compare individuals against their own potential or past achievements. Moreover, the practical implications of moving significantly towards criterion referencing in a multi-grade, subject-based achievement examination system of the kind likely to continue to find favour in England and Wales, have yet to be worked through.

Despite these caveats the shift is significant in large measure because it renders the notion of a target group based upon a normal curve of distribution inappropriate. In so doing it requires those constructing assessment to create a bottom-up model based upon positive achievement in place of the present top-down approach. A much more optimistic environment is thus created that stresses the use of assessment for improving teaching and learning and hence underlines the need for recording systems based on methods other than marks or grades.

Fairness

The second is the emergence, largely as a result of the stress in recent years upon accountability and upon open access to information, of a number of issues relating to fairness, equality of opportunity and parity of esteem. There is a growing recognition that very little has been done in the past to address the major biases, both cultural and sexist, that exist in assessment and that physical disadvantage has not always been treated positively. We have also failed to address adequately the impact of various forms of assessment upon the esteem with which particular courses of study are held. The written essay of itself is not worth more than an oral, or a formal examination worth more than course-work.

If quality is to be delivered within a 14–18 curriculum, particularly if it makes use of modules, both teachers and pupils will need to be involved extensively in assessment throughout the course. Curling our lips superciliously and muttering 'Mode III' will not change this reality. Whether or not there is a need at this stage to set down a formal code for constructing and evaluating assessment along American lines is a matter for debate, but there is certainly a need to enshrine a number of key principles within future practice.

Whole-course Planning

The third is the need to regard assessment as an integral part of 'whole-course' planning, built in from the outset and not bolted on after all the rest of the work has been completed. This should occur whatever the size and length of 'the course' from the smallest unit to the whole curriculum.

When undertaking such planning it is necessary to recognize that a teaching module is not necessarily the same as an assessment module. The extent to which they match will depend upon the intentions of the course and upon the points at which it seems most useful to appraise and discuss student performance collectively or individually. This could be in the middle of a unit or require assessment that runs over several units.

In order to facilitate whole-course planning, three key questions need to be asked and answered:

1. What are the intended outcomes of the course?
2. What evidence is required to ensure that learning relevant to these outcomes has taken place?
3. What teaching/learning activities need to be provided in order to produce that evidence?

The derivation of the outcomes in the first question will vary. Some, like the GCSE criteria, may be laid down externally. Others may result from negotiation and discussion with students and with colleagues. The issue of accountability for both teacher and student has become increasingly significant with the use of smaller units in course structures. A modular structure permits, indeed encourages, quite specific short-term goals to be negotiated within and met within a given period of time. This makes it essential that both outcomes and assessment criteria are shared with students and publicly acknowledged.

When considering evidence it is necessary to recognize the extremely restricted range that is currently regarded as appropriate for assessment purposes. The checklist in Table 8.1 gives some indication of the possibilities. Readers might care to ask themselves how many of these forms of evidence they use in their own assessment and how many form part of the evidence taken into account in public examinations.

The word *evidence* should always be prefixed by the word *minimum*. Over-assessment is a damaging and far too prevalent disease, particularly when, as with modular developments, there is an increase in course-work assessment across the curriculum and in the number of those involved in the assessment process.

Written	3D	Visual	Oral
Report	Models	Picture	Performance
Diary/log	Sculpture	Poster	Role-play
Essay	Produce	Film	Recorded
Story	Artefacts	Video	discussion
Questionnaire		Photographs	Recorded
Letter		Decorations	conversation
Notes/draft		Graph/chart	Interview
Magazine		Printout	Debate
Storyboard			Radio programme
Display			

Table 8.1   Evidence for assessment

In the long run, whole-curriculum planning should be the aim. In assessment terms this will ultimately mean the establishment of an all-through credentialling system for all students from 5 to 19, with formal certification only at the very end. This will, however, take a long time in practice to achieve and may indeed never occur for a whole variety of reasons, ranging from the practical difficulties of whole-institutional and whole-curriculum planning, the implications of pre-service training for teaching styles and cross-curricular developments, to government policies. These last are particularly pertinent at the present time with statements imminent upon modules, national assessment 7–16, possible modifications of GCSE criteria, A-levels and A/S-levels, records of achievement and the future relationship between the National Council for Vocational Qualifications (NCVQ) and SEC. All these issues could be decided independently of one another or as strands of a coherent policy, and thus significantly facilitate or retard modular curriculum developments within a 14–18 framework. There is as yet no clear picture either as to how the new Grant Related In-service Training (GRIST) arrangements will work or what contribution to curriculum development and assessment the MSC's Joint Support Activities (JSA) will make.

The reality, therefore, for most teachers and most institutions is that these questions, at least in the short term, will be applied to subject related courses of study whose outcomes are largely imposed from outside. Here modules or units are likely to play an increasingly important part. Such courses can be used as a springboard for subsequent whole-curriculum development and to play a vital part in encouraging cross-curricular developments, and once again modular developments will be particularly helpful here.

What does all this mean for assessment practice? Earlier in this chapter a number of points are made about the kinds of changes that would be needed to assessment. In particular the need for attitudes to change in relation to the diagnostic use of assessment is stressed. A wider range of techniques and evidence, more informal in-course assessment and increased teacher and ultimately student assessment are also referred to. These, however, are all generalities, and the next section tries to put a little flesh on the bones by looking in some detail at the central issue of positive assessment and how to achieve it. Unless one can show through assessment what all students can do then it is virtually impossible to define progression and make diagnostic use of the information gained from assessment – both vital to modular developments. This chapter then concludes with a section of certification that looks, with particular reference to modular developments, at ways of meshing (with the minimum of tension) the requirements of certification with those of the transcript or record.

POSITIVE ASSESSMENT

What does it mean and what does it look like? Very simply it means that any question (and this is shorthand for problem, enquiry, etc.) must enable all those for whom it is intended to show, through their answers in their own terms, what they can 'do' and be rewarded for doing it. It thus includes both setting and marking. The words 'all those for whom it is intended' are crucial. In the case of GCSE, for example – where differentiation, the term in current use to describe positive assessment, is a key issue – it means 90 per cent of the ability range. There are only two ways in which such differentiation can in practice be achieved. The first is by asking everyone the same questions and the second by asking different questions to different people. In the first case it is the answers that will provide the varying evidence of positive achievement. In the second it is the questions that carry the main weight, but the audience to which they are directed has to be carefully defined.

The implications of this for a public examination such as GCSE are substantial, not least because they destroy the rationale upon which the setting and marking of 'questions' has hitherto been based. It will no longer be possible to use mark schemes, however flexibily interpreted, that are based upon the notion that there is a 'correct answer', or to award marks or grades according to the extent to which students do less well than those awarded more marks or higher grades. What all this underlines is that it was just as correct (and rather more honest) to describe a grade C at GCE O-level as not knowing 55 per cent of what was asked on the day as to describe it as knowing 45 per cent, and such statements are not helpful to anyone. Incidentally, differentiation of the kind required for GCSE cannot of itself be achieved through questions or part questions within the same paper that are progressively 'stepped' in difficulty. There is no difference, except in degree, to exposing students to part questions they cannot answer positively than to exposing them to whole questions.

The construction of such assessment raises a number of key issues:

1. *The need to create questions whose difficulty lies in the tasks they set and not their texts.* Put another way, the capacity to answer a question must not result from an inability to understand it as a question. This is a counsel of perfection since the choice of text, including the wording of the question itself will depend upon both subject and context. Source materials, say, for Elizabethan history may well be inherently more difficult for a 16-year-old than those for a twentieth-century world history topic. There is also the question of technical vocabulary where failure to understand will quite rightly reduce the capacity to answer. There may also be occasions, for example in mathematics, where the nature of a concept is so locked up in the question that the one cannot be understood without the other, and hence common questions over a wide ability range will not work. Despite such problems there is an enormous amount we can do to improve the quality of questioning in assessment.

2. *The inappropriateness of questions that test factual recall as an end in itself and hence can be marked on a right/wrong basis.* This rules out most short-answer questions and all objective items for achieving differentiation. It also makes it extremely unlikely that the majority of essay questions as currently worded and marked will be able to achieve differentiation when used over a wide ability range. Improvement can, of course, be made to the essay, the contexts used in the questions can be widened, choice can be eliminated, the range of communication skills extended and more flexible marks schemes developed. The message, nonetheless, is stark. Many, perhaps most, questions in current use for assessment in both classroom and public examinations and the ways in which they are marked will need rethinking. This requirement will become more marked the wider the ability range involved with common questioning. What is needed instead is as described in issue three.

3. *The construction of questions that pose problems or dilemmas that can be unpacked by those tackling them and answered at differing levels.* In order to achieve this, justification and explanation will need to be stressed at the expense of description, and skills tested in combination and not in isolation. In a sense such questions resemble the wooden Russian dolls to be found in many shops. To some these will appear as single dolls and any questions asked about them will be answered as if this were the case. Other students will explore, experiment and observe the doll and as a result it will turn into a number of dolls of different sizes. The questions used can, of course, encourage such exploration or leave it to the student to decide whether or not to explore. The greater the range of answers generated by the question the more likely it is to differentiate, but the more difficult it will be to mark. Hence the need, already referred to, for setting and marking to constitute an integrated activity. Where common questions are used, mark schemes based upon levels of response are likely to be essential.

The points made in the last few paragraphs can be illustrated by some examples taken from a recent GCSE specimen paper in cricket (Evans, 1986, p. 11). Amongst the eleven questions (all compulsory) are the following three:

6. Name two Minor Counties who have not defeated Yorkshire in one-day cricket.
10. Discuss the relative merits of four chosen 'illegal substances' which can be used to improve the condition of the ball.
11. You are the 'Organiser' of the village cricket club i.e. secretary, treasurer, social secretary, press secretary, transport officer, and groundsman. You are selecting for the first game of the season away from home. Place the following players in order of priority, giving reasons:

(a) The president's grandson.
(b) A mediocre player with a Volvo estate.
(c) An ageing player who is a liability in the field, does not bowl, bats No. 11, but whose wife is an 'absolute treasure' in the tearoom.
(d) A very talented opening bat who does not drive and is extremely loath to pay his end at the bar.

In terms of differentiation there is nothing to be done to improve question 6 (an archetypal short-answer question). It may indeed not be answerable in a few years time! It can only be marked on a right/wrong basis and even if forty such questions are used, student performance can only be described in terms of knowing more or less – the best knows the most the worst knows the least. If it were turned into a multiple-choice item the situation would be the same. The introduction of the words 'explain your choice' after the four or five options would not improve matters either since alternatives do not, indeed cannot, provide different degrees of explanatory power. They are simply right or wrong.

The second (question 10), a typical essay question, is rather better, almost entirely due to the inclusion of the word 'relative'. Its capacity to differentiate would, however, depend substantially on how the mark scheme viewed the importance of that word. Provided that four illegal substances with varying possibilities for improvement were selected and the words 'explain your choice' were added, the question could also differentiate well in a multiple-choice format – although its accessibility might well be restricted by knowledge of illegal substances and what the term meant. It is also worth noting that the more possibilities there were in the options the worse it would be as a multiple-choice item. The essay and multiple-choice formats, moreover, manage the problem very differently. In the essay the choice of the substance lies with the students, in the multiple-choice item it is provided for them. It must be a matter of judgement as to which format is likely to extend the opportunities for positive achievement to more students.

The third question (11) both offers more possibilities and creates more problems than either of the other two, largely because of the more open-ended nature of the problem it poses and the fact there is not a correct answer, only more or less justifiable ones. It is also longer and may create reading difficulties. What the question lacks as it stands is a structure that, while retaining the range of possibilities, renders certain of them more justifiable or more plausible than the others. The words 'away from home' provide a clue as to the nature of the form such a structure might take, providing as they do a positive justification for selecting (b) – who possesses a car – as against either (c) or (d) who do not. In order to exploit the situation more, data would be needed along such lines as 'the club hadn't won a match for two years', or 'it had a high reputation for its hospitality', or 'the president had recently given £10,000 for a new pavilion'. This would both increase and decrease the justification for particular choices. The situation in the question is obviously a relatively trivial one, though not for the organizer, and it may be that it is not capable of useful or valid development as an educational experience. What, however, would such a question look like, say, in history (where there has been several years of experience in their development) and how would it be marked? After studying the example readers might like to construct similar questions and mark schemes in their own subject areas.

The history question reads 'Which of the two sources A and D is most likely to be correct about the total number of defenders at Drogheda? Explain your answer.' It was the second of ten questions (all compulsory) based on a set of five unseen sources on the topic *Cromwell in Ireland*. These were accompanied by a half page of background information that together created the arena within which the students were asked to work and for which they were given one and a half hours. Source A was a letter from Cromwell to the Speaker of the House of Commons, written in Dublin on 17 September 1649. Source D was an extract from a book of biographies published in 1674 by Anthony Wood. Wood's brother, Thomas, was a soldier in Cromwell's army, and he was said by Anthony to have told him. . . . Full details of the extract are not necessary to understand the implications of the question. It is on the face of it a simple question but it has been used successfully for assessment within an ability range of 75 per cent and an age range of 12–25, and for in-service work with teachers. The mark scheme as finally used and published as an open document (Schools History Project, 1982) read as follows (for in-service training purposes a number of sample answers were provided):

> This question may pose difficulties because Source D is reported testimony. Candidates who confuse the author with the participant are unlikely to get beyond level 1. *N.B.* Reward balanced argument on all levels.
> *Level 1* Focuses on
>   – writers: Cromwell present at Drogheda, Anthony Wood not;
>   – date: A written at the time, D later.
>   Confuses accuracy with reliability.
> *Level 2* Conclusion based on the position of the *participants*. Which of Cromwell/ Thomas Wood was in a better position to give correct figure?
>   – Cromwell, because general and got overall picture;
>   – Thomas Wood, because closer to the action.
> *N.B.* Answers which carry clear suggestion that Thomas Wood there and Cromwell not, should be marked at Level 1.
> *Alternatively* – Concerned with *information* given in the Source –
> Conclusion which points to uncertainty expressed in the sources

- Source A: 'I think . . .'
- Source D: 'at least'

Or – Assesses plausibility by looking at information in Source with reference to background information or other sources.

Level 3 Evaluation in terms of interests/motives of the writers and/or participants
  - Cromwell had vested interest in minimising the number;
  - Thomas Wood had no reason not to tell the truth.

Level 4 Evaluation in terms of interests/perspective of recipients. (i.e. Parliament, Anthony Wood)

N.B. To reach this level answers must do more than say A = official document; D = conversation with his brother.

The preparation of such mark schemes whose starting point must always be 'What is the lowest level of rewardable response likely to result from the question?' will require pretesting and marker training in order to determine the levels and to identify them in students' work. It is thus not cheap, particularly in terms of time. The dividends, however, in improved quality of teaching and learning are considerable, particularly where purely descriptive assessment is possible. Where grading is required, as with GCSE, then the problem of the hierarchical nature of the levels and their justification becomes central, and currently too little is known about the nature and patterns of learning within particular subjects to be confident about their validity. Grading also raises issues of question choice (elimination?) and weighting (after rather than before?) that cannot be considered in a chapter of this length. Those seeking more information, both about the paper and the mark scheme, can refer if they wish to an article by the author in *The History Curriculum for Teachers* (Portal, 1987, Chap. 10). External certification and grading may also lead to a reduction in the range of information available to teachers and students for administrative reasons, hence hampering feedback.

So far positive assessment has been looked at largely in terms of asking everyone the same questions. Rather too much stress has been laid upon formal written questioning at the expense of other, less formal means of communication. Public examinations have also loomed larger than teacher assessment. This has been deliberate for two reasons. First, because common assessment appeals more to those seeking comprehensive assessment programmes that are fair to all. Second, because by emphasizing the most commonly used forms of large-scale assessment it is possible to underline more clearly the real need for change in current practices.

Positive assessment can, however, equally well be achieved by asking different people different questions and through in-course, informal, intermittent assessment. Indeed such approaches may be more appropriate for modular programmes that aim to provide alternative but equally rigorous routes for students of differing abilities and interests.

Both approaches to differentiation pose a different but no less demanding challenge to those responsible for 'setting and marking'. The Cockcroft Committee (1982) identified these differences clearly with reference to public examinations when it stated that no grade should be awarded unless a student had demonstrated a 50 per cent mastery of the examination material – an aim that cannot be achieved through common assessment that aims to generate all grades through common questions. In order to do this the outcomes appropriate at every grade level, the number of levels and what constitutes progress between levels will have to be determined and an assessment chain or ladder created from the bottom up (hence Cockcroft's foundation list). Mathematics is the only subject within GCSE that has attempted to date to do this – at least to a degree – with its four-paper overlapping model. It has, however, seriously diluted its potential for differentiation not only by awarding more than one grade upon each paper but also, more significantly, by providing safety nets whereby students putting in particularly good or bad performances can obtain higher or lower grades than a paper was designed to deliver.

There are, of course, graded test programmes in existence, notably in modern languages, maths and music, that go much further along this route but that lock into public examination grades only at certain points, usually at the bottom end. There is a real need to investigate learning/assessment models both within and between subjects that look at progression in this way alongside the current work on GCSE grade criteria. This may well extend to A-level and involve, through the NCVQ, bodies like CGLI, BTEC and the RSA, thus permitting the development of four year progressive programmes. Here the work of the Oxford Certificate of Educational Achievement and modular schemes that involve sequential developments, both vertical and horizontal, would be particularly useful. The logistic considerations involved in banking grades and 'on-demand' testing also need to be investigated.

Such investigations could with advantage concentrate upon programmes that make use of a carefully designed series of assessed assignments. By an assignment is meant a task or problem given to individuals or groups to undertake or resolve within a realistic time allocation. They can be self-contained or more profitably form part of a chain of related tasks designed to meet an overall set of outcomes. This would appear to have a number of advantages both for achieving differentiation and progression within a modular structure. These may be briefly summarized as follows:

1. They can readily be made cross-curricular in scope.

2. They can make very specific and very practical demands and can in consequence pose realistic and manageable tasks.
3. They encourage group work.
4. They provide a useful vehicle for involving students in their own learning and in their own assessment.
5. They facilitate progression and lend themselves particularly well to the assessment of individual programmes based upon sets of common criteria.
6. They encourage students to learn from their own mistakes and make realistic use of advice from others.

It is not possible to elaborate here upon all these points, which, in any case, are substantially inter-related, but a brief reference to some of the outcomes that could be fostered within such programmes will serve to underline the possibilities:

1. Understanding the requirements of problems and breaking them down into their elements in order to assist solution.
2. Communication skills, visual, verbal and numerical.
3. Identification of the strengths and weaknesses of individual contributions to a group.
4. Designing a timetable and sticking to it.
5. Understanding and following instructions.
6. Opportunities to plan, 'do' and reflect.
7. Capacity to learn from others' experience and one's own mistakes and to tolerate others' points of view.
8. Expanding the range of contexts within which learning takes place.

Clearly programmes, which develop a wide range of knowledge, concepts, skills and attitudes of the kind referred to here, lend themselves well to assessment procedures that describe across the curriculum through the use of a record rather than evaluate within subjects through the use of grades. They are, however, perfectly capable of being designed to do the latter and hence of combining summative certification with formative recording, although a great deal of valuable information and potential usage will be lost if the sole outcome is a certificate. Assignments can be particularly valuable in reducing the overall burden of assessment. A range of key criteria within an eight-subject GCSE curriculum could, for example, readily be met through four course-work programmes, say in mathematics, science, the humanities and communications, which carried a 40 per cent weighting for all eight subjects and delivered information technology and a range of general study skills into the bargain! Such an arrangement would not only significantly improve quality but also reduce student overload and permit a re-appraisal of the use of teacher time, thus facilitating the development of whole institutional policies. It would also fit in well with a modular structure that wished to make use of variably timed assessment patterns for different students.

Programmes such as these, and indeed all new curricular and assessment developments, raise significant in-service and management issues particularly where cross-curricular activities are involved. Both are, moreover, increasingly significant when external certification of some kind is sought as it will be for virtually all students at some point during a 14–18 programme.

It is not as yet possible to see exactly how the new GRIST arrangements will work in practice but it is clear that unless assessment is accorded a high priority within future programmes then the changes needed to deliver a 14–18 curriculum along the lines discussed in this book will not take place. It is clear also that pre-service training can only realistically make a small contribution. Two things would, however, be particularly significant here. First, greater emphasis upon the positive uses of assessment and second, the provision of opportunities to establish the connections as well as the differences between subjects. An effective way of achieving both these ends would lie in the programmes by which colleges assess their own students. These all too often establish negative attitudes and reinforce subject boundaries. On the in-service front, assuming that the right environment can be created and sustained, the main issues to which priority might be given are as follows:

1. Whole-course planning, preferably at the institution, and whole-curriculum level, which involves assessment as part of the planning process.
2. The formative uses of assessment.
3. The development of assessment practices that encourage cross-curricular initiatives.
4. Methods of recording and quality control.

Unless the widely-held equation is dismissed that teacher assessment equals lack of rigour or the lowering of standards, then much that is currently essential for curriculum development will be severely constrained and modular developments in particular will suffer.

The preceding points merely serve to underline the importance of managing curriculum change, particularly where the curriculum is based upon themes, activities and cross-curricular approaches rather than subjects. Such a curriculum, which my colleague, Malcolm Deere (to whom I am indebted for the ideas in this paragraph), describes as horizontal, requires much tighter management than the subject-based vertical approach if it is to provide and be seen to provide coherent programmes for all students. In particular, such a curriculum needs to be able to demonstrate

1. to individual students that complete programmes exist that have clear connections with what has gone before and clear pathways to the future;
2. a continuous relationship between process and content within any course of study;
3. a consistent relationship between learning programmes and assessment criteria; and
4. both the necessity and the opportunities for co-operation and interaction between individuals and, where relevant, between institutions.

The thrust between these four points and within this chapter as a whole has lain in the direction of whole-curriculum planning and it is vital that modular developments set themselves – and are seen to set themselves – within this context. Unless they fit together, young people will obtain a fragmented and incoherent experience and it will be difficult to justify existing certification, let alone the kind of over-arching record of achievement needed in order to celebrate adequately the many and varied achievements of all young people. Assessment, as this chapter tries to emphasize, can help significantly to facilitate this fit and make it easier to secure certification, the issue with which this chapter concludes.

CERTIFICATION

The remarks that follow are set within the current context of certification. This, for most youngsters aged between 14 and 18, means GCSE but will also mean for some A-level, A/S-level, CPVE and BTEC, as well as RSA and CGLI courses of varying kinds. The very roll call of initials (and the list is far from exhaustive) underlines the complexities of the problem. It is to be hoped that government policies and public attitudes will lead, and the sooner the better, to a single all-through assessment or credentialling system with a single final certificate awarded against a publicly debated and publicly stated set of outcomes.

Basically, however, the problem of the relationship between the record (the transcript) and the certificate will always remain the same, namely, how to aggregate or how to reduce a great deal to something much smaller and more manageable – currently, usually, a grade. Clearly the degree of match or mis-match between the 'contents' of the record and the requirements of the certificate, which has hitherto carried all the clout, will ease or exacerbate the matter of fit. Particular difficulties occur where horizontal modular developments, which emphasize cross–curricular flexibility, seek certification from the kind of vertical subject–based national criteria developed for GCSE and in a situation where integrating criteria are deemed to be much less respectable than subject criteria. It goes without saying that management along the lines suggested in the preceding section, which must in practice involve guided choice, will avoid unnecessary tensions although it will never resolve the problem completely in present circumstances. For all these reasons, therefore, the main thrust of the remarks that follow will relate to GCSE certification for modular courses. It takes as its starting point the problem currently facing the NEA in its attempt to merge the NPRA unit accreditation scheme with its modular GCSE schemes.

	NPRA unit accreditation	*NEA modular schemes of assessment for GCSE*
Length of module	No length prescribed	Notional length 12 to 20 hours
	No level of difficulty prescribed	Level is that of GCSE
Assessment	By teachers with non-specialist NPRA assessors	By teachers with external moderation
Learning outcomes and assessment objectives	Specified learning outcomes all students must achieve	Each module has assessment objectives which tend to be more generalized than learning outcomes
Hurdles	Each outcome is a hurdle since all must be met. No compensation for failure in one	No hurdle. In general, no specified performance level in any part of a module
Accreditation	Statement of achievement for each unit. Letter of credit listing units at the end of a course	No grade mark at the end of each module. Single overall grade at the end of the course shown on GCSE certificate
Rules of combination	None. Units are free-standing with no accumulation or aggregation	Syllabus includes rules of combination

Table 8.2   Summary of differences between the NPRA and NEA schemes

The differences between these two have been conveniently summarized in *Modular Approaches to the Secondary Curriculum* (Watkins, 1987) – see Table 8.2. It is interesting to note that many of the characteristics of the NPRA scheme are more capable of meeting the assessment needs of the 14–18 curriculum agenda and the moves towards criterion referencing than the GCSE modules, hampered as these are by the necessity to grade and therefore to aggregate. The major problem for combination is created by the existence of a substantial number of GCSE vertical grades in contrast with only a single level in the NPRA scheme. To call the latter levelless, incidentally, is quite incorrect. If learning outcomes are specified that students must master then a decision has to be made as to when that mastery occurs on a simple yes/no basis, and this constitutes a level. Since every outcome is a hurdle with no compensation there are, in reality, more levels in the NPRA scheme than in the GCSE scheme although they are all of a kind. Though it would not be appropriate to grade modules using a GCSE grade scale some indication of levels within modules represents a possible approach to aggregation.

The scheme used by the AEB with the Somerset TVEI, which followed a very substantial investigation into current practices particularly in Scotland, BTEC and the Open University, requires four levels or grades within each module. Combinations of module grades are then specified for the achievement of particular GCSE grades and these rules are published. Each module is thus graded upon completion, the results reported to the school and the combined result reported as a GCSE grade on a certificate. The grades used within modules are derived from two sources, the nature of the subject itself and the GCSE grade criteria, each of which will be modified to some degree by the particular syllabus used. Currently the GCSE grade criteria are being tested operationally and this may well result in some refinements.

The Somerset scheme has a number of disadvantages that, to be fair, are as much to do with what is being attempted as to the proposed solution. It works much better with well–defined subject areas and hence clearer module criteria. It tends to reinforce the requirement for modules of equal length and similar assessment patterns and it encourages over–assessment because it is felt necessary to use both in-course and terminal assessment. It is also not able to take account of the order or sequence in which modules are taken by providing differential weighting. It is also extremely difficult for the certificating body to maintain assessment standards between modules. Existing moderation arrangements need to be replaced by some form of quality control that is primarily concerned with procedures and not detailed practice and that needs to ask questions which are different both in their nature and their timing from those currently asked.

Some of these disadvantages will disappear or become less significant as teachers grow more confident and as in-service training develops. Somerset has undertaken further work at A-level and A/S-level with the AEB, involving the use of a core that may well serve a number of subjects in combination with a number of modules. These last have the function of turning an A-level or an A/S-Level core into an A-level or an A/S-Level subject. This offers interesting possibilities as does the development of a system that places tariffs upon all modules, which can differ in size according to their timing or their assessment. The role of endorsement or enrichment modules and their impact upon grades also needs investigation and it will be interesting to see whether the NEA in its study uses any of these approaches or develops others.

Effective curriculum and assessment management within institutions will, of course, ease the problems of aggregation but ironically will also lessen the need for formal certification as the cachet of success – and here modules have played and will continue to play a significant part in breaking the mould. Ought we not to accept, therefore, that the assessment needed to meet the curriculum requirements of the 14–18 age range is not compatible with grading as currently used and move gradually instead towards systems of validation and accreditation that record achievement progressively over time within a national framework? The notion of levels currently being canvassed by the NCVQ, although quite inappropriate in its detail at present, offers possibilities for such a development as do records of achievement if seen both in a formative as well as a summative context. First, however, we need to secure a cohesive 14–18 curriculum and this must remain the first priority.

REFERENCES

Cockcroft Committee (1982) *Mathematics Counts*, HMSO, London.
Evans, D.P. (1986) 'GCSE (Cricket) 1986 specimen paper,' *Wisden Cricket Monthly*, January.
Portal, C. (ed.) (1987) *The History Curriculum for Teachers*, Falmer Press, Brighton.
National Association of Head Teachers (1987) *Action Plan: A Policy 14–18*, NAHT Publications and Service Dept, Haywards Heath.
Schools History Project (1982) CSE National Examination, Southern Regional Examinations Board, Eastleigh.
Secondary Headteachers Association (1987) *Future Imperative*, Occasional Paper No. 87.1, SHA, London.
Watkins, P.R. (1987) *Modular Approaches to the Secondary Curriculum*, Longman, Harlow (for the School Curriculum Development Committee).

9
CREDIT BANKING
Christine Southall

GENERAL DEFINITION

Credit banking is a means of achieving a certificate, degree or other qualification by accumulating its constituent parts. Each part or unit is clearly defined and delimited and its contribution to the whole certificate is specified. The unit may be recognized and reported in its own right (unit accreditation) or it may have recognition only as a proportion of the whole. Credit banking operates principally in further and higher education, the Scottish National Certificate and the degrees of the Open University being the best-known examples. Credit banking as a means of fulfilling the requirements of GCSE is explored in this chapter.

THE CREDIT BANK OF THE OXFORDSHIRE EXAMINATION SYNDICATE

In 1986 representatives from Oxfordshire's LEA approached the Southern Examining Group (SEG) with a proposal that an LEA consortium – the Oxfordshire Examination Syndicate (OES) – should establish and administer a bank of GCSE credits.

A definition of terms may be helpful at this point. A *credit* is a free-standing unit of learning that may be combined with other credits to form an educational programme leading to the award of a GCSE certificate. Each credit is assessed within the time span allocated to it. This is usually in the region of 20 to 30 hours. A *programme* is a group of five credits that together offer sufficient depth, rigour and quality to qualify for a GCSE title. A *scheme* is the total set of credits that relate to a GCSE title in the bank.

The syndicate is responsible for agreeing with SEG the GCSE titles and the combinations of five credits that are appropriate for those titles. It maintains, therefore, what is known as a module map that indicates the ways in which credits can be grouped to give a GCSE title.

The credit bank is a bank in two senses. First, it is a bank for students as they receive an interim certificate on successful completion of a credit. Students deposit and accumulate their credits, which can be retrieved and submitted for a GCSE award when the requirements for a given GCSE title have been met (i.e. in the agreed combinations of five). Credits can be banked over a number of years and SEG has not specified a time limit. Indications are that five years is acceptable with the possibility of an extension beyond that time. Credit banking holds notable advantages for students: they may accumulate credits beyond the years of compulsory schooling and complete programmes in further or adult education. Students who are dissatisfied with their result on a particular credit may repeat it or replace it with a different credit in order to improve their final GCSE grade. Banking means that individual students may not only defer certification, they may request it earlier – the extent to which modular schemes might lead to premature assessment continues to be debated and is discussed later in this chapter. It is important to note that a GCSE obtained by credit accumulation is indistinguishable at the point of final certification from a GCSE obtained by more conventional means. GCSEs, whether mode I, II or III, modular or non-modular have all been vetted to ensure compliance with national criteria. Standards are therefore guaranteed irrespective of the mode of examination and a GCSE Geography certificate, for example, contains no reference either to modes or modules.

Second, the credit bank is a bank for teachers and lecturers. Credits accepted into the bank from one school or group of schools immediately become available to all other syndicate members. The bank provides a means for teachers to obtain GCSE recognition for curriculum components either to reflect particular circumstances and needs or to support new and changing areas of study and methodology. Prior to the advent of modular approaches, teachers seeking certification for school-based curriculum development had to construct entire mode III syllabuses. The credit bank enables teachers to submit smaller curriculum units for accreditation.

THE ORIGINS OF THE CREDIT BANK

The LEA's initial proposal to SEG, *Examining the Modular Curriculum: Proposals to the Southern Examining Group for an Oxfordshire Framework*, was warmly received in SEG, which published its guidelines on modular GCSE shortly afterwards. The congruence of the LEA scheme and the SEG guidelines generated optimism in Oxfordshire, fuelled also by the knowledge that similar developments were already well advanced in Leicestershire with the Midland Examining Group. The *ad hoc* working party of the LEA, which had made the proposal, was replaced by a more formally constituted body, the OES. The syndicate is the parent organization of the credit bank. Membership of the syndicate is open to all educational establishments interested in the furtherance of modular approaches to GCSE. Member institutions may contribute and borrow credits on whatever scale they feel appropriate. Schools and colleges were invited to become members of the OES and all Oxfordshire secondary schools and most colleges elected to do so at the syndicate's inauguration in September 1986. This level of response exceeded all expectations.

A number of factors may account for the enthusiastic response to the credit bank and these are enumerated here:

1. *Curriculum development and structural change in schools.* Several schools in the county were attracted to modular approaches. Peers School has a 70 per cent modular offer in years four and five. Wantage School has implemented a modular structure starting in year three. Oxfordshire was developing a modular double award in GCSE Science. The motivational benefits to students on credit-based schemes were receiving widespread recognition and were seen to be linked to the setting of clear, short-term goals; assessment within the time span of a credit; assessment against explicit criteria; and assessment closely articulated with learning.
2. *TVEI.* The TVEI scheme operating in six Oxford schools is modular, with two modular mode III GCSEs on offer and a further non-modular mode I GCSE taught in units.
3. *GCSE.* September 1986 was confirmed as the starting date for GCSE. The advent of GCSE was of major significance. If credit-based approaches were to have a long-term future, they needed to espouse the new national examining system. More than anything else credits needed a life inside GCSE not outside it. There were already a few modular mode I syllabuses available. On the whole, though, such syllabuses had not relinquished terminal examining in some form. There was a need for modular GCSE schemes with assessment within the time span of the credit. There are benefits here both for curriculum and for GCSE. Credits accessed into the bank will have been subject to rigorous scrutiny against the national criteria for GCSE. Credits, therefore, have the status and credibility that comes from accordance with national standards. A sense of local ownership of the national examining system is achieved. At

the same time GCSE is seen to be capable of accommodating school-based curriculum development and assessment is demonstrably curriculum-led. The stated intention of GCSE to make the important measurable and not the measurable important gains ground.

4. *Oxford Certificate of Educational Achievement.* Oxfordshire is extensively committed to the piloting of records of achievement through the Oxford Certificate of Educational Achievement (OCEA). The OCEA in Oxfordshire was influential in the establishment of the syndicate. It embraces the notion of assessment against explicit criteria; against absolute not relative standards. Thus far its aims are consonant with those of GCSE. In addition, the OCEA actively solicits the student viewpoint throughout the learning and assessment process. The OCEA 'G' component had at one time promoted short-term objectives for students – the 'G' component had grown out of the graded objectives movement, but had subsequently mutated into a wider, less hierarchical but more complex assessment framework. It now appeared to some of those involved in the OCEA that the credit, not the OCEA 'G', was to be the successor to the graded objective in the promotion of short-term goals. The OCEA had much expertise in criterion referenced assessment. At the same time, GCSE was going to make immense demands on teacher time and effort and could threaten to displace the OCEA work in schools. If the OCEA and GCSE could coexist symbiotically within a credit-based structure, there would be significant gains for both.

THE ROLE OF SEG

The credit bank is based on the premiss that some of the functions normally performed by the examining group can be devolved to an LEA consortium like the OES. This would follow a period of mutual development and pre-supposes a relationship between the LEA and the examining group that is collaborative and consultative. SEG was proposing just such a *modus operandi* during the winter of 1986. The senior committees of SEG were receiving a clear message from the Chief Executive that the long-term interest of the group lay not only in the marketing of board-based syllabuses but in the accreditation of school-based curriculum initiatives. The best way of achieving this was through an LEA/SEG partnership. An LEA consortium such as the OES provided an ideal contact point for the group to ensure convergence of curriculum, assessment and pedagogy.

The extent to which the OES may take on the functions of the examining group is not fully worked out. A gradual devolution is envisaged. At the outset, the OES and the group work together to achieve a system of operating the bank, which is as simple and economical as possible and compatible with the maintenance of standards. Ultimately it is likely that the syndicate will take over the management of the credit bank under licence from the group. When fully operational the syndicate will be responsible for the issue of credit results, and the maintenance of all records, monitored only lightly by the group. The group will issue GCSE certificates on receipt of the appropriate information from the syndicate.

CREDIT BANKING IN GCSE
Aggregation not Accumulation

A GCSE credit bank operates within the parameters of GCSE national criteria. The latter pre-date widespread interest in modular approaches as do the mode I, II and III regulations of examining groups. GCSE was designed with two-year, 180-hour courses as the norm. The relationship of GCSE to credits has been described as 'credit accommodation' as opposed to 'unit accreditation'.

This is not just a pedantic distinction but highlights a very real issue within GCSE. This may best be illustrated by constrasting GCSE credit banking with the type that operates in the Scottish National Certificate. In the case of the latter, SCOTVEC modules are accumulated by the student and contribute towards a Scottish National Certificate. Modules are listed on the certificate, which may contain only one module or dozens! In the GCSE credit bank, on the other hand, units are not accumulated to achieve the certificate, but rather, the syllabus requirements for the certificate are divided up to achieve the units. A credit in GCSE is, therefore, a fraction of the whole GCSE. The question is often asked, 'How long is a credit and how many credits make a GCSE?' This is like asking how many slices there are in a cake. The answer is, of course, that it depends on how many slices you want to cut it into! The Somerset TVEI modular scheme cuts GCSE into quarters, the OES cuts it into fifths. (It is not clear how far uniformity is either possible or desirable. SEG is prepared to consider schemes with between three and seven modules.)

How can the task of fashioning one-fifth of a GCSE be accomplished? Each GCSE scheme or title has a number of aims and assessment objectives. The knack (the word is used deliberately, as compliance with GCSE requires all manner of technical ingenuity) is to carve the assessment objectives into fifths and to apportion them to credits. The cake example is useful here and Figure 9.1 offers a tentative illustration of how this can be done. In Figure 9.1(a) a cross-section of objectives is addressed in the credit.

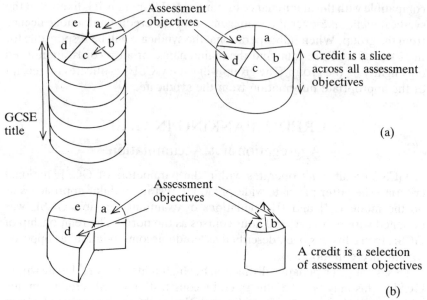

Figure 9.1   Carving assessment objectives to apportion them to credits

The credits are then truly free-standing and can be stacked in any order in fives to achieve the title. This method lends itself to a humanities title, for example, where there is no hierarchy or sequence of credits.

In Figure 9.1(b) a selection of objectives is addressed in each credit. The credits must then be very carefully assembled to achieve the 'whole'. The rules of combination or credit map are essential to show how credits interlock and which permutations are permissible. This approach might lend itself to a scheme in which the later credits contain a design project, for example, that requires greater attention to the application of skills acquired in previous units or in which certain synthetic and evaluative objectives are best left to the end of the sequence.

There are certainly other ways of cutting the cake. Combinations of Figures 9.1(a) and (b) are possible. The overriding principle is that any combination of five put forward for certification demonstrates coverage of the assessment objectives. The carving of knowledge skills and values is not as artificial as it may at first appear. The reality is that in tackling a whole syllabus, teachers are constantly selecting and sub-dividing. There is merely a more systematic attempt to do so in the credit-based approach.

There is also a fear that the GCSE cake, when sliced, may crumble – the accusation of fragmentation and lack of coherence that surfaces in any teacher audience when modular approaches are discussed for the first time. The answer is that credits are as coherent as GCSE, no more and no less. Fragmentation is not a danger where the scheme (the whole), the credits (the parts) and the module map and rules of aggregation (the interlocking of the parts to form the whole) are addressed together at the outset as is the case with the OES. Good credits derive from good schemes with a valid educational purpose and valid and reliable assessment.

The Nature of GCSE

It is worth devoting some time, at this point, to acquiring an understanding of GCSE, the nature of assessment in it and the relationship between assessment and certification in GCSE. Assessment in GCSE is directed at the stage of syllabus construction by the statement of aims and assessment objectives. Assessment objectives prescribe the kinds of abilities that candidates are required to demonstrate, for example, to know, to evaluate, to look from the perspective of people in the past, to analyse, etc. A scheme of assessment defines the assessment components that represent the most effective means of collecting the evidence of those abilities described as assessment objectives. Differentiated assessment opportunities are devised so that a candidate awarded grade G, for example, has performed well on an appropriate task, not badly on a task that was too demanding. Assessment objectives and the criteria for allocating marks must be 'visible' and discernible on the entire continuum that stretches from GCSE national criteria, through the syllabus of the scheme and the credit descriptor, into the assessment components and the marking schemes or reporting scales. Wherever assessment takes place in GCSE, the assessor asks the same questions:

- Which objective is assessed here?
- To which level can it be assessed here?
- What are the criteria for giving credit?

These are searching, pertinent questions that need to be addressed by every teacher involved in GCSE assessment and they generate much information about an individual candidate's performance.

At the point of certification, however, the assessment information is boiled down and down, into a grade. Assessment is elaborate and ambitious in its intention to give all candidates an opportunity to measure their performance against known objectives and agreed standards. Certification remains crude – grades A to G and unclassified. The major defect of GCSE, therefore, is that the certification does not do justice to the quality of assessment envisaged. How has this situation come about? Users (employers, educational establishments) it is argued, require concise indications of a candidate's attainment. Would a publisher, to construct an analogous situation, think it acceptable to distribute the novels of a Nobel prize-winner as blocks of compressed paper waste? Of course not, so why apply this reductionist mentality to assessment? The mis-match between process and product is nowhere more acute than in the relationship between assessment and certification in GCSE. This is what is bedevilling the attempt to devise grade criteria – the fairer and more valid the assessment, the greater is the ingenuity required to marry it with reductionist certification.

INTERIM CERTIFICATION

The tension between assessment and certification has been discussed at some length for the bearing it has on credit banking. Since interim certificates are to be issued on completion of a credit, there is a risk that certification will interfere with assessment not once in the course of a GCSE programme but five times. The nature of the interim certification is consequently highly significant and was the subject of prolonged debate by the OES. The following principles were established:

1. GCSE is objectives-led – on the interim certificate candidates are entitled to receive information about their attainment in relation to those objectives. They should be able to make inferences about their learning and their strengths and weaknesses from the credit certificate.
2. The contribution of the credit to the final GCSE grade should be evident from the certificate. The formula for calculating the final grade from the programme of five credits should be public. Thus candidates can look at an interim certificate and deduce that if they obtain the same score on subsequent credits, they will gain a grade C, or that by obtaining a one-score improvement on two subsequent credits they will gain a grade B, for example.
3. The aggregation formula for determining the GCSE grade should permit some compensation so that the higher module performances are acknowledged in the final grade. The reason for this is that maturation has been cited as a concern in modular GCSE. A credit acquired in the third or fourth year of secondary school by a 13- or 14-year-old has been assessed at post-16 standard and counts towards the GCSE grade. Students on credit-based schemes have a lower average 'assessment age' than those following syllabuses with a greater emphasis on terminal examining. There is a possibility, therefore, that such students may be disadvantaged by premature assessment.

The aggregation formula should be used to counter-balance this so that the effect of an uncharacteristically weak performance in a single credit can be minimized in the final grade. The case for maturation as a significant factor in candidate performance is not proven and it remains to be seen whether any pattern will emerge of weaker performance in the early credits of a programme.

Having established these three principles, it was necessary to consider what should be recorded on the interim certificate and what is best recorded on the curriculum attainments section of a record of achievement. How much can the OCEA accommodate GCSE and vice versa? Similar issues have been faced in the north of England by the NEA and the NPRA in their considerations of the extent to which NPRA units are compatible with GCSE (see Chapter 8). A first paper to the executive group of the OES proposed that assessment objectives or grouped assessment objectives should be listed on the interim certificate and that a score from one to seven, effectively a G to A grade, should be recorded alongside each objective. The aggregation formula took the profile of scores across the programme of five on each objective that acknowledged the higher performances. The final accumulation formula had to take into account the relative weightings of the objectives. A five-credit, five-objective conversion scale looked as follows:

32–35 = grade A
27–31 = grade B
22–26 = grade C, etc.

The above proposal was in line with the three principles outlined above. However, the formula and its rationale looked too complicated for public release and the 'assessment' objectives became invisible where the 'certification' arithmetic took over.

By May 1987 the modular approach had become much more firmly embedded in the educational scene, and local pragmatism was quickly being superceded by regional and national solutions to issues encountered by those working on mode III modular schemes. SEC had published working paper 4, *Assessing Modular Syllabuses*, the Joint Council for the GCSE had discussed issues of mutual concern with regard to modular syllabuses, MEG had issued a second set of modular guidelines and SEG was compiling a definitive document on the regulation and operation of modular schemes. The AEB had undertaken development work in connection with the Somerset TVEI scheme. SEG convinced the OES that the best way to ensure that GCSE fulfilled its intention of being criteria-driven was to report results on interim certificates as levels and that levels should not be aggregated arithmetically but using rules of combination as follows.

Levels and how they are Combined to Give a GCSE Grade

Credit results are reported on the interim certificate as levels. The levels are one to four with four as the highest level of attainment that can reasonably be expected on the credit and one as the minimum requirement for successful completion of the credit. For each level, level descriptors are written that derive from the assessment objectives. They are written in positive terms and describe in general terms what the candidate knows, understands and can do at each level. The level descriptors are used as the basis for marking course-work and tests, either directly or by using conventional mark schemes and matching these with the levels so that scores are assigned to one of the four levels. Interim certificates record, among other things, the credit title and the level attained by the candidate as well as the level descriptor. For each scheme a set of combination rules is devised that compares all possible permutations of levels against the grade descriptions for the scheme and assigns each permutation to a grade. This is a lengthy process requiring thoughtful matching and adjusting of level descriptors in the design stage of schemes and credits. A five-credit and four-level scheme would generate 56 possible combinations of results ranging from IIIII – grade G, to 44444 – grade A. A decision must also be made about the influence of an unclassified result on the grade.

A COMMON ASSESSMENT FRAMEWORK

During the autumn of 1986 the syndicate explored a number of alternative directions that the credit bank might take. These were reported in a series of position papers to the executive group. Papers on assessment, moderation, aggregation, the administrative structure of the bank and interim certification were approved and eventually compiled in a handbook, *The Credit Bank: Guidelines for Users and Designers of Credits,* (OES, 1987). One idea that was not taken up was the notion of a cross-curricular framework governing all credits in the bank. A cross-curricular taxonomy was trialled in workshops and was the focus of a fascinating in-service training exercise for those involved. The idea was abandoned in the end and the following paper (*see page* 193), as well as summarizing the deliberations around this issue, typifies the kind of debate prevalent within the syndicate.

CONTRIBUTING CREDITS TO THE CREDIT BANK

The administrative structure of the OES is designed to permit rapid inclusion of school-designed credits in the credit bank. A centre wishing to contribute a scheme or credit sends a notice of intent to the OES, which offers assistance from a team of seconded teachers. A list of credits and schemes in preparation is published regularly to maximize the potential for co-operation and shared development. Advisory groups for each GCSE title are established. Their brief is to vet credits against the relevant national criteria and the regulations of SEG. Advisory groups also invite an injection of curriculum energy from the LEA. It is hoped that the groups will eventually develop positive strategies for combatting gender, ethnic and other forms of bias and contribute expertise in readability and differentiation, for example. The composition of each advisory group is the OES co-ordinator; an officer of SEG; an LEA representative; a subject specialist who is not a member of the applying institution; and two other members, one of whom is an employer representative. The OES also consults advisory groups to evaluate existing credits on an annual basis and to recommend amendments.

Access to Credits in the Credit Bank

A full list of credits is distributed to member schools and colleges each autumn term. A short description of each credit is included in the catalogue and the GCSE titles and other certification outcomes for which the credit may be used. Since many credits are valid for more than one title – a local studies credit can contribute to a Geography or a Humanities GCSE, for example – entry procedures have been adjusted so that candidates may enter for a credit rather than a title. Clearly, there can also be many routeways to a given title and the best way to hold these is on computer.

Credit Descriptors

Each credit is recorded in standard format on a credit descriptor (see Notes and Illustrations) the purpose of which is to demonstrate that all GCSE regulations have been satisfied and to assist with the mapping of routeways to GCSE titles. The descriptor is a syllabus and assessment skeleton only, so that individual institutions and teachers can realize the assessment objectives in different ways. The credit bank intends eventually to make available teaching syllabuses, support materials and suggested teaching and learning strategies, but must be careful to distinguish between the mandatory and voluntary aspects of a credit when it is loaned to a centre. Guidelines and workshops in credit design are provided by the OES.

MODERATION

Modular schemes call for revised moderation procedures, particularly in the case of banks issuing interim certification. A situation may arise in which a popular credit is 'borrowed' by several centres. Centres do not have to synchronize credit start and completion and all want a moderated result (interim certificate) for candidates as soon as possible after completion. SEG moderates centre-assessed components by inspection. The following moderation procedure was agreed.

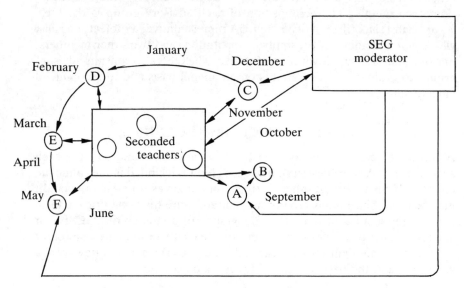

Figure 9.2   A model for the moderation of credits

A SEG moderator is appointed for each scheme in the bank. Centres notify the OES of their intention to offer a credit during an academic year. Agreement trials are held amongst participating centres, the moderator and teachers seconded to work on the scheme. Syndicate-based in-service activity ensures that the credit descriptor, assessment instruments, reporting scales and level descriptors are understood. Seconded teachers 'link' with the moderator, the advisory group and centres.

Figure 9.2 shows a model for the moderation of credits. Centres A, B, C, D, E and F offer credits under this title in the course of an academic year. The external moderator inspects A, C and F. A teacher from centre A moderates centre B's candidates. A teacher from centre C moderates D's candidates and so on. Figure 9.2 is a model. The frequency of its application should decrease over time to be reviewed in the first years of operation of the bank.

The long-term policy of SEG is for teacher accreditation. Teacher accreditation is the authorization of teachers to undertake with only a low level of monitoring any of the following: syllabus construction, assessment and awarding grades. The centre-based assessment work in GCSE makes this the only feasible long-term option for GCSE. The OES with its secondment provision (three full-time equivalent secondments and ten × 36-day secondments for 1987–8) is able to promote precisely the kind of assessment in-service activity that is needed for teacher accreditation.

CONCLUSION

The concept of credit banking is an exciting one. Very few people have been encountered inside or outside education who have not appreciated its prodigious potential. Students can bank credits and build programmes of study regardless of age. Modular curricula give students the opportunity to attain a long-term target like GCSE by making a series of short-term commitments and in many cases determining their routes to that target. Credit banking offers a further benefit. Its intention is simple and powerful – students receive a credit reporting not only their present attainment level but also how that relates to their final grade. The formula for combining credits to give a GCSE grade is public information.

Some progressives in education have been too quick to condemn GCSE. Its flaws have not been minimized in this chapter. However, those who have not looked beyond the grades should reconsider. Modular structures and modular banking combined with an assessment system for GCSE that is sensitively differentiated, where targets are explicit and it is clear what constitutes attainment of a target will lead to real improvements in educational practice and in the attainment levels of individuals. The national criteria for GCSE are regarded by some as a means to greater curricular proscription and circumscription, but they also hand over assessment to public ownership. The publication of the 'rule book' can be seen as an opportunity for locally devised initiatives and diverse curricular perspectives to obtain GCSE status.

In Oxfordshire the notion of credit banking received support and enthusiasm from many quarters. The New Learning Initiative (NLI, Oxfordshire's version of LAPP) recognized that it had a useful contribution to make to GCSE. GCSE requires assignments and assessment components on which those receiving foundation grades can register positive achievement. By actively engaging in the design of such components for the bank's credits and ensuring their readability and accessibility, the NLI could accomplish within GCSE something of lasting benefit for the young people who are the focus of that initiative. A local nature reserve plans to accredit its conservation course through the bank and teachers of health and fitness and sport science also intend to construct a modular scheme. Other LEAs are seeking similar partnerships with SEG. While different banks within SEG may well remain separate for the purpose of administration and moderation, they can collaborate on particular titles or set up reciprocal arrangements to exchange and share credits. This will necessitate some degree of standardization on matters such as the essential features of a GCSE credit and the number required for certification.

In its first year the OES focused attention on understanding the nature of GCSE and how it could be modularized, administrative arrangements, aggregation and moderation. There is still much to refine and to decide – What is the optimum achievable degree of criterion referencing? How can the issue of interim certificates be managed smoothly and economically? The LEA and SEG show continuing support for the scheme and a willingness to work to improve it. Perhaps the day is not so far distant when the effective secondary school is no longer the school with the highest number of A–C-grade GCSE passes. A school's effectiveness will be judged on the extent to which its students improved their performance between their first interim certificates and their final GCSE grades.

REFERENCES AND BIBLIOGRAPHY

Adams, R.M. and Wilmut, J. (1985) *The Somerset TVEI Scheme: An Approach to Modular Assessment* (paper to BERA Conference), (unpublished) AEB, Aldershot.

Cambridgeshire TVEI (1986) *Modular A-Level Guidelines*, University of Cambridge Local Examinations Syndicate.

Moon, B. (1985) 'A modular framework', *Forum*, Vol. 27, No. 2, pp. 48–50.

Oxfordshire Examination Syndicate (1987) *The Credit Bank: Guidelines for Users and Designers of Credits*. Oxfordshire County Council, Oxford.

Scottish Information Office (1985) *The 16+ Development Programme*, Fact Sheet 31.

Southern Examining Group (1986) *Guidelines for the Preparation and Submission of Modular or Unit-based Curriculum Schemes*, Tunbridge Wells.

Turner, J. (1986) *Designing the Modular Curriculum, Part 1, GCSE Assessment*, Leicestershire TVEI.

Walter, P. J. (1986) *An Investigation into the Aggregation of Grades as Proposed for GCSE Results*, paper to Oxfordshire Examination Syndicate (unpublished).

Watkins, P. (1987) *Modular Approaches to the Secondary Curriculum*, Longman, Harlow (for the School Curriculum Development Committee).

Wilmut, J. and Owen, S.J. (1985) *Assessment and Certification for a Modular Curriculum*, Associated Examining Board, Aldershot.

ACKNOWLEDGEMENTS

Bob Moon and Peter Walters of Peers School, Oxford. Bob Eggleshaw, Michael Jones and Nick Young of Wantage School, Oxfordshire. Peter Burke, John Wilmut and Stephen Vickers of SEG.

NOTES AND ILLUSTRATIONS

A CREDIT DESCRIPTOR

Oxfordshire Examination Syndicate   Southern Examining Group

GENERAL CERTIFICATE OF SECONDARY EDUCATION

CREDIT DESCRIPTOR

Credit Title	Leisure, recreation and tourism

Credit Code	Scheme Title(s) HUMANITIES	Scheme Code(s)

Preferred entry level	Candidates may take this unit at any stage when constructing a course in Geography or Humanities.

Rules of Combination/ Module Map	As for the scheme as a whole.

Aims of Credit	To acquire knowledge and understanding of the growing importance of leisure in modern life, the ways in which it can be classified and the patterns of distribution and use which may develop at different scales.
	To develop skills such as data collection and communication through the use of both primary and secondary sources.
	To develop an awareness and understanding of forces causing change and possible conflicts related to differing values and attitudes.

Assessment Objectives	1a. To recall evaluate and select knowledge relevant to the context and apply it to specific locations at a variety of scales.
	1b. To make use of, understand and apply geographical concepts (whilst appreciating their limitations) appropriate to the physical, economic, environmental and social context of the unit and appreciate interrelationships between human activities and the total environment.
	2. To demonstrate the skills necessary to acquire, study and communicate a wide variety of geographical material from a range of sources.
	3. To demonstrate an awareness of the significance of values and attitudes in issues relating to leisure, recreation and tourism.

Content and Context	1. The importance and growing part played by leisure in modern life, considered at a variety of scales.
	2. The classification of leisure facilities and activities, related to criteria such as range, formality, seasonality and age range.
	3. The variations in the character and distribution of facilities related to factors such as environment, history, culture and politics.
	4. The variations in the pattern of use of facilities, related to factors such as accessibility, mobility and wealth.
	5. The dynamic nature of both demand and supply of leisure; the causes, patterns and possible conflicts arising from such developments.

	Objectives	Relative weighting %
	1a	25%
Weighting of Assessment Objectives	1b	25%
	2	30%
	3	20%
	Total	100%

	Assessment Component	% Allocation	Duration (of Test)	Timing
Scheme of Assessment Summary	Coursework	70%	—	During
	Unit test	30%	50 min	End

Statement of Differentiation	Coursework differentiation will be achieved by presenting candidates with tasks appropriate to their individual levels of ability.
	Unit test differentiation will involve:
	a. differentiation by outcome related to stimulus material.
	b. structured questions.

	Assessment Objectives	Assessment Component Coursework	Test	Total
Specification Grid showing Relationship Between Objectives and Assessment Components	1a	15	10	25
	1b	15	10	25
	2	25	5	30
	3	15	5	20
	Total	70	30	100

Grades Available	Full range

A MODULAR OFFER

The modular offer of one Oxfordshire School accredited through the OES's credit bank

Ref.	Title	Geog.	Hist.	R.S.	Hum.
H 1	HISTORY AROUND US: Transport		●		
H 2	HISTORY AROUND US: Change in the local area		●		●
H 3	MODERN WORLD STUDY: Super power conflict		●		
H 4	MODERN WORLD STUDY: C20 Dictators		●		
H 5	STUDY OF SOCIAL CHANGE: U.S.A.		●		

H 6	STUDY OF SOCIAL CHANGE: India	●	
H 7	STUDY OF SOCIAL CHANGE: C20 Britain	●	
H 8	STUDY OF SOCIAL CHANGE: Changing role and status of women	●	●
H 9	IN DEPTH STUDY: Study of an industry	●	
H 10	IN DEPTH STUDY: C19 Health Issues	●	●
H 11	IN DEPTH STUDY: Nazi Germany	●	
H 12	STUDY IN DEVELOPMENT: C19/20 Social and Economic	●	
H 13	STUDY IN DEVELOPMENT: Persecution and Prejudice	●	●
G 1	LANDSCAPES AND WATER	●	
G 2	AGRICULTURE AND INDUSTRY	●	
G 3	POPULATION AND SETTLEMENT	●	
G 4	DEVELOPMENT	●	●
G 5	LOCAL STUDIES	●	●
G 6	TRANSPORT	●	
G 7	ENERGY	●	
G 8	LEISURE RECREATION AND TOURISM	●	
R 1	BELIEFS AND VALUES	●	●
R 2	EQUALITY: COMMUNITY AND PERSONAL ISSUES	●	●
R 3	JUDAISM: THE HOLOCAUST	●	
R 4	JUDAISM: BELIEFS AND PRACTICES	●	

R 5	FAST FESTIVAL AND PILGRIMAGE		●	
R 6	PERSONAL AND FAMILY DEVOTION		●	
R 7	CORPORATE WORSHIP		●	
R 8	SACRED WRITINGS AND RELIGIOUS LEADERS		●	
R 9	MORAL TEACHINGS		●	●
R 10	GOSPEL OF MARK: LIFE OF CHRIST		●	
HU 1	CONFLICT			●
HU 2	URBANISATION			●
HU 3	LAW AND ORDER			●
HU 4	POLITICAL MOVEMENTS AND AWARENESS			●

UNIT COMBINATIONS

It will be possible to combine units in a variety of ways, as indicated in the table below, to allow G.C.S.E. certification of the subject titles indicated.

Table indicating unit combinations

TITLE	UNIT COMBINATIONS/REQUIREMENTS
GEOGRAPHY	Candidates must study G1 G2 and G3 and any two other Geography units.
HISTORY	Candidates must study one unit from each of the following: (a) History around us H1/H2 (b) Modern World Study H3/H4 (c) Study of Social Change H5/H6/H7/H8 (d) In depth study H12/H13
RELIGIOUS STUDIES	Candidates must study any five of the units R1 to R10
HUMANITIES	Candidates must study any five of the units indicated as being suitable for certification under the subject title

AN ASSESSMENT FRAMEWORK FOR THE CREDIT BANK : A DISCUSSION PAPER

A discussion paper prepared by Christine Southall for the Oxfordshire Examination Syndicate.

One of the most attractive features of credit banking is that, as a free-standing unit of learning, a credit can be combined in a number of ways with other credits to form a student programme. Students and teachers can construct coherent courses with credits as building blocks. If the outcome of such credits and programmes were expressed as criterion referenced statements of student achievement and certificated by records of achievement, the task of the credit bank would be relatively simple. However, since GCSE accreditation is central, there are a number of issues that the syndicate is trying to resolve.

It is important that the Oxfordshire Examination Syndicate should stimulate:

1. the construction of interdisciplinary and cross-curricular programmes where skills from a number of areas are brought to bear on a task
2. student initiative and problem-solving.

The syndicate has, as one of its functions, to discern and generate the criteria for schemes additional to national subject criteria.

Many credits need to conform to GCSE national subject criteria which means, to continue the building-block analogy, that to combine a GCSE science credit called 'Corrosion' with a GCSE geography credit called 'Erosion' is like trying to cement a paving slab to a housebrick. How can the syndicate facilitate the building of coherent courses across subjects?

The Leicestershire Modular Framework syllabus seemed initially to point a way forward. In this the characteristics of problem-solving are indentified:

RECOGNITION, LOCATION, APPLICATION,
COMMUNICATION, EVALUATION

All credits are framed in relation to these five objectives, which are always equally weighted. The scheme of assessment provides a neat mechanism for the final aggregation of marks. A degree of standardization, compatibility and equivalence in and between credits is achieved. So the Leicestershire scheme facilitates cross-curricular development and the framework has a unifying effect. There still remains the difficulty of negotiating titles for programmes, and if the titles stray near to national subject criteria, then these come into play.

However, the Oxfordshire credit bank has as its objective the sharing and dissemination within the syndicate of all kinds of credits. If a unifying framework were to be constructed it should be comprehensive enough to admit subject-based and cross-curricular credits and possible sources have been investigated and trialled. It would need to take account of cognitive, physical and affective criteria. Any attempts to allow differential weighting of objectives to match the aims of particular credits diminishes compatability and starts up the paving slab/housebrick problems again. A comprehensive framework would be a complex unusable structure; a simple, usable framework would be a curriculum straitjacket.

What is clear from the workshops trialling assessment frameworks is that teachers take readily to credit writing and are increasingly comfortable with objectives-led credit design. Problems arise when conflicting sets of criteria have to be reconciled.

Following the workshops and discussions with Roger Murphy of the Assessment and Examinations Unit in Southampton, John Hanson from Oxfordshire Advisory Service and Henry Mcintosh from the TVEI Assessment Unit, I would offer the following suggestions:

1. That a single over-arching framework, while ostensibly facilitating equivalence and compatibility between credits from a variety of curriculum areas, is neither practicable nor desirable and will ultimately prove inhibiting to curriculum development.

2. That a sounder way forward is for the OES to negotiate GCSE titles with SEG. Where appropriate cross-curricular units are perceived then syllabus titles are generated and the syndicate provides a series of guidelines that help teachers to formulate educational and assessment objectives.

3. That frameworks such as the problem-solving grid and the Oxfordshire Skills Programme's analysis of operational ability should be further explored as helpful in stimulating schemes under GCSE general criteria.

10
TIMETABLING
THE MODULAR CURRICULUM
Martin Taylor

INTRODUCTION

It is clear that the introduction of a modular curriculum requires, at the very least, some alterations to the standard secondary timetable pattern. The purpose of this chapter is not to provide a blueprint for such changes nor to give detailed advice on the mechanics of timetabling, but rather to outline some possible approaches to the timetabling of what is perhaps one of the most important areas of current curriculum development. This approach is one that goes beyond the immediate requirements of a modular curriculum to offer considerable scope for future developments.

BACKGROUND

It is not so many years ago that the author attended an LEA seminar intended to assist timetablers in planning for falling rolls. This was clearly a sensible and positive initiative yet the reality consisted of little more than how best to calculate the years in which particular subjects would have to 'drop off' the bottom of the option columns. It was also noticeable how it did seem to be the essentially non-academic, non-traditional subjects that were listed at the bottom of the columns in the examples used.

Of course any timetable must work in educational as well as in purely structural terms. It must ensure that properly grouped pupils are undertaking relevant learning with an appropriate member of staff in an appropriate space for an appropriate length of time with appropriate frequency. Unfortunately, the traditional timetable structure often places severe limits on the degrees of relevancy and appropriateness that can be obtained. The word *subject* has been deliberately left out of the list of criteria. It is the traditional concept of subject that dominates, and – it is believed – severely restricts the efficiency of many timetables and this is one area in which in timetabling terms a modular curriculum has much to offer. The basic unit of the standard timetable is made up of four elements, a group of pupils, a subject, a room and one teacher – and it is usually considered axiomatic that this unit, once established, should remain inviolate throughout the school year. This basic unit is controlled by the subject and the school year and it is not easy for those connected with secondary education to break away from the concept that all pupils must receive (and that is too often the verb used) certain amounts of particular subjects, the amount being defined by quantity of subject-matter and/or time. The standard timetable simply reinforces and hardens this principle.

The secondary timetable is a complex jigsaw and it is the relationship between the shape of the pieces and the quality of the final picture that this chapter is primarily concerned.

THE ROLE OF THE TIMETABLE

The function of the timetable must be to facilitate and encourage curriculum developments that in their turn must enable all students (and increasingly that will include members of the wider community) to be offered learning experiences that are relevant to them. Inherent in its structure should be a devolution of genuine control to the teams of teachers responsible for the actual delivery of the curriculum – control that is, over the grouping of students, the duration of courses or at the least elements within courses, as well as the style of delivery. It should also offer the students greater control over the nature of his or her learning experience by providing for student negotiated pathways through a range of possibilities.

In other words, the timetable should be enabling rather than restrictive, flexible rather than rigid. At Peers School the curriculum and timetable planning documents made frequent reference to these key aims and at T.P. Riley School we have given our developments the title 'An Enabling Structure' in recognition of what we are seeking to achieve. The modular curriculum is a cornerstone in all this, provided that the timetable is so designed as to enhance rather than restrict its many possibilities.

THE PRACTICALITIES
Terminology

The following working definitions are based on those gaining increased currency in examination group thinking, though there is still a confusing lack of unanimity:

1. *Module* A free-standing unit of learning with its own learning outcomes and assessment objectives.
2. *Programme* A series of modules that together form a whole for certification purposes.
3. *Scheme* The total set of modules offered in a curriculum area from which students may select.
4. *Cycle* A set of modules timetabled at the same time and for the same length of time.
5. *Modular curriculum* A curriculum design that contains within its structure the facility to organize courses on a modular basis wherever appropriate. It does not mean that the whole secondary curriculum is organized on a modular basis. Even if this were mechanically possible it would raise immense organizational problems and have serious implications for the coherence and continuity of the students' experience. In general terms, somewhere between 30 and 50 per cent of the total curriculum would seem appropriate in years four and five with probably a smaller proportion in the first three years.

BASIC PRINCIPLES

The modular curriculum requires that the timetable be made up of larger basic units or blocks than the standard unit referred to in the opening paragraphs. This is hardly a new concept but has often been restricted to the first one or two secondary years and/or to English, maths and games in years four and five, the main purpose being to enable setting or banding, see Figure 10.1.

Each block would consist of a whole or half-year group, a set of appropriate teaching areas and a team of teachers with complementary interests and expertise. The length of time allocated to each unit would be sufficiently long, e.g. 60–80 minutes to enable its sub-division into shorter learning activities as decided by the teacher team and thus altered to suit a particular topic or other need. The teacher team is also able to decide upon the make-up of teaching groups to suit the particular need of their curriculum area and, if appropriate, alter the groupings for a particular occasion or section of work. Thus the maths team could have setting, whilst the expressive arts team operate in flexible mixed-ability groups.

The teacher team itself can be made up in a variety of ways as suits the staffing structure and curriculum balance in each particular school. It can

Fourth year Wednesday

Periods

	1	2	3	4	5
	Option 3		Option 2	Option 4	
1	ART	ENGLISH*	ART	ART	CAR
2	FRENCH	ENGLISH	GEOG.	GEOG.	R.E.
3	FRENCH	ENGLISH	GEOG.	GEOG.	CAR
4	HISTORY	ENGLISH .	HISTORY	CHEMISTRY	R.E.
5	HISTORY	MATHS*	HISTORY	CHEMISTRY	ENGLISH*
6	CHEMISTRY	MATHS	BIOLOGY	PHYSICS	ENGLISH
7	CHEMISTRY	MATHS	BIOLOGY	PHYSICS	ENGLISH
8	G.Sc.	MATHS	G.Sc.	G.Sc.	ENGLISH
9	G.Sc.	M.I.S.†	C.D.T.	G.Sc.	MATHS*
10	T.D.	M.I.S.	T.D.	L'WORK	MATHS
11	Tcgy	M.I.S.	Tcgy	P.D.	MATHS
12	Comm.	M.I.S.	Nwk	H.E.	MATHS
	O.P.		TYPING	H.E.	CAR
				TYPING	R.E.

* Limited ability related blocking to allow for setting or banding. Movement of students between these blocks requires a change of teaching group in three subjects.
† M.I.S. = Modern industrial society, a core human studies course.

Figure 10.1   Setting and banding in the timetable – fourth year Wednesday

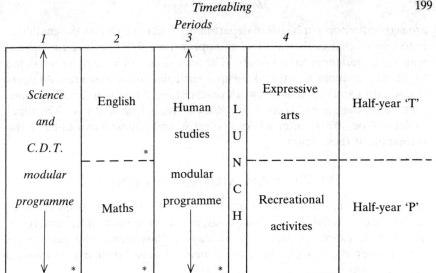

Half-year blocks are parallel in ability.
The possibility exists for co-operative developments between expressive arts and recreational activities.
* Member(s) of the special needs department available for support as appropriate.

Figure 10.2   Fully-blocked timetable – fourth year Wednesday

consist of staff with a single-subject specialism such as maths or English or could bring together staff from several departments such as a humanities team.

This larger basic unit also enables the staff to develop a wider variety of courses reflecting more closely the needs, abilities and interests of the pupils. In a whole-year science and technology block in years four and five, there could be two-year GCSE courses in the separate sciences running as part of a modular structure offering pupils a wide variety of modules also building up to accreditation at GCSE or other level.

The difference that this brings can perhaps best be illustrated by contrasting the outline of a typical day's timetable for a fourth year, Figure 10.1, with a fully-blocked structure, Figure 10.2. At this stage the internal details are not particularly relevant. It can be seen from this example that a considerable range of possibilities is immediately opened up for the types of development explained elsewhere in this chapter and in more detail in other chapters. The teacher teams responsible for each curriculum area block are immediately involved through their teacher-team leaders (e.g. head of department, head of faculty, area co-ordinator) in timetabling, which becomes to some extent a continuing process rather than a yearly exercise.

The composition of these teacher teams is mainly the responsibility of the area co-ordinators (or heads of departments, etc.) and clearly the challenge is to ensure that each team has an appropriate make-up in terms of the learning experiences to be offered. The team does not have to be restricted to the subject departments making up a particular curriculum area. At Peers School, for example, a needlework teacher taught textile technology modules within the science/technology block in years four and five. The timetabler will be able to offer advice, expertise and practical assistance in the formation of these teams.

MODULAR ARRANGEMENTS

If we look more closely at a curriculum block that, it has been decided, should be organized on a modular basis, a number of possibilities emerge of which three examples can serve by way of illustration. The parameters within which the modular system will operate must be clearly established and will include

- the length of each module (this will almost certainly be affected by certification requirements);
- the number of staff in the teacher team;
- the range of specialisms that can be offered by the teacher teams and are considered relevant;
- the nature of special needs support;
- teaching space availability; and
- the number and length of the blocks (periods) allocated to the curriculum area.

For example, Figure 10.3 shows how a fourth year science/C.D.T. modular programme could appear in simple timetabling terms. Students would, through a proper course-planning process, take three modules in parallel and at the end of the 12-week cycle move on to a further three, and so on. Modules could link in various ways to provide, for example, a continuous single-subject course leading to a GCSE certificate or to a multi-subject modular certification such as those currently being developed by SEG, the NEA and MEG amongst others. Where a TVEI or similar project is in operation students would follow a particular TVEI-module pathway.

Some modules are offered more than once in each cycle to ensure flexibility for individual course planning. For example, to offer the first module of a single-subject course in only one module block could be very restrictive and, if in demand, could necessitate expensive (or impossible) duplication of equipment, facilities or teacher expertise. Conversely, the structure enables popular modules to be offered as frequently as necessary

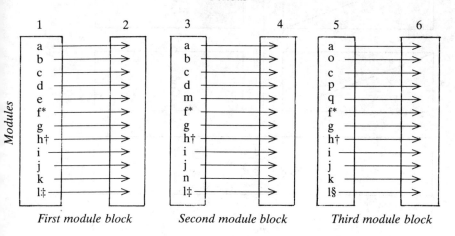

First module block   Second module block   Third module block

Size of year = 240, whole-year blocked in science/C.D.T.
Number of periods per week = 6, length of periods = 60 minutes.
Teacher teams = 12, plus some special needs support.
Module length = 12 weeks (24 periods).
* First module of GCSE Biology course.
† First module of GCSE Chemistry course.
‡ First module of GCSE Physics course.
§ First module of GCSE Technology course.

Figure 10.3   Fourth year science/C.D.T. modular programme

thus maximizing facilities and expertise. The same principle would certainly apply if it was decided that, for example, module 'a' – *Human Nutrition* – and 'c' – *Domestic Electricity* – were general core modules to be taken by all students. In this case there might be more than one group taking these modules in each module block during the first and second cycles. The range of modules offered in the second and subsequent cycles would need to be planned in advance, but are certainly capable of being altered in response to student demand, the success or otherwise of particular modules in educational terms, the availability of specialist facilities, and staff changes, etc.

Indeed, the development of module banks by a group of schools or LEA will enable such changes to be made on an 'off-the-shelf' basis, thus making expertise and experience available well beyond the originating institution.

There are many possible variations to this basic organizational pattern for timetabling a modular curriculum. Each school will have its own particular views on curriculum balance and day patterns as well as its own existing

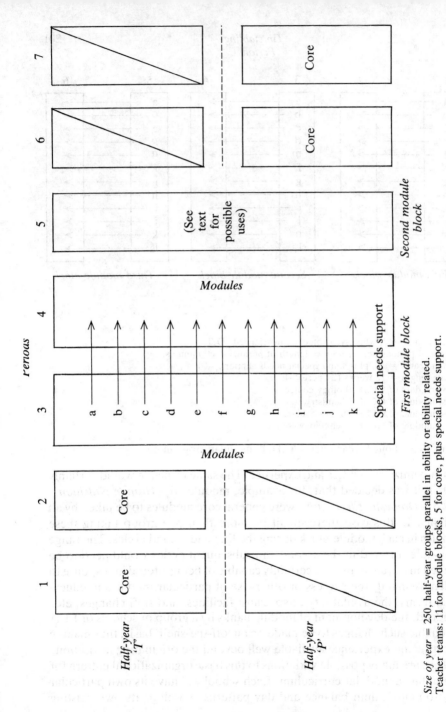

Size of year = 250, half-year groups parallel in ability or ability related.
Teacher teams: 11 for module blocks, 5 for core, plus special needs support.

Figure 10.4 Timetabling with half-year blocks

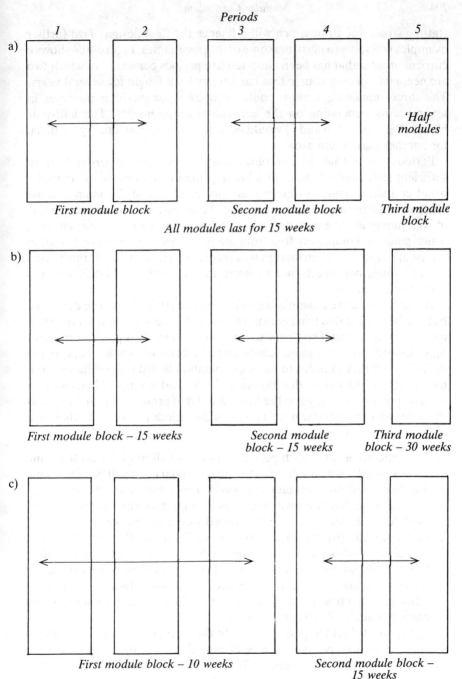

Figure 10.5 Flexible timetabling of a modular curriculum

staffing structure, all of which will influence the final design. Two further examples will serve to illustrate some of the possibilities. Figure 10.4 shows a curriculum area that has been allocated five periods per week, of which two are needed for a core course that has already been taught for several years. The three remaining periods could be utilized for modular purposes in several ways depending on the curriculum requirements. The half-year blocks (Periods 1, 2, 6 and 7) would be timetabled against a half-year block for another curriculum area.

Periods 3 and 4 need to be blocked as a whole year in order to have sufficient staff available to offer a broad programme of modules. Period 5 could contain modules extending the range offered in the main module block or could introduce a different type of experience such as a programme of community involvement activities, project work, work experience, etc., which could be completely free from the pressures of external certification but be an important contribution to a record of achievement. If this period was in a single period afternoon pattern the range of possibilities becomes even more interesting.

A third illustrative example is given in Figure 10.5. This curriculum area has also been allocated five periods, all of which need to be used for the main modular programme if students are to be offered the best possible range of opportunities. For this same reason all the blocks are whole years. It has been decided that in order to meet examination board requirements modules must be of 30 periods duration though a limited number of half modules are also possible. Clearly it is the fifth period that presents the challenge, as the other four can be operated in pairs for 30 periods (15 weeks). There are at least three solutions:

1. In Figure 10.5(a) the fifth period is used for half modules on the same 15-week-cycle, which will mean that the modular cycle will be of the same duration for all students and all periods. This solution has the advantage of simplicity, but the probable disadvantage that the number of half modules that would have to be offered would be excessive.
2. In Figure 10.5(b) the fifth period is used for the third block of full modules also of 30 periods duration. In this case the cycle for this module block would last for 30 not 15 weeks. This obviously has implications for the organization of the course-planning process for students but has the advantage that it would only be after every 30 weeks that students would change modules in all three blocks.
3. In Figure 10.5(c) the periods are split three and two. Thus the modules occupying three periods each week would last for 10 weeks whilst the others would be for 15 weeks. This has the virtue of simplicity for the

timetabler but is less likely to recommend itself to his or her colleagues responsible for organizing the assessment system or course planning. It also reduces the range of modules and courses that can be offered.

These examples should serve to illustrate the considerable flexibility that is offered by the type of timetable structure required to facilitate a truly modular curriculum. Not only does the bringing together of the twin concepts of teacher teams and whole- or half-year blocking enable consideration of a variety of modular patterns, but also curriculum developments are to a large extent freed from the rigidity and restrictiveness of the traditional subject-dominated timetable.

HALF-YEAR AND WHOLE-YEAR BLOCKS

The flexibility of timetabling in these larger units is related to the number of whole-year blocks required. In general, it is only the modular parts of the curriculum in years four and five that demand whole-year blocking. Full core courses, while they may be taught and even assessed in units, do not usually benefit from whole-year blocking – indeed to attempt to provide it would almost certainly put intolerable strain upon the composition of the teacher teams. It is, however, equally true that certain modules within a modular pattern can be made compulsory or core for all students and be offered at whatever stages in the course were most appropriate. At Peers School, whole-year blocks occupied seven periods out of 20 in the fourth and fifth years, and at T.P. Riley School a similar pattern is emerging. In the lower years all blocking is in half years.

The flexibility inherent in this type of structure does also mean that where different curriculum areas are blocked against each other, interesting, co-operative developments can take place (see Figure 10.2) but it is not appropriate to go into further detail here.

SPECIAL NEEDS

One of the principal benefits of a modular system is that the need for completely separate options courses for students with special needs is removed. The provision of an appropriate range of modules offering appropriate learning strategies should enable all students to have access to the main curriculum. There will, however, clearly be a continuing need for individual support work employing whatever methods are most appropriate. In a modular system special needs teachers can be added to teacher teams to assess need and implement the appropriate support. In essence this means de-timetabling these specialist staff to give them the flexibility to meet need wherever, and in whatever way is most appropriate. This is illustrated in Figures 10.2. and 10.3. An additional and significant further benefit from this approach is that it encourages interaction between the curriculum area team and the special needs teacher or teachers – perhaps one of the most important aspects of staff development.

THE INTRODUCTORY PHASE

The benefits and possibilities created by modular strategies and their supporting timetabling structures are becoming more and more evident. Once in place across the appropriate years in a school or college (and it is argued strongly that in a secondary school this should be all years if the fullest range of possibilities is to be created), the emphasis for development can at last be shifted away from the timetabler and on to his or her role as a consultant to the teacher teams. There are, however, very few senior management teams today who can start with a new school and a blank timetable free from the problems posed by introducing a significantly different timetable structure into an already well-established pattern.

In the same way that each school or college is unique, so the process and strategies for introducing a modular curriculum will vary – all it is hoped to do here is to offer some general principles for consideration illustrated from experience in the two schools where the author has been closely involved in the conception, design and introduction of the type of timetable and curriculum model outlined above. A very brief outline of the situation in these schools is relevant as background.

Peers School, Oxford (see Chapter 2), is a 13–19 upper school that, in 1982 when the initiatives began, had 1,000 students and a rapidly falling roll. The curriculum was traditional and the timetable was conventional, i.e. in year three (the intake year) there were three horizontal bands, with minor variations on a standard subject-based curriculum. In years four and five there was a core of English, maths, P.E. and R.E. with six mixed-option columns with some choice restrictions intended to produce a balanced curriculum. In year six there were A-level courses, plus a one-year secretarial course and a mixed programme of O-level, CEE and CSE courses.

T.P. Riley Community School, Walsall, is an 11–19 split-site community school that, in 1984 when the initiatives began, had 1,500 students and a falling roll. The curriculum was also mainly traditional, i.e. in years one to three there were three horizontal bands with a subject-based curriculum. In years four and five there was a core of English, maths and P.E. with leisure and modern industrial society courses, plus four options with choice restrictions and a subsidiary courses programme intended to redress imbalances resulting from the options programme. Year six was mainly A-level with a mixed programme of one-year courses.

Stage One

The need for a new timetable framework to enable significant initiatives in the development of the curriculum and in particular to facilitate modular systems was discussed by senior management. An ideal curriculum model was designed in outline including the balance between the various curriculum areas. This clearly demonstrated that a fully-blocked timetable was needed – a considerable change for both schools.

Stage Two

The composition of the curriculum areas was established. This had to be based on the existing staffing pattern, departmental organization and facilities as well as educational principles. The size of the teacher teams had to match the numbers of students in either the whole- or half-year blocks as well as being able to offer a relevant programme whether modular or not. In both schools the availability of appropriate teaching areas has proved to be as big a problem as the staffing situation.

Stage Three

A prototype timetable was produced to show how (and indeed whether!) the proposed curriculum would work when in place in all years, and how the sixth form curriculum would be affected. This is a *relatively* straightforward timetabling exercise as it mainly involves the strategies necessary to get the optimum arrangement of the blocks. It also revealed where particular staffing and rooming issues were most likely to arise. At this stage, the model deliberately took little account of the current timetable – it was very much a conscious attempt to put the timetable back into its rightful position as the servant of the curriculum.

Stage Four

After appropriate modification this timetable prototype was used as the objective for the production of a timetable for the interim phase of the introduction of the new curriculum structure. This, not surprisingly, was the most complex exercise, but it is clearly essential that before any concrete curriculum proposals are put to staff generally the senior management team has established that the plan is feasible both in its introductory and fully-established stages.

The most interesting challenge was to devise option columns for the last two years of the old options system that could be blocked against the new curriculum areas as they were introduced. The more that these option columns could reflect the new curriculum areas, the easier the introductory phase would be, provided always that the students were able to follow courses relevant to them. (At Peers School the simultaneous change from a 48 × 60-minute period, 10-day pattern to a 20-period week, 15 × 70 minutes, 4 × 80 minutes and a 45-minutes tutorial, produced additional considerations.)

It was not felt necessary to include every detail of staffing and rooming as the groundwork undertaken in stage two, along with the timetabler's knowledge of the existing situation, enabled more detailed studies to be produced where difficulty was likely to occur. What emerged from this process, therefore, appeared in the form shown in Figure 10.6. This example is based on the outline produced for the first year of the new structure's introduction at Peers School in September 1983. The fifth-year pattern showed very few changes as it had to be a continuation of the existing fourth-year curriculum. The mixed block was a one-year compromise to allow some additional time for certain option subjects following the change in the number and length of periods mentioned in the preceding paragraph.

The fourth-year pattern contained features of both the old and new systems with some half-year blocking and the option blocks showing as much similarity to the new curriculum areas as staffing and rooming permitted. Thus option block 'e' contained a high proportion of science and technology subjects, whereas 'a' and 'b' were biased towards the humanities.

The third year was blocked entirely in half years. As this pattern rolled through into the fourth year, some whole-year blocking was introduced in science and technology and community studies to facilitate modular systems. Languages disappeared as a separate block, foreign language courses being offered in a variety of ways including placing some language modules into other curriculum area programmes.

Stage Five

The curriculum proposals, with the educational philosophy they expressed, were now presented to the staff and governors and contained outlines both of the interim and final timetables so that decisions could be taken on the basis of an understanding of how it would all work. Further information on

Figure 10.6 Timetable based on first year of new structure at Peers School, Oxford

Column span headers: ← 70-minute periods → | ← ≤80-minute periods → | 45 min.

Vertical label (right-hand 80-minute block): T U T O R I A L

	A	A	A	B	B	C	C	C	C	C	D	D	D	D	Gen.	A	B	C	D
U/L6th A-level																			
BTEC	F.E. link element ——————————→														St.	F.E. link			
C & G 365	↓ ——————————— City & Guilds 365 course ——————————— ↓																		
Sec. 6th	↓ ——————————— Secretarial course ——————————— ↓																		
Year five	d	a	a	f		c	c	Eng. / Maths R.E./P.E.	R.E./P.E. Eng. / Maths	R.E./P.E. Eng. Maths	Maths / R.E./P.E. Eng.	b	b	Maths / R.E./P.E. Eng.	e	Eng. / Maths R.E./P.E.	R.E./P.E. / Eng. Maths	R.E./Maths / P.E. Eng.	mixed block
	Eng. / Rec. acts.	Eng.	a	Maths	Maths	Maths/Eng.	b	b	Rec. acts.	c	c	c	Rec. acts.	Maths	d	e	f	f	d
Year four			a	a	Eng.	Eng./Maths	Maths	Maths	d										
Year three (intake)	Maths	Maths	Lang.	Lang.	Sc./Tec.	Sc./Tec.	Sc./Tec.	Maths	Sc./Tec.	Sc./Tec.	Eng.	Sc./Tec.	Sc./Tec.	Exp. arts	Comm. Comm. / Exp. arts	Exp. arts	Rec. arts	Sc./Tec.	Comm.
	Lang.	Lang.	Maths	Maths	Comm.	Comm.	Comm.	Sc./Tec.	Maths	Sc./Tec.	Eng.	Eng.	Sc./Tec.	Sc./Tec.	Eng.	Comm.	Sc./Tec.	Rec. arts	Exp. arts

A, B, C, D = A-level blocks.   Comm. = Community studies.
a, b, c, d = option blocks (traditional).   Exp. Arts = Expressive arts.
– – – = year divided into parallel halves.   Rec. Acts. = Recreational activities.

Sc/Tec. = Science and technology.

how the blocking system could be used for modular and other strategies was provided. Throughout, the emphasis was and still is on the flexibility the system offers and the control it delivers to both teachers and students.

ALTERNATIVE STRATEGIES

Of course, it is not necessary to move the whole school on to a fully-blocked timetable structure in order to introduce some aspects of modular organization into a curriculum. Option systems can be modified to operate on a modular basis but it is not easy to achieve a system that offers the full benefit of modular organization without at least having some elements of a curriculum area framework. Indeed, it is likely that unless the restrictive hold of the standard timetable is broken the pressure of the traditional areas upon the modified ones might well prove irresistible and the modular curriculum will eventually be reduced to nothing more (or less) than traditional subject courses taught in units. As an introductory strategy, however, creating limited modular arrangements within an options system may have attractions to schools not wishing to make the wider changes suggested here.

FURTHER POSSIBILITIES

It is not within the scope of a chapter on timetabling the modular curriculum to explore in detail other opportunities that might arise from the type of structure described. It is, however, hard to resist giving just one example of how the introduction of this type of structure does offer considerable scope for what are essentially timetabling initiatives by the teacher teams themselves.

Figure 10.7 shows a third year of 210 students that have two periods per week for expressive arts blocked in half years of parallel ability. The teacher teams are drawn from the art, music, drama and P.E. (movement) departments and there are four staff in each team. The teacher team, having discussed the nature of the learning experience and outcomes they wish to offer, are able to propose their own programme for the grouping of students, and the use of the staff time and rooms allocated, knowing that it will not affect other areas of the curriculum and that it can be modified at any stage. It will be noted that this particular scheme, which is loosely based on one devised and operated successfully by staff at Peers School, is not restricted to the length of the school year but is a continuum leading into a range of specialist courses in the fourth and fifth years that could be of either traditional or a modular nature.

Passing reference should also be made to several other possibilites:

Weeks

1	10	12	20	28	36	Year four
ART						Two-year
DRAMA	Main	First	Second	Third	Main	modular programme offering
MUSIC	co-operative	module	module	module	co-operative	specialization to GCSE
MOVEMENT	presentation	cycle	cycle	cycle	presentation	level where appropriate

Pattern shown is for a half-year group of 105 students with a teacher team of four.

The teaching groups can remain the same throughout year three.

The module blocks operate on a 'circus' basis to give students experience in all four course elements. Each cycle could conclude with small-scale presentation of work done.

The main presentations could take the form of productions, exhibitions or other displays.

Figure 10.7 A possible expressive arts organization: years three to four

1. Basing the timetable on curriculum areas creates the opportunity for arranging the block release of teacher teams, particularly in the post-examination weeks in the latter part of the summer term when planning and development time for the coming year is at a premium.
2. An imaginative approach to the day pattern (i.e. distribution of periods, tutorial time, etc.) can produce the possibility of creating a block of extension-study time in which a wide variety of modular courses could be developed, ranging from those that reinforce or enhance a student's main studies to those offering a completely different type of learning experience. If it were possible to create a situation in which this extension period was part of the normal working week for the staff but was optional for students, still further opportunities would be opened up.
3. The particular alignment of curriculum area blocks can provide opportunities to break the rigid hold that student age has on the composition of teaching groups. This could, for example, mean ability groupings going across two school years or the enhanced use of short-term facilities and expertise. The flexibility of a modular system can only extend such possibilities.
4. For any community school or college, or an institution wishing to move in that direction, modular systems offer considerable scope for increasing the community accessibility of the curriculum. The shorter duration of the modules enables far more people to participate (two years is impossible or unattractive for many) and the increasing variety and relevance of the modules offered should benefit school and community students alike.
5. In LEAs where flexible or split contracts are already in operation or envisaged, consideration of a three- or four-session day based on a modular curriculum could add another dimension to future developments.
6. The apparently imminent emergence of a coherent framework of pre-vocational and vocational qualifications would seem to add weight to the arguments for a modular curriculum in schools and other post-16 institutions. It is very much easier to establish relevant timetable links with the type of structure argued for in this chapter for a student's course that includes modules taken at more than one institution.
7. The moves already underway in several areas to establish module banks will, as has already been mentioned, add considerably to the range of modules available to schools and ease the process of development.

USE OF COMPUTER TECHNOLOGY

The work undertaken by Peter Walter at Peers School and by David Allsopp and Roger Nelson at T.P. Riley School in the use of computers to improve the timetabling and other aspects of the modular curriculum has amply demonstrated that the general simplicity of the blocked timetable is almost ideally suited to computer application. A suitable programme can produce the optimum blocking pattern with far greater speed and consideration of possibilities, thus releasing the timetabler to develop the suggested consultative role. The computer can be used to record modules and courses taken by the students and their performance on them. In turn this information can be processed and extracted to supply up-to-date information for students, teachers and parents – perhaps eventually feeding directly into a record of achievement. When students involved in a modular programme make their choices for subsequent cycles, appropriate computer use cannot only match student demand to the available modules, but can inform the student – whose first preference is full – of the date on which he or she will be able to start on that particular module in a later cycle.

It is not unrealistic to envisage that timetables of the type under discussion will, with computer assistance, be produced in a fraction of the time currently required. The beneficial implications of such a situation will not be lost on timetablers nor their colleagues!

INDEX

215